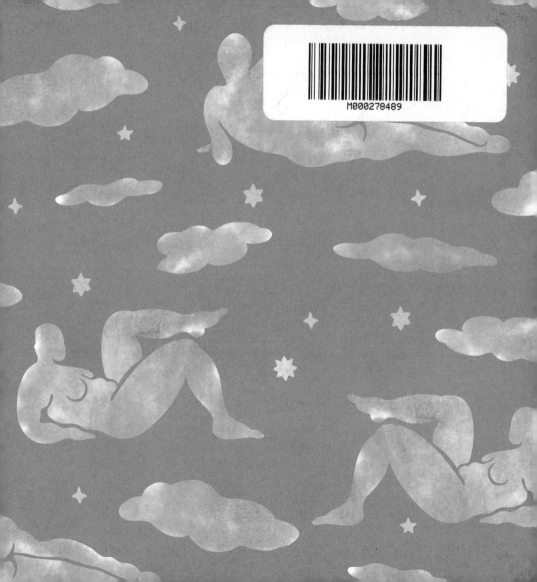

SEX ED

With illustrations by

Ruby Rare   **Sofie Birkin**

A Guide for Adults

BLOOMSBURY PUBLISHING
LONDON · OXFORD · NEW YORK · NEW DELHI · SYDNEY

cont

Introduction
6–11

1 Re-thinking Sex
12–23

2 Your Brain
24–51

3 Your Body
52–81

4 Solo Sex
82–107

5 Partnered Sex
108–171

6 Sex and Society
172–191

7 Sexy Extras
192–215

Cumclusion
216–217

ents

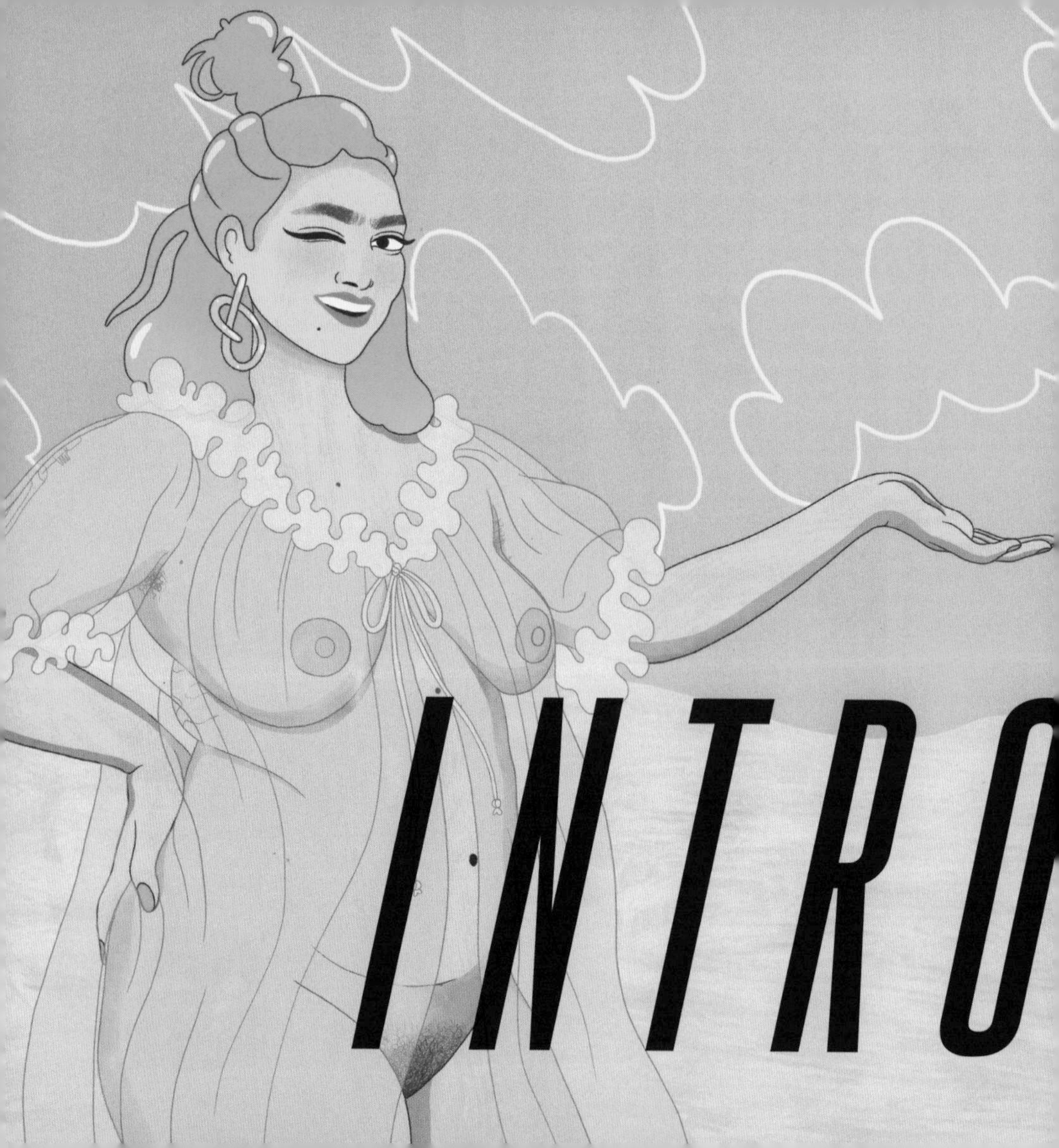

INTRO

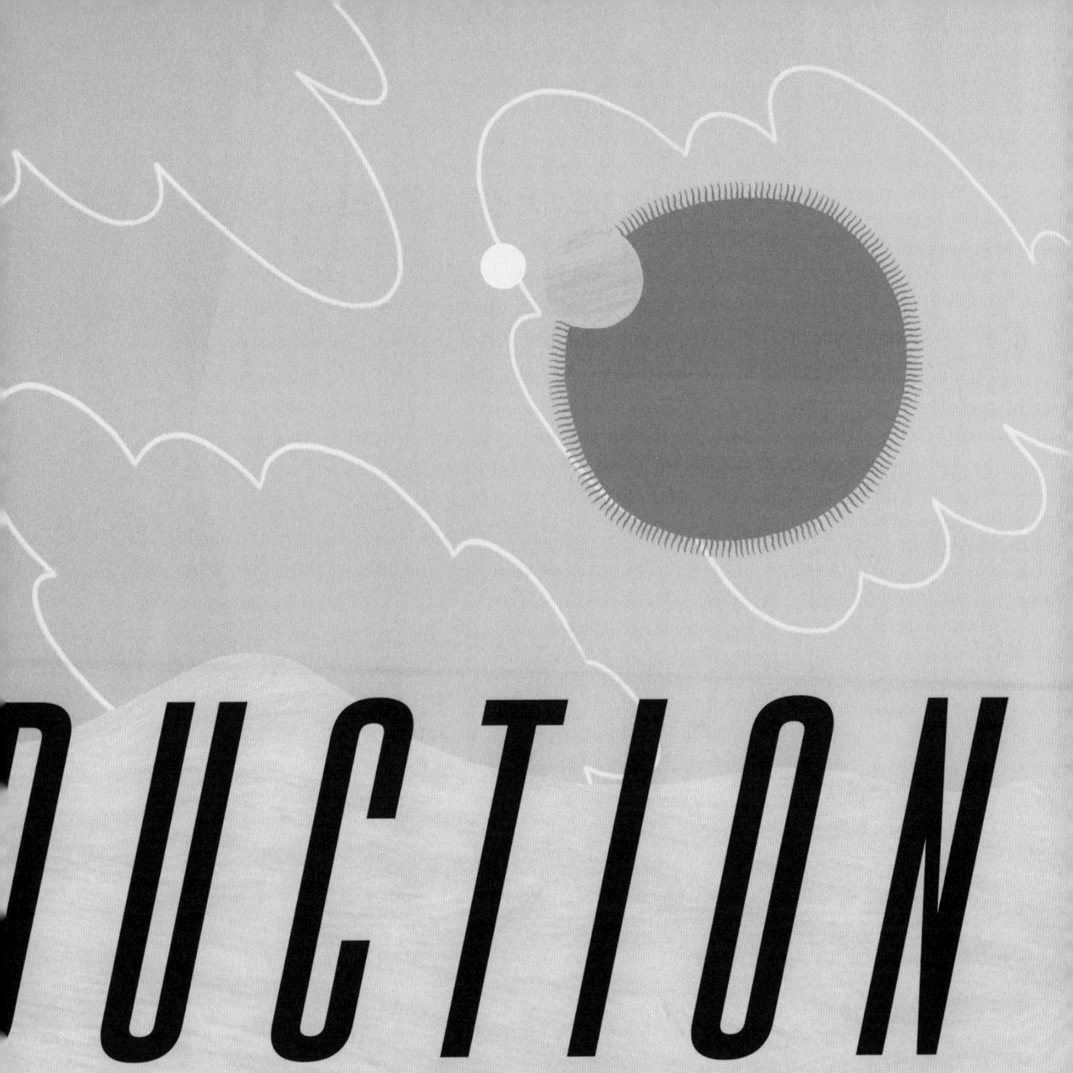

DUCTION

We don't talk about sex half as much as we should.

It's the most entertaining topic of conversation – the fact we grind our genitals into one another is hilarious. But more importantly, sex impacts all areas of our lives. Whether you like it or not, we live in a sexualised world, and learning about sex and discussing experiences with others is an act of empowerment.

Since we're going to be spending some very intimate time together, let me introduce myself. Hi! My name's Ruby. I'm a queer, non-monogamous sex educator, and I love sex. I love having sex, but I equally love talking about sex and helping others feel more confident about their own pleasure. I've taught thousands of sex ed lessons in schools and to adult audiences, from wide-eyed 12-year-olds who've never heard of a clitoris to pleasure workshops with a group of women in their 70s (I'm delighted to report that grannies are just as horny as the rest of us).

Wherever you're at in life, there's always time to become more informed about sex. And it's so important to create kind and encouraging spaces to learn and talk openly, and this is one of those spaces!

Welcome to *Sex Ed*, where everyone is invited to the party, and the party is very, very sexy.

Also, how incredible are Sofie Birkin's illustrations?! Sex is sexy, and we wanted to reflect that in the illustrations. No more euphemistic drawings of 'couple gazing into each other's eyes longingly'. This book is full of people fucking, and I feel really proud of that.

The *Sex Ed* Manifesto

1

This is the pleasure-focused sex ed you deserved to get at school (but probably didn't). And now we're all grown-ups, I can share this information in a more explicitly sexual way. I don't just want you to feel safe, I want you to get as much fun and pleasure out of sex as possible!

2

My aim is to demonstrate just how broad and varied sex can be, and it's up to you to pick and choose the information that's right for you. I'll present alternative ways to think about sex, and invite you to investigate further and form your own opinions.

3

We'll give space to the challenging aspects of sex. As much as I'd love sex to always be rainbows and orgasms, there's a lot of difficult, painful shit we have to wade through, and I'm not shying away from that.

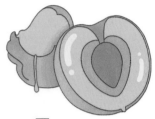

4

My hope is for you to finish this book feeling celebrated for who you are, proud of what your body is capable of, able to communicate what you want, and curious to expand your sexual horizons.

Things to bear in mind as you read

Remember you are OK. OK?

This book isn't about making you feel you should be constantly pushing the boundaries. You don't need to have the 'wildest' sex, or have sex at all for that matter – whatever's right for you is OK. In fact, if there's one phrase you'll read more than any other in this book, it's this: it's all OK!

Here you'll find guidance, and perhaps new ways of thinking – but please remember that you are the best person to give yourself sex advice, because you're the ultimate expert when it comes to your body and your desires.

The winding road to pleasure-town

There's a bit of cultural heavy lifting we need to do in order to get the most out of sex, to peel away the onion layers of shame and expectation that we inherit from previous generations. If you're in a hurry and want to skip to the 'how to improve your sexytimes' chapter, be my guest, but I think it's valuable to take stock of where you're at right now and how you got here before diving into the juicy stuff.

More lust than love

Great sex starts with the relationship you have with yourself, which we'll be focusing on a lot. I'll also be talking about the way we communicate with others through sex. But this book doesn't cover dating, love or the non-sexual aspects of relationships. (I'll save that for another book.)

Language

I've written this guide with the aim of being as inclusive of all gender identities, sexualities and relationship styles as possible. I use gender-neutral phrases when describing body parts, as genitals don't define gender, and sometimes use the terms 'people with a vulva/penis', and 'afab' and 'amab', which stand for 'assigned female/male at birth'. Unless specified, when I use the terms 'woman' and 'man' I am including everyone who identifies with those terms – not just cisgendered people.

I use 'partner' to refer to whoever you're having sex with. I like the vagueness of 'partner', not only because it applies to all genders, but because it could mean someone you just met, the person you've been in a relationship with for ten years, or maybe even your partner in crime, you cheeky little criminal.

Intersectional sex ed

Sex advice shouldn't need to change depending on the audience, because we all have sex in different ways and we all have the right to access basic inclusive information. However, I'm mindful of how race, faith, class, ability and so many other factors shape our experiences. If there's an aspect of your identity that impacts the way you have sex – for example, if you live with a physical disability – the advice in this book will apply to you, but you may also benefit from education that's specific to that component of your identity. I've recommended some further reading on page 220.

A choir of sexy angels

I've provided a broad spectrum of voices in this book. I'm not gonna lie, there is a lot of me talking (which I hope is to be expected, it is my book ...), but I've included accounts and insights from friends spanning a range of sexualities, genders, ages and ethnicities. I'm lucky to have them in my life, and I'm very grateful to them for contributing to this book in such an honest and open way.

Hey boys

If you are a man reading this book – hello! Thanks for picking this up. I really think you can learn a lot and hope you stick around. The sex-positive movement (which I talk about in more detail on page 21) is led by women and queer folks, which is obviously brilliant, but I'd love to see more cis men engaging with these ideas. In order for cultural attitudes to shift, we all need to be part of this conversation.

Kindness is cool

Sex can be a challenging topic for many reasons. Perhaps being sexually vulnerable in the past has led to emotional pain; perhaps aspects of your body cause you to feel dysmorphic; perhaps your health impacts your ability to feel sexual; perhaps you've experienced trauma which complicates your relationship to sex. Sex is not always an easy thing to enjoy. These are all factors we may need to investigate in order to have pleasurable sexual experiences. I wrote this book kindly, and I encourage you to be kind to yourself as you read.

This book aims to leave you feeling like a more confident sexual being. And I really hope you have fun reading it! **Now, let the sex ed begin ...**

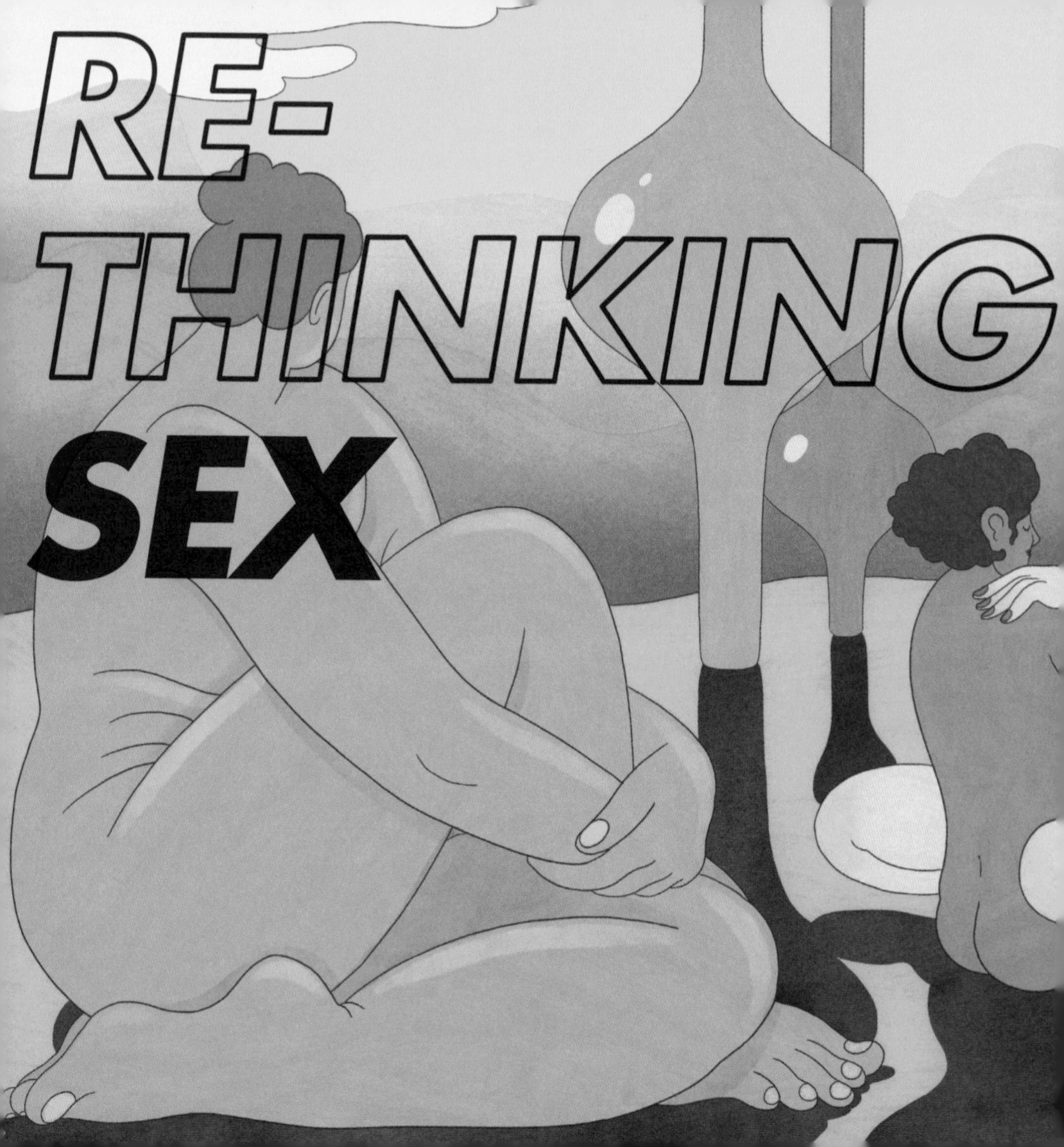
RE-
THINKING
SEX

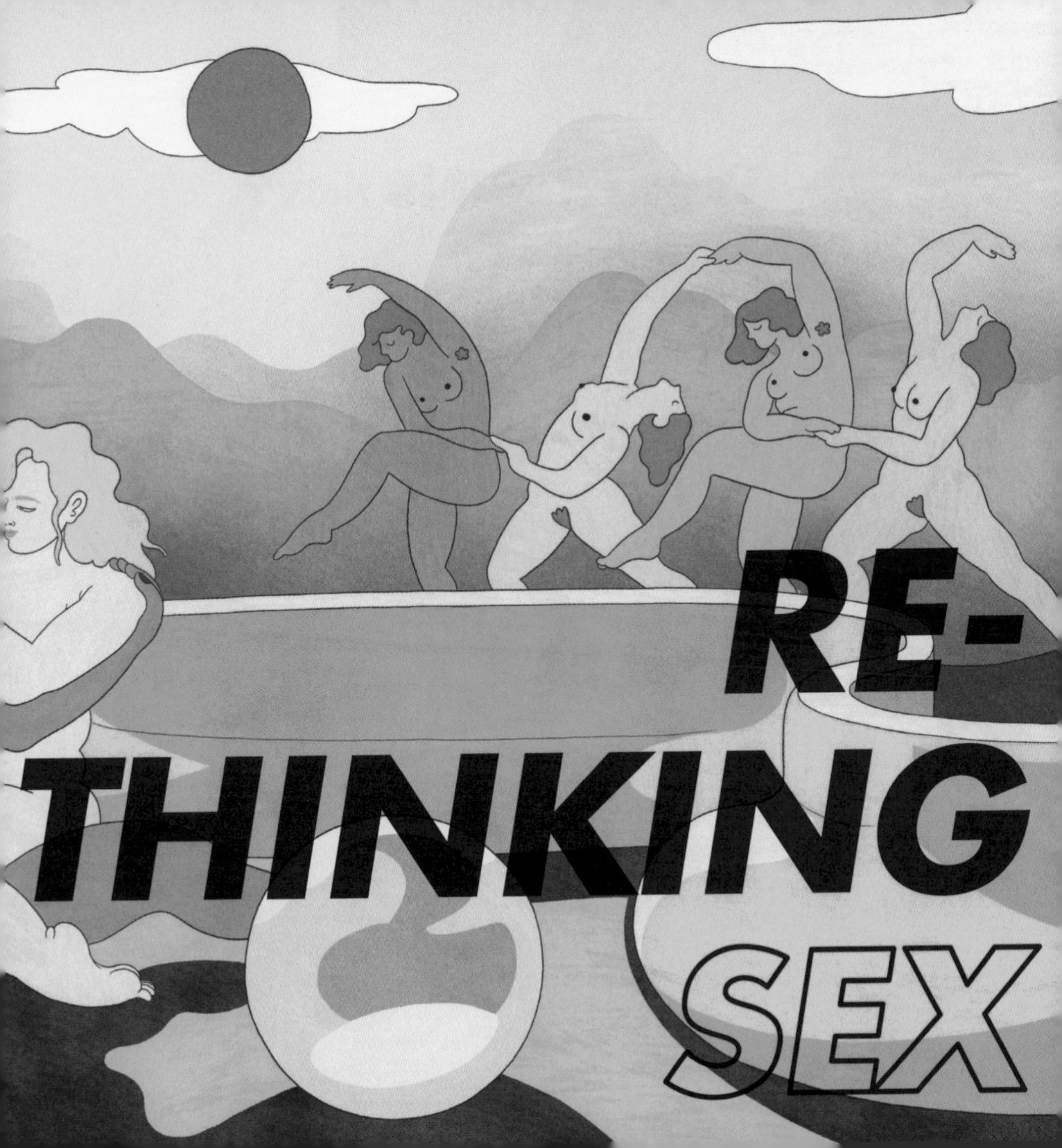
RE-
THINKING
SEX

'A complicated bodily release: in equal parts wonderful pleasure and shame.'

'It's how I earn a living.'

What even is sex?

What does good sex mean *for me*?

The short answer is that it's safe, and it's fun. Here's the long answer.

Good sex can happen on my own, with one partner, or with a whole fun group. It's a space to be playful, to indulge all of my senses. It's a space for shared vulnerability; it encourages me to exercise my curiosity and think of new ways to explore my body.

Queerness is at the heart of my good sex. Breaking away from heteronormative ideals and writing my own rules about how I experience pleasure has been a massively rewarding process, and continues to influence the way I talk about and experience sex.

Trying acrobatic positions or wild novelties can be fun, but it's not a priority. Good sex is about feeling at home in my body, and creating a space to explore and connect with partners and myself.

We each get to define what sex means to us, and this varies widely. To demonstrate this, I asked some friends to share their definitions, which you'll see all over this page.

'A very intimate union between two people, who are fully seeing and experiencing each other in the present moment.'

'Sex is exploring my own body in a way that feels comforting. It's like giving my genitals a hug.'

'Sex is a way of transcending my body and connecting with my spirituality; a way of healing and deep exploration of myself.'

'Something I have very little interest in!'

Write your own definition of sex

'Sex is a form of expression. Whether it's self-expression of my own sexuality, expressing deep feelings for someone who is dear to me, or expressing an insatiable desire for a hot lover.'

'It's just another way to communicate and share with another person, so the depth and meaningfulness of the sex depends on the connection.'

'An emotional connection that requires trust, patience, exploration and laughter.'

....

....

....

....

....

....

....

....

....

....

....

There's also space for you to add your own. None of these definitions are better or worse. We all approach sex differently, and that's OK. But there's value in seeing how others define sex, as we can learn a lot from each other.

At the end of the day, you have autonomy over how you define sex.

How do we learn about sex?

Messages about sex are everywhere: from advertising, to porn, to your Twitter feed. Yet these messages frequently fail to talk about sex in a way that's inclusive, informative and welcoming. We tend to take on messages about sex from quite a young age, and often the earliest ones we receive come from the things that *aren't* said, rather than the things that are.

16

Sidenote: We don't start feeling horny when we hit puberty – humans are sexual from birth. Sexual curiosity, such as holding or playing with your own genitals, or curiosity about other people's genitals, is a perfectly normal part of children's development. But because we rarely speak about this it's easy for adults to freak out and shut down this behaviour, in turn passing shame on to the child. If you'd like to learn more, there's a brilliant resource called the Traffic Light Tool which identifies behaviours that are a healthy part of development, and those which may indicate cause for concern for specific age groups.[1]

Take a moment to list where you've received messages about sex. This could be specific people in your life or community, professionals you've engaged with (teachers, doctors), media outlets and creative industries. You can be as broad or specific as you like; I've given a few examples to get you started.

You may find there are more negatives than positives on your list – there are on mine. This can feel disheartening. When we start questioning the beliefs we've held, it's easy to feel guilty for carrying them for so long. But it's important to remember that we aren't to blame and that we've all received a hell of a lot of flawed conditioning that we didn't ask for. I hope you feel proud that despite the bullshit messages you inherited, you're here now, ready to learn new things and embrace a more positive attitude to sex.

But before we get to the positive stuff, let's look a little closer at some of these messages.

1. 'Sexual Behaviours Traffic Light Tool', Brook [sexual health services for young people], <https://legacy.brook.org.uk/brook_tools/traffic/index.html?syn_partner=>

Let's start with the positives:

- TV & films (*Sex Education*, *Booksmart*, *Big Mouth*)
- Following sex-positive people on social media
- Sexual health websites

....

....

....

....

....

Now ask yourself:

- How have these messages shaped your sex life?
- When did you start receiving and noticing these messages?
- Was it easy to find positive messages about sex, or did you have to seek them out?

Now on to the negatives:

- Conservative family members
- The '2 Girls 1 Cup' video being sent around school
- Seeing how sexual violence is portrayed in the news

....

....

....

....

....

Now ask yourself:

- Were these messages meant with good intentions?
- Was your identity, sexual or otherwise, represented in these messages?
- How did they make you feel? Have they had a lasting impact on your attitudes to sex?

The problem with sex ed

My sex education was pretty terrible. They tried, bless them, and it was better than nothing, but it was still terrible. This is what I took away from my girls' school sex ed:

- Wet dreams and wanking are for boys, periods are for girls (and btw, periods are gross).
- There's a fine balance between being a slut and being frigid, and your job is to stay bang in the middle of the two.
- 'Losing' your 'virginity'[2] will cause you pain and not much else.
- You haven't had 'real sex' until a penis has gone into a vagina.
- IT'S ALL ABOUT THE PENIS!

That was pretty much it. Isn't that depressing?

My sex ed lessons were delivered by my religious studies teacher and her best piece of advice about sex was her explanation that 'while intercourse has been extremely sexually rewarding for my husband and me, it is also physically exhausting for us both'. Looking back now, I am genuinely happy she was having pleasurable sex, and she's right, sex can be bloody knackering at times. But was this useful advice to receive as a teenager? Did it fill me with the

2. This truly infuriates me. We'll get to how virginity is a pointless bullshit concept in Chapter 5, so I'll save the rant for then.

confidence to communicate clearly in sexual situations? Did it make me think better of her as a teacher? No. No to all of these.

A lot of sex ed has some valuable advice at its core. But by packaging it up in a truly unhelpful way, we often

CONSENSUAL SEX IS MEANT TO BE FUN!

miss those core messages. Many sex-negative messages are conveyed with a sense of fear, disgust, embarrassment or shame. The content of your school sex ed may have been accurate, but if it was presented to you by an embarrassed teacher who would literally rather be anywhere else in the world than in that classroom, their delivery is likely to impact you as much as the content itself.

My sex ed was more heteronormative than a his 'n' hers matching towel set. It didn't equip me to navigate consent, and it failed to mention the fact that my own pleasure is valid. I deserved better than that. We all do.

That's not the sex ed you'll be getting in this book.

For one thing, I'm not a religious studies teacher with a penchant for orthopaedic footwear, passing down sage (aka questionable) advice. I'm a lady with neon pink hair and exquisite taste in shoes, whose job is to know a lot about sex, and I deliver what I know in a way that's inclusive, inquisitive and FUN.

So much of sex ed forgets to emphasise the fact that CONSENSUAL SEX IS MEANT TO BE FUN!

This should be one of the first messages we receive, yet for many of us it's heard far too late. And things can get even more complicated once we step into adulthood ...

Sex Ed for Grown-Ups
(forget everything we said before)

So you've probably spent your adolescence being told sex is bad and something to avoid at all costs. Then you become an adult in a relatively sexually liberated part of the world and you're catapulted into sex. Not only are you expected to become a sexual being, you're expected to be *fucking amazing* at it. Sex is everywhere. It can make or break a relationship, and it can feel like playing the world's most complicated board game without ever seeing the rules.

And even though sex is everywhere, the examples of sex and relationships available to us are often just as crap as the education we received as teenagers – with much of it othering or outright ignoring those with identities and sexual preferences that sit outside social norms. Now don't get me wrong, there are a lot of amazing educators and resources out there, and sex ed for adults is becoming less of a taboo, but you have to actively seek out this stuff. With more mainstream sex ed there's still an airbrushed quality to depictions of sex, with many shying away from the real nitty-gritty.

This is echoed in our social interactions: I've overheard countless conversations where a group of friends manage to talk about sex while simultaneously avoiding the mention of anything directly sexual. It's a true art form. They discuss the flirting, the date, the build-up to going home together, what the flat looked like, neglected houseplants and all. But then, like a gentle fade to black in an '80s romance film, the conversation jumps to 'the morning after'.

I want to talk about the mechanics of sex. None of this 'down there', 'we did *it*', 'they were good at, you know ... [winky face]'. Here, we are going to fill in the gaps. All the gaps.

Introducing the
SEX-POSITIVE MOVEMENT!

So school sex ed let you down, and adult sex ed can feel just as confusing. But fear not – the sex-positive movement is here to save the day! OK, that's not entirely true – I'll get into my criticisms later – but it's significantly better than the other crap we've discussed so far.

Want to know if you're sex positive? Tick the statements that apply to you:

- ❏ I believe consensual sex is a healthy part of life, and that we have a right to experience pleasure if, when and how we choose to.
- ❏ I believe everyone has the right to access inclusive sex education and sexual health services.
- ❏ Provided they're done safely and consensually, I support other people's sexual desires and practices, even if they differ from my own.
- ❏ I believe we each have the right to take ownership of our bodies and sexual choices.
- ❏ I am committed to having a healthy attitude towards sex, even if I don't feel like I'm 100% there yet.

If you ticked all these boxes, you have a sex-positive mindset. Hurray!

The sex-positive community is where I call home. It's a broad term used to describe a positive mindset. For me, it's about encouraging myself and others to enjoy our sexuality, which involves lots of fun chats about pleasure, but it's just as much about fighting for better education and access to services for all. There's still so much inequality and injustice surrounding sex (we'll come back to this in Chapter 6).

You don't need to have a 100% positive relationship with sex, your body or your relationships in order to be sex positive (does anyone?). It's about recognising the challenges and feeling confident to ask for support to face them. Embracing sex positivity doesn't happen overnight – it's a gradual process.

= women's sexual autonomy = a fair few hippy orgies), which was happening at the same time as the rise of the gay rights, feminist and civil rights movements.

Since then, it's continued to grow, and in the last decade it's really taken off. This is in no small part due to the prevalence of social media in our lives – although the platforms themselves are absolutely not sex positive, censoring sexual expression and the bodies of marginalised groups left, right and centre. I'll never understand what's so shocking about a bloody nipple.

My criticisms of sex positivity

- There can be the sense that in order to be sex positive, we should be ready to dive into kinky orgies at a moment's notice. If this is what you're into, that's wonderful! Go forth, you have my blessing. But when this is the sex-positive headline, it can be intimidating and result in people feeling like the space isn't for them. There's room for all sexual practices here, and I'm keen to see that reflected more.

- There's still so much we need to do to include everyone in the conversation. Most sex-positive events still have a largely white and middle-class audience. Effort needs to be made from within the community to create spaces that feel truly inclusive and accessible.

Sex positivity is *not*:

- Wanting to have loads of sex (or *any* sex, for that matter)
- Wanting everyone to share the same values as you
- Having no boundaries
- Having an uncomplicated relationship to sex
- Being in a 'who can have the wildest sex' competition

Sex positivity isn't new; it first emerged in the 1920s with a guy called Wilhelm Reich, but the movement as we know it began in the 1960s with the rise of the sexual revolution (birth control pills

If you'll allow me to get anti-capitalist for a sec, sex positivity has turned into a buzzword, co-opted by large companies to rebrand and appeal to more leftie audiences. This does help to raise awareness and counteracts traditionally sexualised advertising, but slapping a sex-positive message onto a product fails to address any deeper issues. It dilutes the core message and repurposes it to boost sales for massive (and potentially unethical) companies.

OK, rant over.

Sex positivity exists because of the vast amount of sex negativity we continue to be surrounded by.

There are still ~~utter fuckwits~~ people who fear the power we gain from sexual liberation, because it doesn't fit their own values and because they believe it benefits them to continue living in a world that oppresses so many of us. It's also our job to challenge them, if and when we feel able to.

The sex-positive movement provides a sanctuary, a space to learn and grow and play and shed harmful beliefs. Remember that you are worthy of sexual pleasure, and by addressing the crappy messages you received and actively taking on more positive ones, sex can become a more nourishing component to your life.

This chapter in a sexy nutshell[3]:

- Sex is so much more than reproduction. The way we define it is subjective, and each of our definitions is valid.
- The messages we receive about sex are incredibly formative. Unfortunately the negative messages can stick with us just as much as the positive ones (sometimes even more). A lot of the sex education we receive at school and as adults is a bit crap. By acknowledging this, we can start to unpack the messages, engaging with them consciously and critically, and learn to recognise negative ones whenever we come across them.
- The sex-positive movement fights against this negativity, with the aim of providing us all with the tools to have consensual, pleasurable experiences. It's not perfect, but it's a space to shed negative messages and take on positive ones. You're very welcome here.

3. I tried to find a term that wasn't so testicle-specific, but there's just no equivalent – soz.

RE-THINKING SEX

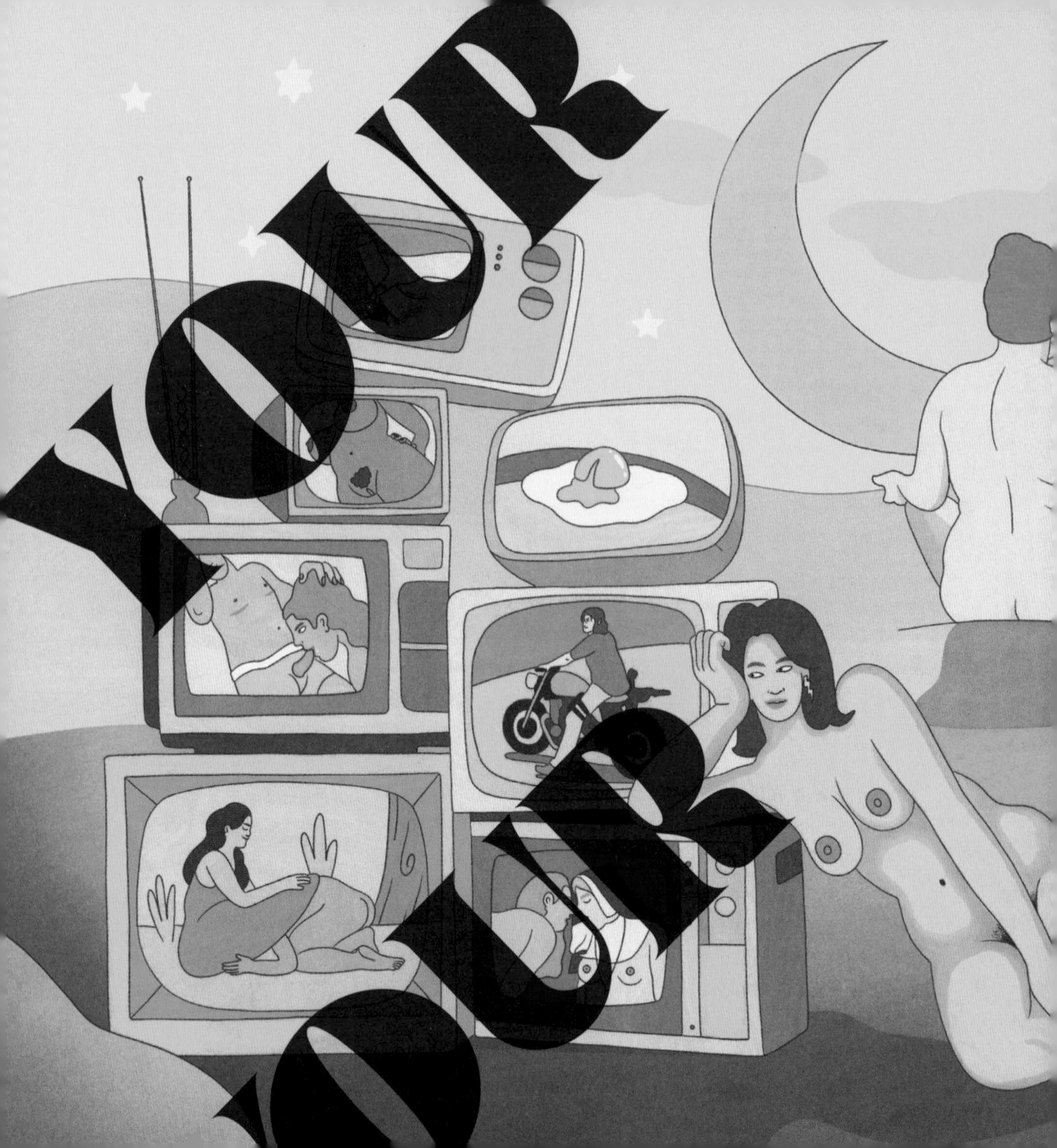
YOUR
OUR

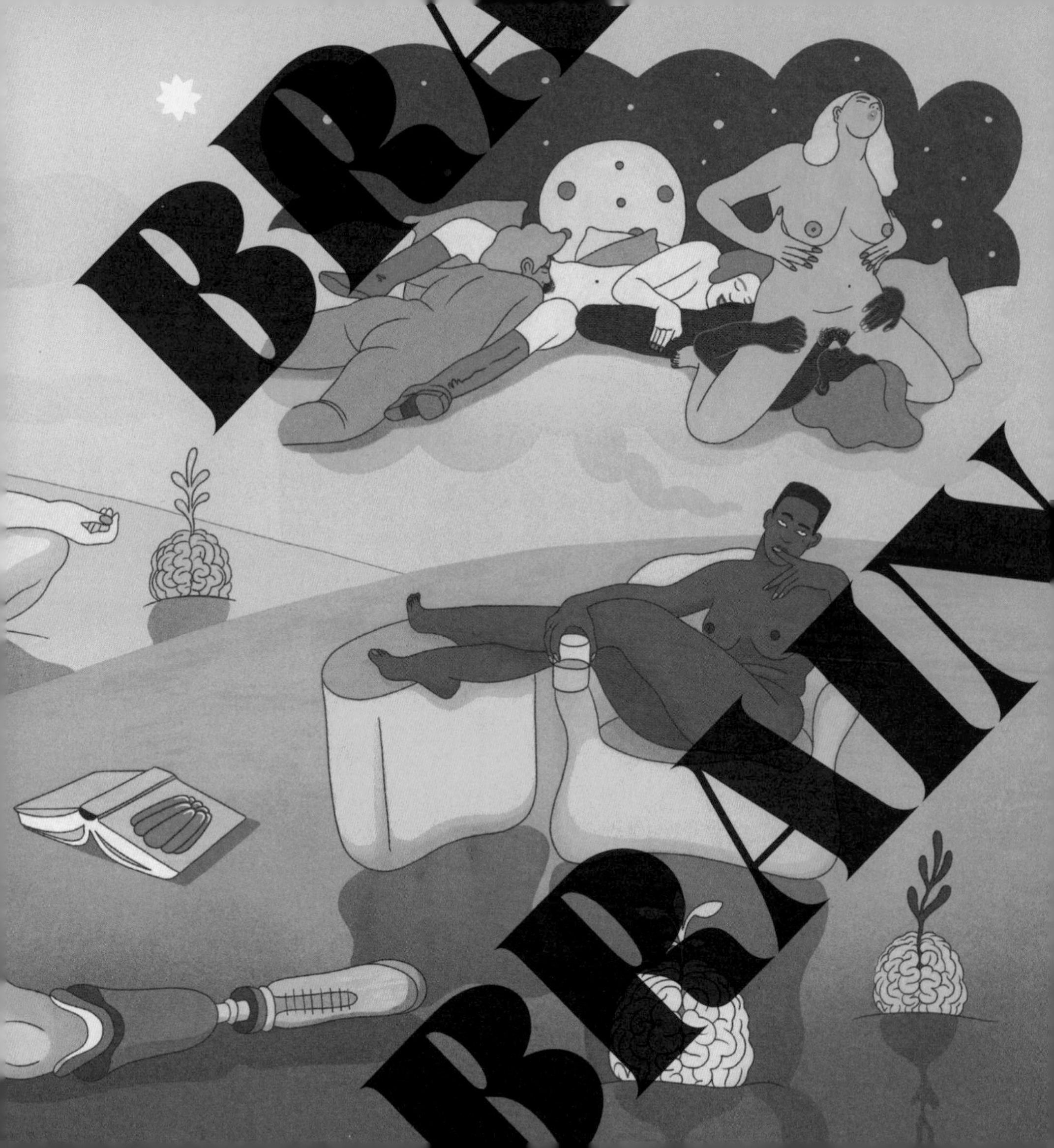
BRAIN

If I asked you what the sexiest organ in the body is, you'd probably feel spoilt for choice. There are so many sexy organs, how could you possibly choose just one? Well, there's one front-runner, and it's probably not what you're expecting (perverts).

That's right – it's the brain!

Sex starts in the brain, and without it we'd be unable to process, feel or communicate anything going on in our bodies. If you think of the body as a whole orchestra, the brain is the conductor; it always takes centre stage.

Which is why it's important to start up here, instead of diving straight down into your pants.

My favourite brain fact: The primary somatosensory cortex (that's right, the fancy words are coming out) is where the brain processes tactile stimulation (i.e. touch). It runs along the top of the brain, and maps out the entire body. But rather than being scaled to size, the map is scaled to the sensitivity of each body part. A cortical homunculus is a distorted model of the body as it's perceived through the brain, and it is fucking WILD.[4] Look it up right now – you will not be disappointed.

---

4. Two annoying things to flag here. Firstly, all the models and diagrams depict white men (yawn). And secondly, MOST OF THEM EXCLUDE THE PENIS! The massive genitals all homunculi deserve have been censored by the scientific community – yet another example of the sex-negative attitudes that surround us. I demand to see the hugely distorted genitals our brains compute!

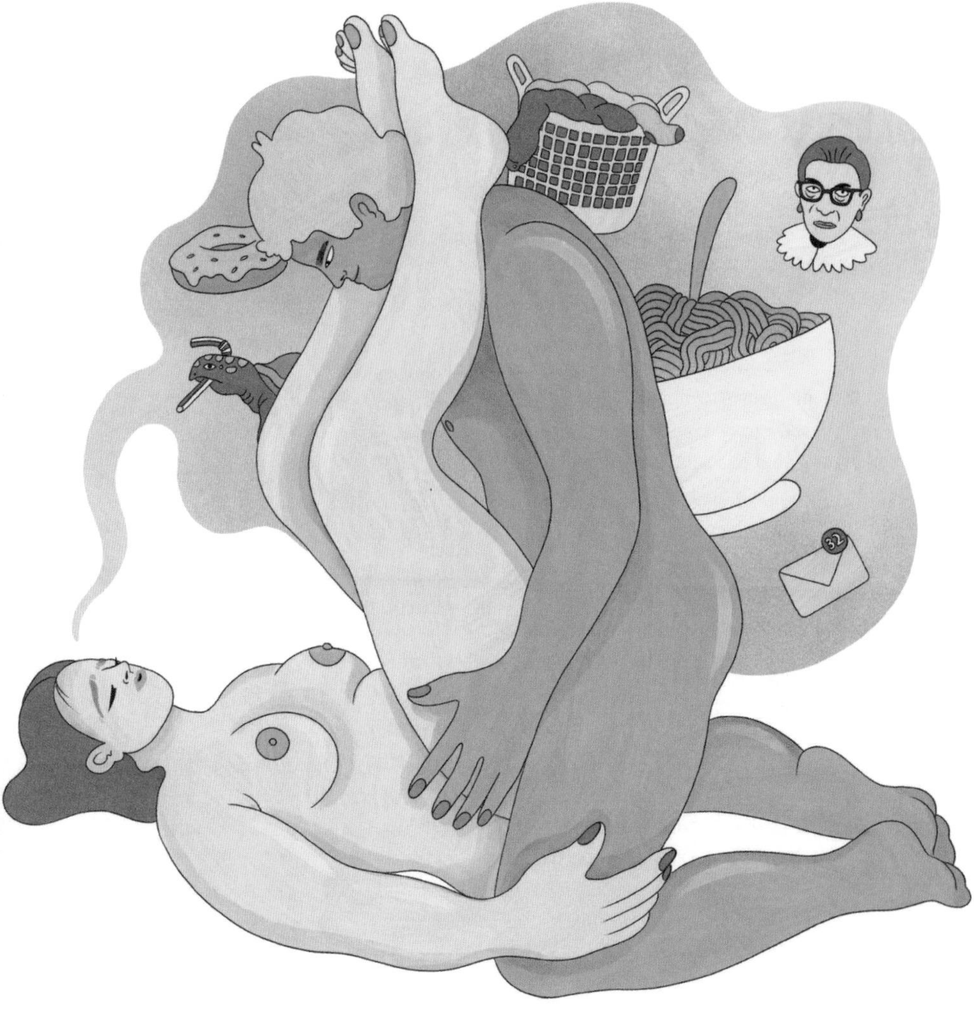
32

There's NO such thing as a sex drive

If we're getting technical (and we are), sex isn't a drive. It's a motivational system.

We're drawn to sex because it's fun and enjoyable, rather than being biologically driven to it to keep us alive in the short term – like we are with eating, hydrating and sleeping. There's also the procreation thing, but this is a book about pleasure, not baby-making.

IT'S TIME TO MOVE ON FROM THINKING OF SEX AS A DRIVE.

This isn't to diminish the importance of sex; it's one of the things which gives meaning to our lives. But (to my knowledge) no one has died of horniness.

The trouble with seeing sex as a drive is it implies that it's something we need day-to-day in order to survive. This allows people to interpret that as a right to sex, which is a subtle way consent is complicated by culture. Sex, especially involving others, is always subject to change and should only happen when everyone is in the right headspace. Feeling an urgent desire to have sex does not give anyone the right to force someone else to be sexual.

And there's another important reason why we should ditch this misleading term. For many people, sex itself isn't a driving force – you need to be in the right frame of mind and environment to even want to have sex.

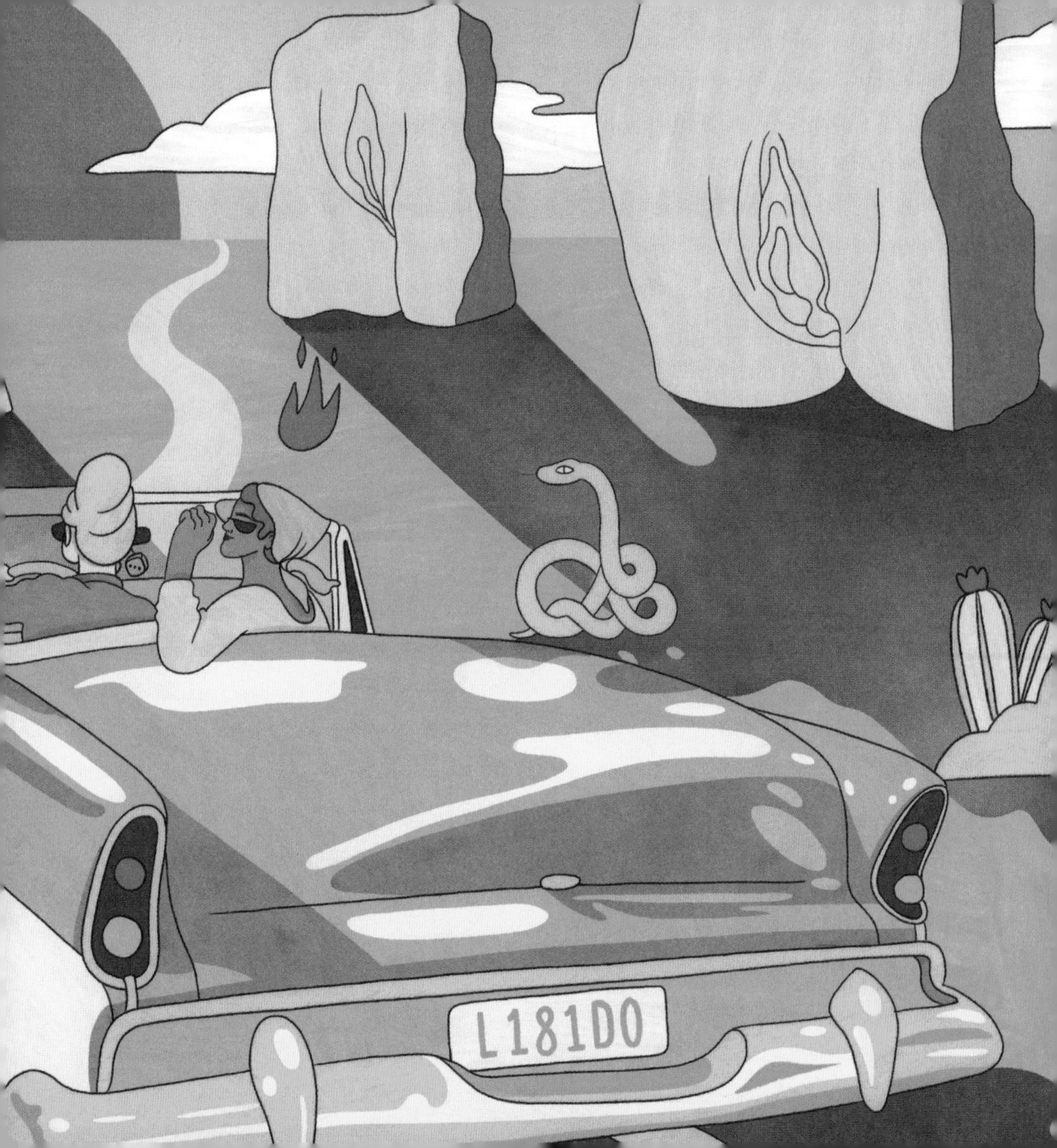
L181D0

A new driving-related metaphor

I'd like to introduce you to the dual control model. It completely changed my understanding of desire, and I hope it does the same for you.

It was developed in the 1990s by Erick Janssen and John Bancroft at the Kinsey Institute, and unlike earlier arousal studies, it goes beyond what physically happens to our bodies when we get turned on. The model is made up of two systems:

The accelerator.

The excited one! Whenever the accelerator picks up something sexy, be that a thought or something happening in the real world, it sends signals from the brain to the genitals telling them it's ON.

The brake.

The inhibited one! This sounds negative, but it's actually incredibly important. Your brake is working most of the time, noticing all the things around us that are unsexy, be that danger, risk, discomfort or an inappropriate setting.

Culturally, we see the accelerator as the only component to sexual arousal, but without considering the role of the brake we're missing out half of the story. It's not as simple as turning the sexy things on; you also have to turn the unsexy things off. Isn't that fascinating?

Sexual Desire Bingo

Here's a selection of the ways your dual control model could be triggered to turn you on or off. Cross out any that you've experienced and add a few of your own.

(There's no 'correct' amount of things to tick off, because we're all different and that's all good. Everyone's a winner!)

Listening to a particularly sexy song	....	Sitting on the bus and feeling the vibrations from the engine in your nether regions	....	Hearing your partner moan when you kiss
....	Someone playing with your hair (I'm convinced this is catnip for humans)	....	When your partner cleans the flat without you asking	....
Sexual tension building in a film	....	**TURN -ONS**	....	The feeling of sun warming your skin
....	A musky sexy smell of your choosing	....	Brushing arms with the dreamy person at work	....
Putting on your favourite pants	....	Feeling sexy in yourself	....	Intense eye contact with a stranger

Working on a tight deadline	....	Hearing *The Walking Dead* through the thin walls of your houseshare as you start wanking	....	You don't like how your date smells. They don't smell bad, it's just not your vibe
....	Bad breath (your own or someone else's)	....	A partner trying to move wayyy too fast — woah there cowboy	....
You've not showered in 3 days and are fairly sure you smell like a small wizened cabbage	....	**TURN -OFFS**	....	An email from your boss popping up on your phone
....	Your date starts talking to you like they're Gollum*	....	Your partner saying a phrase that reminds you of your dad (SEXY)	....
Mansplaining	....	Finding out someone has terrible music taste	....	Noticing all your partner's houseplants are dying

*Yes, this did happen to me. No, I do not want you to refer to me as 'my precious'. My vagina has never clamped shut quite so fast.

The sensitivity of the accelerator and brake varies from person to person, and learning about how your dual control functions is such a gamechanger.

Someone with a sensitive brake and a less sensitive accelerator will be very responsive to all the reasons not to feel sexy, and it can take time and effort to tune into sex. Whereas someone with a sensitive accelerator and a less sensitive brake will respond easily to sexual stimulation, and may find it more difficult to prevent feeling sexy (although as we've discussed, that doesn't always mean acting on it).[5]

For instance, I have a medium accelerator, so I respond to the sexy stuff easily if the context is right – but I have an insensitive brake, meaning I'm not as responsive to the reasons not to be aroused.

So it's not that I'm easily turned on ... it's more that there's less turning me off.

These levels of sensitivity can change from day to day, depending on our mood and surroundings. My brake becomes incredibly sensitive if I'm having a shit time with my mental health, or memories of trauma resurface. Remember: your sexual identity isn't static!

Mental Health

Mental health affects all aspects of life, and sex is no exception. Day-to-day stresses and anxieties can easily creep into your sex life, challenging self-esteem and preventing sex from feeling like a safe space.

Your interest in sex can increase and decrease depending on your mental health, and some medications have the side effect of altering your libido. If you live with post-traumatic stress disorder, or tend to dissociate during sex (where you disconnect from your current surroundings), your sexual response may reflect that. Remember that so many of us face challenges due to our mental health – you are not alone. It can really help to talk to a loved one about what you're experiencing, and if your mental health is getting in the way of your sex life, it's worth seeking professional help.

5. In her excellent book *Come as You Are*, Emily Nagoski provides a test to give you an idea of the sensitivity of your dual control model, which I highly recommend.

Breaking down the brake

If our internal monologue includes worries and concerns, it's going to impact the brake.

These can fall under a few categories:

- **Concerns about ourselves:** 'What if they think I'm bad at sex?', 'I don't like how my belly looks when I'm on top', 'My vulva looks so different to other people's', 'What if they think my orgasm face is disgusting?'

- **Concerns about health:** 'What if they have an STI?', 'What if I get pregnant?', 'I'm really worried about getting cystitis again.'

- **Concerns about your partner:** 'Do they like me as much as I like them?', 'Can I trust them?', 'Are they going to ghost me after this?'

- **Concerns about society:** 'If my parents found out they'd be so disappointed', 'If this gets out everyone will think I'm a slut', 'I'm not really into oral but I feel like a weirdo because everyone else loves it.'

Not to mention the worries we have that are completely unrelated to sex!

There can be an internal battle going on when we try to avoid thinking about these things. By acknowledging our worries and concerns, we can see them for what they really are, rather than building them up in our head. There may be something you can do to ease these worries. This could be practical – using a reliable method of contraception, communicating how you feel to a partner or friend, or making adjustments to the sex you're having. Some things are beyond our control, but by communicating honestly with ourselves and others, we can minimise the risk of getting hurt.

And it's not just what's happening internally that determines if we're turned on, it's our environment as well. In a calm, safe environment, our brake has less potential risks to flag, which in turn allows the accelerator to pick up the sexy stuff. But if our environment is unfamiliar, chaotic or feels unsafe, there's so much for the brake to pick up on that the accelerator may not be able to kick into action.

Improving the context around you is one of the best ways to tune into your sexual arousal.

Re-learning Desire

There are two ways we start to feel desire:

- **Spontaneous desire:** where you feel sexy without much external stimulus – it's less about the environment being explicitly sexy, and can feel like your desire pops up out of nowhere.

- **Responsive desire:** where you begin to feel sexy only once some of the things that turn you on – physical touch, an explicit shift in environment – start to happen.

Many of us will have experiences of both of these, but there may be one you tend to align with more. Both of these are completely normal, but, much like the emphasis on the accelerator, culturally there's still way more emphasis on spontaneous desire. Hollywood sex scenes have a lot to answer for here. We've become accustomed to seeing scenarios go from 0 to 60 on the sexy scale in seconds, with all the dramatic, 'I simply must have you now' crap. And we see this in porn too (more in Chapter 6). Rarely do we see depictions of responsive desire, which is a big reason why it doesn't get the attention it deserves.

Challenging life events can impact sexual desire: parenting and other care responsibilities, bereavement, trauma, stress, mental and physical health. We often jump straight to thinking that these always decrease our capacity for sexual desire, but it really depends.

After the UK voted to leave the EU, I had some of the most intense sex of my life. I was a complete mess and would have predicted I'd have no capacity for desire while I mourned the country as we knew it, but instead sex made me feel alive and connected. In times of great change, sexual desire can spike up, completely diminish, or anything in between.

Sexual Response

Desire is emotional: it's your brain wanting to have sex. Sexual response is physical: it's your body's response to sexual desire.

When you become sexually aroused, a number of physical things can happen. Your heart rate, blood pressure and body temperature rise, and your skin can become flushed. Your genitals self-lubricate and erections are caused by blood storing in areas of the body. While the whole bloody world knows about penises becoming erect, there's very little awareness that the same process happens to the clitoris (more on this later!), nipples, ears and lips. You heard me: ears get erections.

DESIRE IS EMOTIONAL. SEXUAL RESPONSE IS PHYSICAL.

In the 1950s, the iconic research team Masters and Johnson identified four stages of sexual response: excitement, plateau, orgasm and resolution. While this was pioneering work at the time, I think it's more important to recognise your own sexual response than focus on fitting into this linear pathway. You won't always respond the same way, even if it's exactly the same source of stimulation. And the significance of our dual control model in how we each experience sexual response differently is huge.

Your sexual response may not be completely synced up to how your desire unfolds. If you experience spontaneous desire and are super turned on, but the physical signals of arousal take longer to come into play, that's OK! And if you find yourself getting hard and wet before you're mentally turned on, that's also absolutely OK. And if there are moments in your life (ranging from a few weeks to years) where desire in either form is just not knocking at your door, that's also OK. The ebbs and flows of your sexual desire are totally normal.

Mapping Your Own Arousal

Take a moment to think about the last time you became aroused – on your own or with a partner.

We all have different things that tend to get us hot under the collar.

Identify how each of your senses were engaged:

Touch

Sight

Taste

SOUND

Smell

66 *Words do it for me more than anything else – hearing or reading them."*

66 *I really, really like having my ears kissed – it feels a bit like ASMR."*

66 *Slow, playful, unhurried touch that builds."*

Did this follow a similar pattern to how you usually become aroused, or were there any notable differences?

By working out what turns you on, you can return to these stimuli whenever you fancy, though much may depend on the context – where you are and who you're with. If you love being massaged, but the person you've brought home can't massage for shit, it's not going to hit the spot like it usually does.

Attachment style

Attachment theory, developed by John Bowlby and Mary Ainsworth, looks at the ways our childhood experiences impact how we connect with others. Whether we experience a chaotic or calm family environment as we grow up has a lasting impact on our behavioural patterns and how we form relationships.

This theory isn't all about sex – but recognising which of the four attachment styles you fall under may help you navigate your sexual relationships in a more mindful way. The more we know about ourselves, the better we can see our healthy and unhealthy patterns, which can lead to greater openness, initimacy, and ultimately better sex!

The first attachment style is secure, where people feel comfortable getting close to others and with others getting close to them. This style doesn't generally impact your sexual relationships in unhealthy ways, but that's not to say there can't be unhealthy habits expressed by a 'secure' individual – more on this soon.

Then there are three insecure attachment styles:

- **Avoidant:** this manifests as a fear of getting close to others, of opening up to someone only to be let down, so the tendency is to show less vulnerability and be more self-reliant. Partners may want more intimacy – sexual or otherwise – than someone with this style feels comfortable giving. There may be more of an emphasis on the physical sensations than the emotional connections linked to sex, and the idea of spooning or gazing into each other's eyes could feel more vulnerable than sex itself. If this sounds like you, trying to open up and get closer to others will help to combat this style. Recognise the fear of abandonment, and rather than shying away from intimate situations, ask for support to navigate them in a way that feels safe.

- **Anxious:** people with this style long for intimacy, and fear being alone. Their desire to feel needed by others can be expressed through sex, but there's a risk that feelings of connection and acceptance generated by this can be fleeting. They may also prioritise their partner's sexual desires over their own. To combat this, try to embrace a more self-reliant attitude towards affection. You can do this through exploring solo sex, or conciously figuring out what you want from sex and asking for it, instead of going along with what your partner wants.

- **Disorganised:** this style stems from experiencing trauma or abuse in childhood. Because of these early experiences, loved ones can represent nurture and danger simultaneously – positive emotions are very closely linked to negative ones. People with this style experience the stress and uncertainty of bouncing between fear and a need for closeness. They may feel disconnected from their bodies in sexual situations (which can involve dissociation), or may find their experiences of sex unpredictable. Here, the goal is creating some stability. I'm not talking monogamy and a white picket fence, but working towards some structure may help regulate the changeable pattern associated with this attachment style. Communicating your fears and asking for patience from partners can really help, as it may take longer for you to get to a place where you feel safe.

You may already have an idea of the attachment style or styles that resonate with you; there are free tests available online if you'd like to learn more. It's also helpful to know your partner's attachment style, as it may mean you see things from different perspectives and require different support from each other in order to feel secure. Acknowledging these tendencies creates greater awareness, and this can make a real difference in how they shape your actions.

But while attachment theory is useful in deepening our understanding of human behaviour, we should be careful with how it's used.

♦ The theory works off how our past plays into the present, but if we're not careful, learning about our attachment style can become a self-fulfilling prophecy. The styles can feel fixed and, without the right information and support, it can be difficult to maintain a sense of agency.

♦ The idea of being secure or insecure can create 'winners' and 'losers' in our minds. The goal for many of us is to gradually move towards the secure style, which is an ongoing process. But it's easy to feel hard done by if you currently identify more with an insecure style, which is something I'm wary of. Remember, this is a useful tool, but don't hang onto it too tightly. This is not the only thing that defines us.

♦ Deep down, we all carry fears of being let down and being alone, and this manifests in different ways for each of us. When looked at in isolation, these four styles can feel like an oversimplification of our inner fears.

At the end of the day, if we're being honest about our wants and needs and are communicating openly, we all have the capacity to develop deeper and more balanced sexual connections. Whatever attachment styles you resonate with, it doesn't define who you are – we're all flawed, but there are always ways we can improve how we engage with others.

Sex and Gender

Biological sex is determined by our chromosomes, genitals and hormones (more in Chapter 3). Gender identity is a whole different thing. It's about how each of us feel on the inside, as well as the social roles we play in relation to others. 'Male' and 'female' are biological sexes, 'masculine' and 'feminine' are ways of acting and presenting that play a part in our expression of gender.

We put so much emphasis on gender, in some ways it's the most important performance of our lives. I'm far more interested in how our gender impacts the sex we have than the biological sex we're assigned at birth. Personally, my sex life has greatly improved now I've stopped obsessing over 'this person has a vulva and this person has a penis'. We're all so different, and sex and gender goes way beyond whatever genitals we have.

A person's gender identity shouldn't be defined by their genitals, but sadly this is still the presumption. Even before birth, most babies are stamped with a gender, and the assumptions their parents make as a result of that stamp play a huge part in that baby's life. This begins with their grand exit from the womb; well before they have a chance to develop a personal attitude towards their own gender. The fact that many boys play in a way that's boisterous, and many girls play in a way that's more delicate is in large part down to the way children are taught how to perform gender. You can see how this feeds into the messages we receive about how different genders should perform during sex as we grow up.

Your parents don't get to choose your gender; no one does. It's down to you. Gender is nuanced and our perceptions of it are ever changing, and there's growing recognition of this now.

The terminology used to describe gender identity is vast, but the three big 'uns are:

- ◆ **Cisgender** – where your gender identity matches the biological sex you were assigned at birth. Male = man, female = woman.
- ◆ **Trans** – where your gender identity differs from the biological sex you were assigned at birth.
- ◆ **Non-binary** – where your gender identity sits outside the man-woman gender binary (which can fall under the trans category).

Perceived gender identities have a huge impact on sex – if you're cis, you're expected to fall in line with the role your gender is expected to play in the bedroom. You know the drill: men = the macho aggressors; women = dainty passive receivers. Whereas if you're trans, the fact that you sit outside the norm is constantly questioned and politicised. These inherited roles prevent us from exercising our agency and accessing a full range of human emotions and experiences.

~~~~~~~~~~~~~~~~~~~~~~~~~~~~~~~~~~~~~~~

I like the word 'agency' because it emphasises making your own choices. For me, the words 'power' or 'control' make it seem like your actions are at the expense of others, when I believe it's possible to exercise our own agency while respecting someone else's. It's about recognising what's best for you (without being a dick to others), and having the confidence to express that and take actions to make it happen.

~~~~~~~~~~~~~~~~~~~~~~~~~~~~~~~~~~~~~~~

If you're cis and/or straight, it can be easy to stick to the rules without questioning if they actually work for you. If your gender and/or sexuality falls outside heteronormativity, you have an opportunity to create your own rules when it comes to experiencing pleasure. Of course, this has its downsides – it's exhausting to have to question everything – but I try to think of this as a positive: it's liberating to build a structure that works for you. This feels like a lot less of a burden when you're part of a supportive community.

A way of challenging these roles is through sex that subverts, challenges or plays with traditional gender roles. Rather than breaking down in tears over how fucking bleak it is to live in such a gendered world, it can be fun, sexy and healing to fuck with gender through sex. This can be explored through actions (pegging, fantasising, role play), but it's more about the attitude you bring to sex. If you're usually the more passive partner, try exploring what it's like to be more dominant. I enjoy tapping into my masculine energy through sex, and through this exploration I've become more playful with how I navigate gender roles across other areas of my life.

66
    Sex while trans is not particularly straightforward. Feeling male is an instant turn-off, and it's far less to do with my anatomy but by other small things: the way I am touched by someone, the dynamic, how I feel I look to them, what they expect from me. Some of this is within my control and some isn't.

    I have a lot to work on before I can fully lose myself in a sexual scenario. I look forward to that. Most of my sexual partners have been very supportive. It helps when people are sensitive and thoughtful and make it clear to me that they are into me (very paranoid my flirting comes across as creepy, thanks TERFs). Regardless of medical changes, being intimate with a trans person is different to being intimate with a cis person. I really don't want my body to be touched like a cis male body, but I'm aware that it does not function in the same way a cis female body does. The ideal scenario is for the pair (or more) of you to have a fun, sexy time inventing and building a whole new intimacy that works for everyone involved. The thought of that is as revolutionary as it is hot."

66
    Coming out as genderqueer allowed me to openly play with my gender identity, which changed my relationship with sex. I spent my early 20s dating in heterosexual dynamics, and struggled with the way sex fell into gender roles so easily – especially when PIV was involved – because it didn't feel true to who I am. I have always loved playfulness and silliness around sex, and try to keep that at the core. Now, my partners and I make an effort to play with gender roles and expectations rather than feeling constrained by them."

Trans Experiences

'Transgender' is an umbrella term, with lots of identities sitting within it: trans women (can also be known as MtF – male to female – or amab), trans men (FtM, afab), non-binary, two-spirit, genderqueer, genderfluid ... the list goes on. Language around gender identity is constantly evolving – it's good to be aware of the basics, and open to adapting to new language as it shifts.

PSA: a person's 'trans-ness' is no more valid if they take steps to transition medically through hormones or surgery. For some there may be structural and financial barriers to accessing these services. Many trans people have to be on waiting lists for years before they're able to talk to medical professionals. For others, this simply isn't an important or essential step in their transition.

Regardless of gender, all bodies are different. But trans and non-binary people's bodies face disproportionate scrutiny. If you're cis, imagine how inappropriate it would be if every time you met someone new they asked what your genitals were like? This is what the trans community experience all the bloody time, and it's draining.

The only time it's appropriate to ask someone about their genitals is when you're a health professional and it's medically necessary, or if you're going to be sexually intimate with that person (but this doesn't mean you have the right to ask someone what's going on in their pants the minute you start chatting on a dating app!). You should always talk to a sexual partner about what they like before getting intimate, but the conversation should be about establishing boundaries and sharing the ways you both like to touch and be touched. For some trans folk, touching parts of the body may cause a sense of gender dysphoria. It's also worth discussing how best to support a partner if they do start to feel dysphoric. The conversations I see about transitioning are often quite clinical, but incorporating pleasure, sexual or otherwise, into your transition can be an act of empowerment. I highly recommend reading Juno Roche's brilliant book *Queer Sex* for more on this.

All trans identities are valid and beautiful. You are worthy of love, care and respect, and wonderful sex! I'm sorry we still exist in a world where your identity is questioned and where you face discrimination. Part of being a proactive ally to the trans community is fighting for the rights and respect all trans people deserve.

YOUR BRAIN

Sexuality

Sexuality covers your sexual orientation (the people you're into), as well as your broader capacity for sexual feelings.

Your relationship with your sexuality can have a huge impact on your sex life and your attitude to your body. Your sexual attraction can be different from your romantic attraction; making a distinction between the two can help you express, and therefore understand, the way you form relationships.

For example, a person can identify as bisexual, where they're sexually attracted to all genders, and could also identify as homo-romantic, meaning they tend to develop romantic feelings towards people of their own gender. An asexual person may identify as hetero-romantic, meaning they are interested in pursuing romantic relationships with people of the binaried opposite gender, but they're not sexually attracted to anyone.

Each identity is unique, with its own set of challenges and prejudices, which many of us may not experience and may never have considered.

Regardless of your own sexuality, it's a good idea to engage in conversations about the whole spectrum of sexual identities (and genders). We have so much to learn from each other! Here are a few examples:

66 *My queer friends have helped me see I don't always need to play the more 'feminine' role during sex."*

66 *Sex doesn't have to include genitals."*

66 *I learnt that despite the popular debunking, some people do really enjoy scissoring."*

66 *Before I came out as bi I asked my friend what it felt like to kiss a woman, and her answer soothed me and made me feel happy in my want to do that."*

66 *I had a gay male flatmate, who told me he only really liked hand and oral play. At that time I was so surprised, I loved any and all play, why would anyone not love something that is so good! Now it's obvious, people simply love what they love."*

While sexuality can't be 'changed' by external factors – you can't be turned straight; a person, object or activity can't make you gay – queerness can evolve over time. Processing and acknowledging aspects of your sexuality can be a lifelong journey and it's always OK to be figuring it out.

It's OK to have known from a very early age who you're attracted to, and for that not to have been challenged or altered throughout your life.

It's OK to have identified with one sexuality, but for that to change at some point in your life.

It's OK to be figuring out your relationship to your sexuality and to be trying on different sexuality hats to see if any of them fit. And it's OK to resent the need to wear a hat!

It's OK to shout about your sexuality from the rooftops, or to be completely private.

It's OK to be attracted to people of multiple genders, but not to have dated or had sex with some of those genders – yet or ever.

It's OK to ....

It's OK to ....

It's OK to ....

It's OK to ....

It's OK to ....

It's OK to ....

Swimming in the Bisexual Soup

Some people are 100% straight, some are 100% gay, and that's wonderful! But there are many people who sit somewhere in between.

I like to think of this as a big lovely soup. And I reckon there are more people in this ambiguous soup than there are people who consider themselves to be 100% gay or straight. This doesn't mean that 'secretly everyone's bi' – that invalidates those who are only attracted to one gender – but there's a good chance far more people reside somewhere in the soup than those who choose to publicly identify as queer soup-dwellers.

There's the idea that bisexuality is bang in the middle of gay and straight, but I don't see it as being one fixed spot along a spectrum. Plus this spectrum presupposes a gender binary, and once you start to question the very notion of gender, it can be difficult to identify as explicitly gay or straight.

Because we're raised in a heteronormative environment, it can be incredibly easy to disregard your attraction to other genders, dismissing it as a 'girl crush', or telling yourself

you're watching Disney's *Hercules* again purely for the love of the songs, when in reality all you want to do is gaze at Meg and her incredible hips (seriously, how can a cartoon character be that sexy?).

I define my bisexuality as being attracted to my own and other genders, which includes non-binary and intersex folks. I tend to use this term because it has the most immediate recognition (plus I like the colours of the bi flag more), but personally my definitions of bi, pan and omnisexual are very similar.

If you think you're bi, you are! You don't have to prove how bi you are to anyone. And it doesn't make you greedy or indecisive. Your sexuality is valid regardless of your sexual and romantic history, and if you're in a straight-presenting relationship, it doesn't make you any less queer.

The soup is warm and welcoming, and if it feels right for you, you are welcome to exist within it without having to find a definitive spot along a sexuality spectrum. It's a space where you can feel truly nourished.

Regardless of your sexuality, my hope is that you are attracted to yourself. Not in a narcissistic 'staring at yourself in a mirror as you cum' kind of way (although that can be fun), but I really hope that you can see the value you hold as a person. Work towards validating yourself before seeking the affection or adoration of others. We don't get there all the time, and this is a constant work in progress, but my aim is always to feel self sufficient with my sexuality, to know that I can cater for myself and provide joy, sexual or otherwise, for me, before I seek out encounters with other people.

Fantasies

When it comes to desire, imagination and fantasy play a big part. With a great fantasy, sex can happen entirely in the brain.

While the world of fantasies is never-ending, most of our fantasies tend to fall into three categories: power & control, group sex, and novelty. (And some fantasies will hit more than one of these at once.) We tend to enjoy fantasising about sex we may not be having IRL – grass is greener and all that – as well as scenarios that wouldn't be possible outside of our imagination.

What do you fantasise about?

What we fantasise about is incredibly subjective. The issue is we're often told what we should think of as sexy by the culture that surrounds us, instead of having the opportunity to figure it out for ourselves.

Porn and erotic content play a large part in fantasy (to be discussed in Chapter 6). But it's nice to generate your own fantasies every once in a while.

Most of us have things that turn us on sexually, but which we have no interest in exploring in reality. There are fantasies you may be happy to discuss with partners or friends. Perhaps because they're relatively common, or feel funny or 'tame enough' to be shared. I talk about my fantasy of being set in a giant bath of jelly to anyone who'll listen, because while I find it a legitimate turn-on, I also acknowledge it's weird and funny, and it opens up an interesting conversation.

But there are other fantasies that we might not want to share. Perhaps the most common of these is ravishment. This used to be called rape fantasy – the change in language has been made so as not to trigger flashbacks for sexual assault survivors, as well as to distinguish these fantasies from the horrors of rape in real life, and make it possible to explore these themes in a safe environment. If you fantasise about being ravished, it doesn't mean you secretly hate yourself or think you 'deserve it'. If you fantasise about being the ravisher, it doesn't mean you secretly hate your partners or want to cause them harm. And having a ravishment fantasy does not make you a bad feminist!

If you enjoy ravishment fantasies, but engaging with them brings on a sense of guilt, making time to reflect and unwind after you fantasise can help you form a more conscious relationship with them.

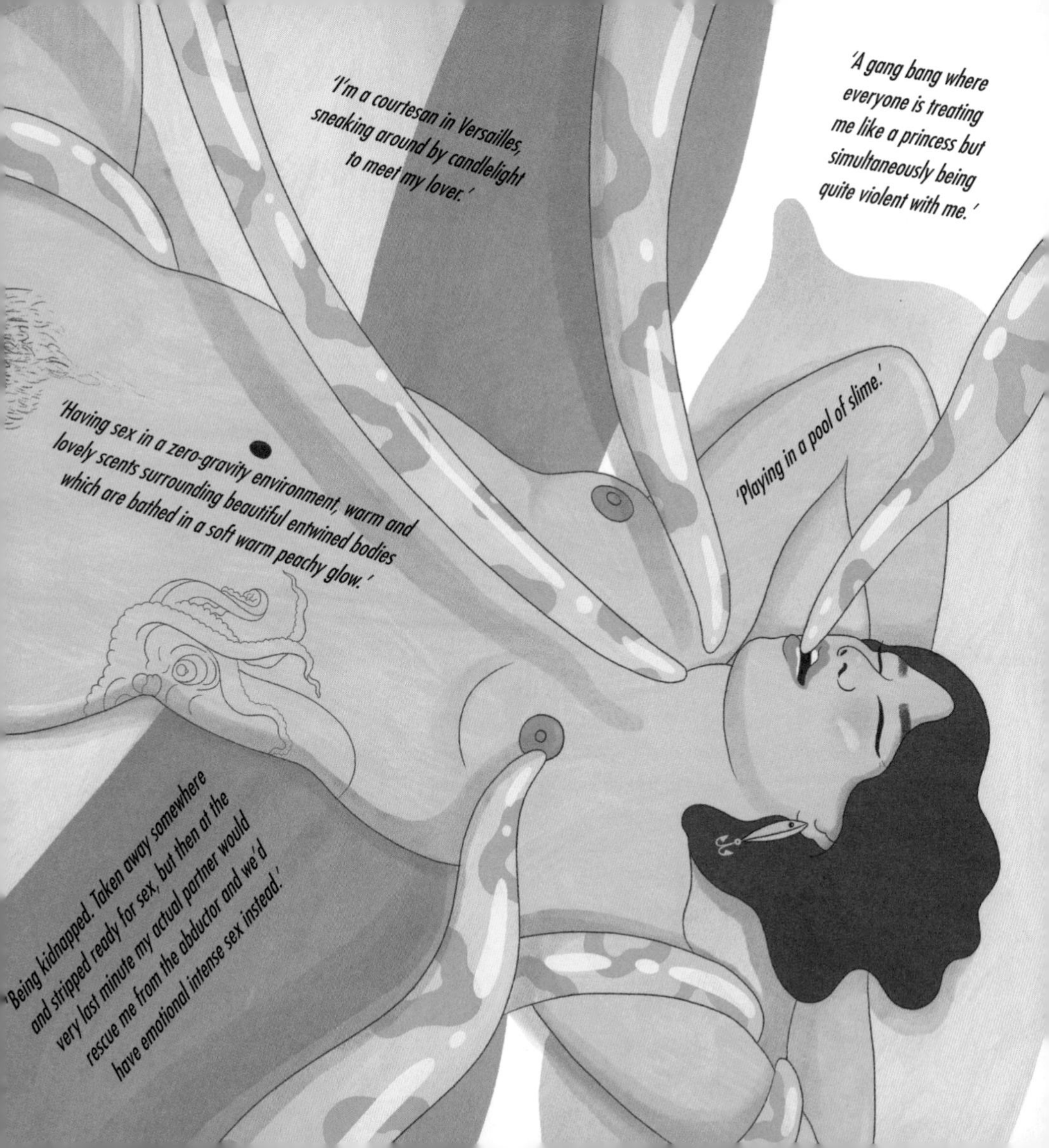
'I'm a courtesan in Versailles, sneaking around by candlelight to meet my lover.'
'A gang bang where everyone is treating me like a princess but simultaneously being quite violent with me.'
'Having sex in a zero-gravity environment, warm and lovely scents surrounding beautiful entwined bodies which are bathed in a soft warm peachy glow.'
'Playing in a pool of slime.'
'Being kidnapped. Taken away somewhere and stripped ready for sex, but then at the very last minute my actual partner would rescue me from the abductor and we'd have emotional intense sex instead.'

Shame

Urgh, sexual shame is the worst. It's thrust upon us from an early age, and unless we're given tools to unpack it, we can carry it and its BFFs, guilt and denial, around for the rest of our lives. Shame can be experienced in all aspects of our sexuality, and fantasies are no exception.

Something that's helped me with overcoming shame is acknowledging the difference between a shameful secret and a conscious secret.

A conscious secret is kept out of choice: you're acknowledging the desire to engage with it privately, rather than shrouding it in shame and trying to keep it secret from yourself as well as the outside world. It's completely OK to choose not to share some or all of your fantasies with others, but that shouldn't mean you have to feel shame about them. Remember that the vast majority of people have these more private fantasies: you are not alone. Solo sex is a great space for you to safely form relationships with the fantasies that you don't wish to share with others.

If your fantasies feel more extreme, a good way of engaging with them without taking on guilt or shame is to consume porn and erotica that doesn't involve real people. When you're imagining something, or reading a story, or looking at illustrated/animated content, everybody involved has consented. But if the porn you're consuming contains real people, there's a chance it might not have been produced consensually, or it may feel unethical because of the nature of the content. If you feel a great sense of shame about your fantasies, I advise speaking to a professional who'll be able to help you unpack this in a safe environment.

From fantasy to reality

It can be useful to take a moment to consider where your fantasies come from, not only to better understand your own sexuality but to spark ideas about how elements of these can be incorporated into your real-life sex. It might be best to think about them individually at first, but you may find you can draw interesting patterns from your wider repertoire.

- ◆ What is the fantasy?
- ◆ What specifically do you enjoy about it?
- ◆ Why do you think that is?
- ◆ Are there ways you could incorporate similar sensations or experiences in your

real-life sex? Obviously if you are super into tentacle hentai porn, it's quite difficult to incorporate that into your sex life literally, but are there sensations and things that you can do to mirror your fantasies?

We cannot control our fantasies – they may differ greatly from the morals we as regular people live by (in fact, the best fantasies often do). That's totally normal! We are all weirdos when it comes to fantasies, I promise. The shit my brain has conjured up is alarming; it's from the depths of my subconscious and I can't pretend to understand it

all. But I've made an effort to acknowledge these fantasies, in all their bizarre glory, in an attempt to shake off some of the shame we carry round if we simply shove them to the back of our minds. Shame is an extra burden we just don't need.

When you're analysing your fantasies, remember to be kind to yourself. The rules of fantasy land differ from the real world and it is the ultimate sexual playground. It's a space to play with all the sexual norms we've been handed down, to embrace them or subvert them. Fantasies are an invitation for us to unleash our inner perverts. How delicious.

In a sexy nutshell:

◆ The brain is where all things sex begin. There's no 'one size fits all' when it comes to desire and arousal, and understanding your dual control model can revolutionise your approach to sex.

◆ Biological sex is what's going on in your pants; gender identity is what's going on in your brain. Whatever your gender, you are worthy of respect and pleasure.

◆ Sexual and romantic attraction aren't necessarily the same. It's OK to be figuring all this out slowly. The way you understand and express your gender and sexuality can be a lifelong journey.

◆ Fantasy land is the ultimate sexual playground. What you fantasise about doesn't abide by the same morals we stick to IRL – give yourself permission to indulge in them like you're at a Roman banquet (great location for a fantasy, btw). We're all perverts when we fantasise; I promise you're not alone.

Now let's take a look at the rest of the body.

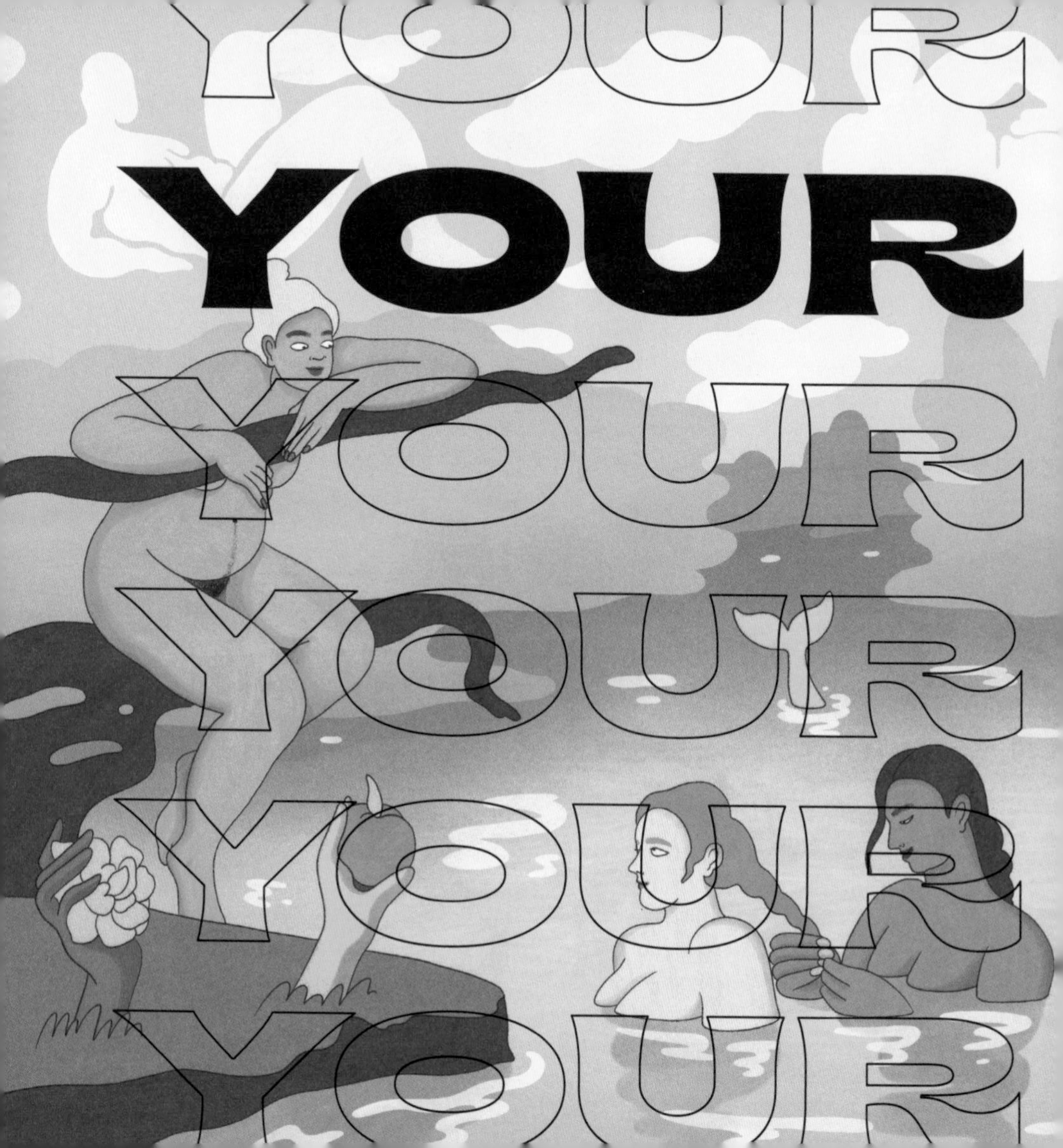
YOUR
YOUR
YOUR
YOUR

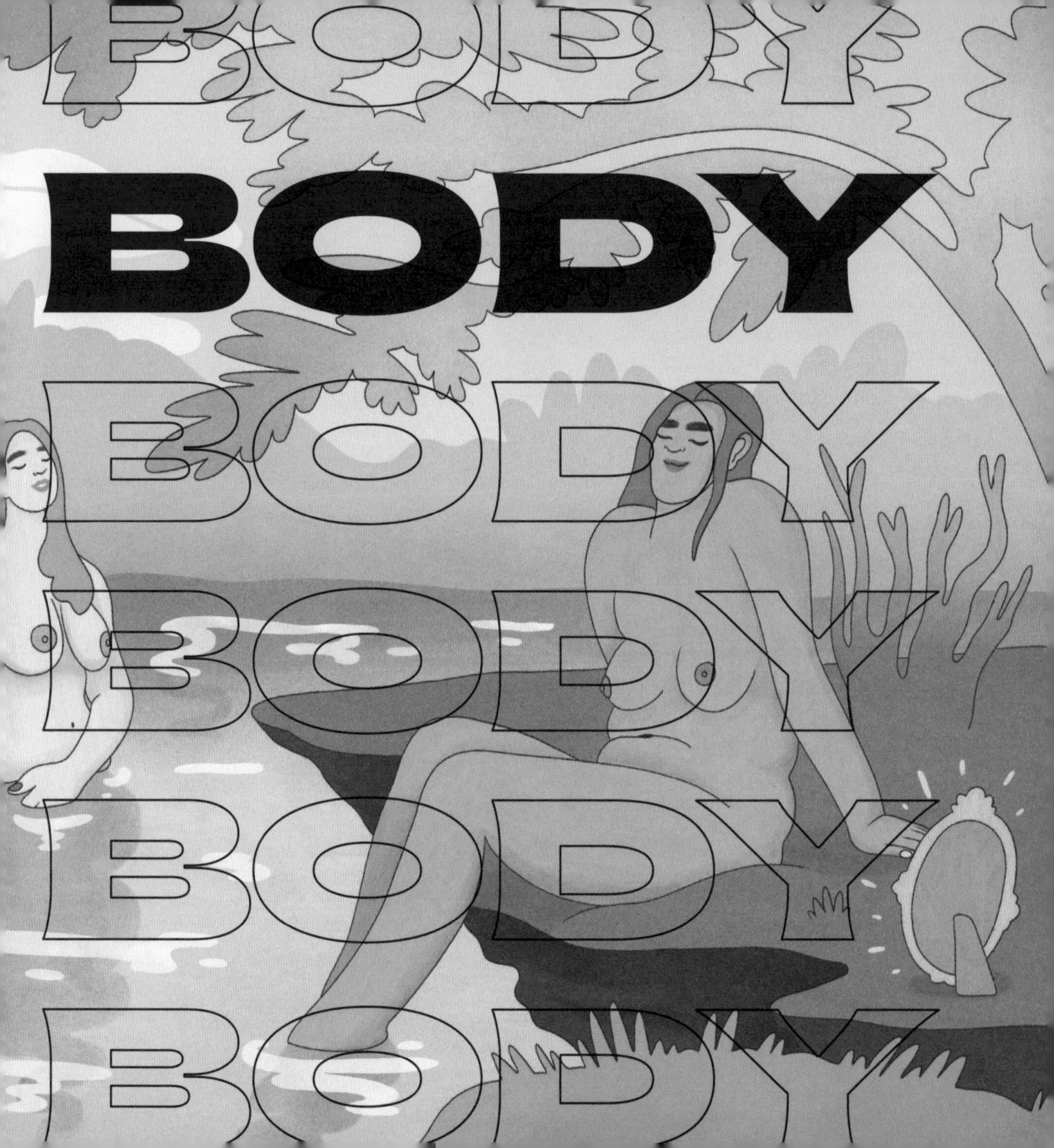
BODY
BODY
BODY
BODY
BODY
BODY

Your Wonderful Genitals

Genitals are fucking incredible. They can be a source of endless pleasure; they can birth life; they're squishy and hairy and warm and endlessly exciting.

But there's a lot of negativity surrounding genitals. We rarely see detailed images of them outside of porn and medical textbooks, both of which generally fail to reflect what our own bodies look like.

I love the word 'beautiful'. I was brought up on the Roald Dahl definition of beauty, how it comes from within and beams out into the world. To me, beauty is powerful, courageous and raw. It's not about something fitting into a certain category or looking a certain way. It's about finding ways to see beauty in all things. Using 'beauty' and owning it is a superpower, which is why I've chosen to use the word in this book.

A Note on Language

The attitudes we have to our bodies and sex are completely tied up in language. Sadly, there's a lot of shame embedded within the language of sex, because the idea that sex itself is dirty and sinful is still prevalent in many cultures. The less confidently we discuss our bodies, the more difficulty we'll have embracing our pleasure and ensuring the sex we have is safe.

Being able to accurately identify body parts and sex acts opens up our ability to communicate our wants and desires, or describe something accurately if we're seeking help. It's empowering!

In this book, I mostly refer to body parts and sex acts using medically accurate terminology, so we're all on the same page and can become familiar with this language. But I will stray off the medically correct path sometimes to use other words that I particularly like, because adapting language is an important part of exercising your agency.

Babe, that's <u>not</u> a vagina

How many times have you heard the word 'vulva'? Until well into my twenties, I could count the number of times on one hand. It was all vagina vagina vagina.

Don't get me wrong, I love vaginas. I like the word, I love my own and I'm very fond of a few other people's. But I also think vulvas are fucking fantastic, and want everyone to know that these two things ARE NOT THE SAME! We'll get to discussing anatomy soon, but, simply put, the vagina is the tube on the inside and the vulva is everything you see on the outside.

This may not feel like a massive deal to you – sure, they're different parts of the body, but they're next-door neighbours, so what's the harm? But as wise woman Emily Nagoski said, 'You wouldn't call your face or your forehead your throat, right?'[6] The ability to distinguish between these two parts of the body has changed the game for me and my sex life.

By recognising the correct terms for biologically female anatomy, we make it clear that there's more to sex than just penetration. Having sex that involves the vagina is great: penetrative sex gets a big thumbs up from me. But the majority of pleasure lies in the vulva and can be enjoyed with no penetration, so we do ourselves a disservice by erasing all that pleasure in the language we use. Why limit yourself to one lovely word, when you can have two words and double the fun? Viva la vulva!

6. E. Nagoski, *Come As You Are* (2015), p. 29

Genital-naming ceremony

Across the world there are thousands of words used to describe genitals. Adapting language so you have celebratory words to use is an act of empowerment (and it's also quite fun).

Here are some of my favourites:

Crown jewels
(there's no need for it to be dick-specific; very into my genitals being likened to such magnificent jewellery)

Mrs Vag
(my sister came up with this and it's one of my faves – it makes your genitals sound like a rich aristocratic lady, which I'm very into)

VULVA
(sounds so silky)

Unicorn
(um, hello, this is adorable)

Cunt
(powerful AF)

My particulars
(comes from the 1940s; really helps if you say it in an old-school Hollywood accent)

Now it's your turn! Write down some terms that make you feel sexy, silly and above all JOYFUL about your genitals. These could be words you already use, or new terms you've just come up with:

....

....

....

....

....

....

....

On to the **Sciencey Stuff**

Everyone's body is different and everyone, regardless of their identity, uses their body in different ways.

Genitals do not define gender. Having a penis ≠ man. Having a vulva ≠ woman. Breaking away from heteronormative ideas of which genitals belong to which gender and what genitals should 'do' when it comes to sex has peeled back my expectations of what genitals should look like. Culturally, we're still obsessed by the differences between genders. While there are certainly biological differences, there are many similarities as well!

Let's take a look at how similar our genitals really are.

Sidenote: For those who napped through biology lessons, chromosomes are tiny structures that store our DNA. Humans have 23 pairs of chromosomes, and one pair is the sex chromosomes. Two X chromosomes make someone biologically female, and an X and Y pair of chromosomes makes someone biologically male (although remember biological sex is separate to the way we express gender!).

Fun fact: The sperm determines the sex of a foetus! While eggs always carry an X chromosome, sperm live on the wild side and can bring an X or Y chromosome to the table. So when Henry VIII was pissed at Anne Boleyn for not having a son, IT WAS DOWN TO HIM ALL ALONG!

Homology is a biological term for two or more structures (in this case, sexual organs) sharing a common origin – they may be structured slightly differently, but at the core they're really quite similar.

The basics of our genitals are all the same, because they're made from the same stuff. For the first six weeks, all fertilised eggs develop in the same way. Then, a wave of hormones causes the egg to begin developing reproductive organs depending on the chromosomes.

Every part of the biologically female genitals has a homologue in biologically male genitals:

XX chromosomes	XY chromosomes
Clitoris	Penis
Labia Majora	Scrotum
Ovaries	Testicles

You read that table right: **the clitoris and penis are basically the same thing!**

Both the clitoris and the penis are made of erectile tissue, which fills with blood and swells when we're aroused. They both have glans, a sensitive area containing the highest concentration of nerve endings, and they both extend into the body from the base. All of these parts of the body are formed from the same foetal tissue.

Like all parts of the body, the genitals can change as a result of treatment and surgery relating to physical health. These changes can also happen non-consensually, the biggest example of this being female genital mutilation, a traumatic procedure which has a huge impact on health and pleasure.

Sidenote: Biological sex isn't binary either. Intersex folks have hormones, chromosomes and genitalia that can differ from typical male or female bodies. Notice I said 'typical' here, because while it's most common for people to fall into the biological female or male categories, that doesn't mean intersex folks aren't normal – they absolutely are! Like everyone else, they are born with all the same parts, just organised in a slightly different way. As part of this, intersex folks may have genitals that aren't classed as either 100% a clitoris/vulva or a penis/scrotum.

Other people's genitals may look and function differently because of changes made to their body. If a trans person is on HRT (hormone replacement therapy) the appearance and function of their genitals may change, and genitals can be altered as part of gender confirmation surgery (but remember, these are not essential parts of transitioning for everyone).

Isn't all of this fascinating? I wish this was something we were taught at school. Think of the impact this knowledge would have on gender equality if it was something we grasped from an early age.

Outdated Biology Diagrams

Even though it's what's on the inside that counts, our main fascination with genitals, our own and others, is how they look. You've probably seen diagrams of genitals in a biology textbook. And by that I mean, one diagram of a vulva and one of a penis. These diagrams tend to show:

● The genitals of someone who's white and young
● Little/no pubic hair
● Symmetrical labia and testicles
● Little/no colour variation
● Zero imperfections – not a spot or ingrown hair in sight
● Very 'average-sized' clitoris, labia, penis and testicles

But, as I'm sure you've realised, there's a whole glorious diversity of genitals out there, and this is just one way genitals can look.

I spent my teenage years with this crappy diagram (and porn) teaching me what my genitals 'should' look like. As a result, I thought my genitals were wrong and gross. All it would have taken was someone to explain that, like literally all other parts of our body, the appearance of genitals varies and that's exciting! I would have felt so much more confident in myself.

If you turn over the page there is a beautiful display of genitals, and I'd like you to take a moment to look at them and reflect on your emotional reaction. Have you seen this diversity of genitals in one place before? When you look at them, how do you feel: in awe? Overwhelmed? Nervous? Turned on? How do they make you feel about your own genitals? Recognising any uncomfortable feelings you have is useful, as it's only by directly addressing shame and negativity that we can start to overcome it.

Falling for Your Genitals

All genitals are unique and that should be celebrated. Think of me as your genital fairy godmother, encouraging you to see the beauty in them.

Here are some ways to become more familiar with your genitals:

1 First up, look at them. I'm particularly speaking to women and people with vulvas here – it's considered relatively normal for boys to ogle their penises, but girls are shamed for checking out their genitals. You're never too old to crack out the mirror and have a proper look, say hi and get to know yourself better.

2 Don't just stop at looking. Draw it, take photos to refer back to later, or ask partners to take photos from angles you may have never seen before.

3 If you find a safe suntrap, let your genitals get some sun (although not too much – I can confirm a sunburnt vulva is not a good idea).

Feeling comfortable and confident about your genitals is not always the easiest mindset to shift into, but it's time to start on that journey. And an important step is learning more about your anatomy.

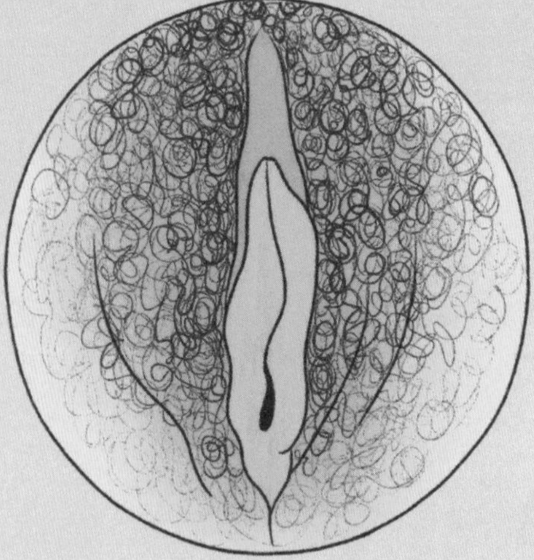
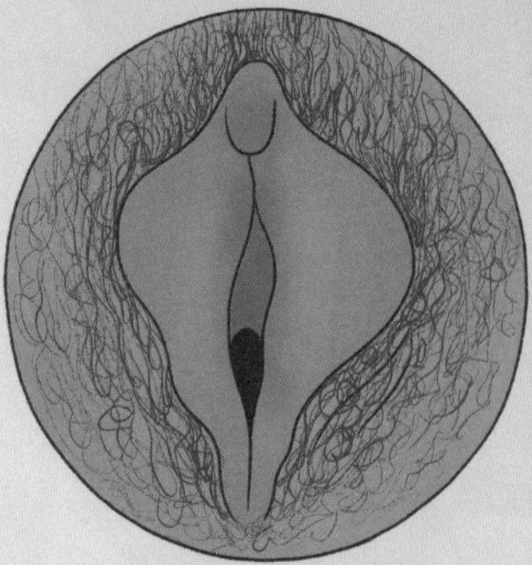
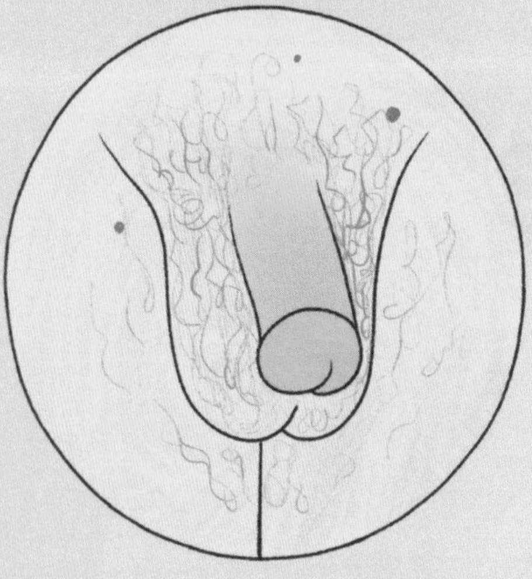
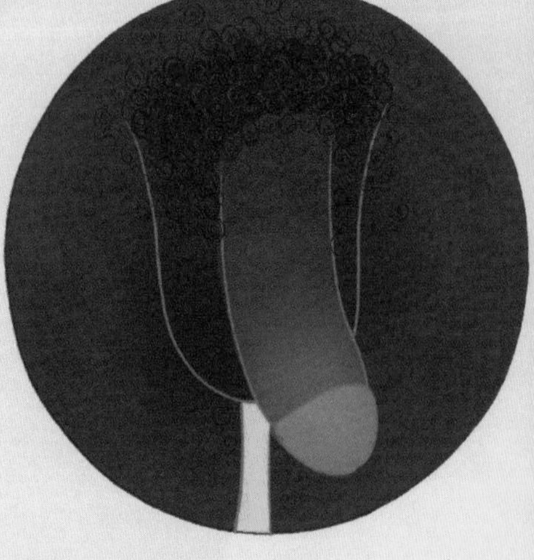

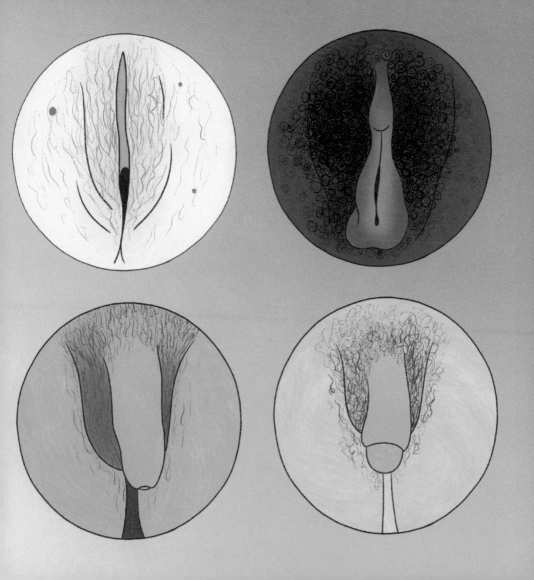

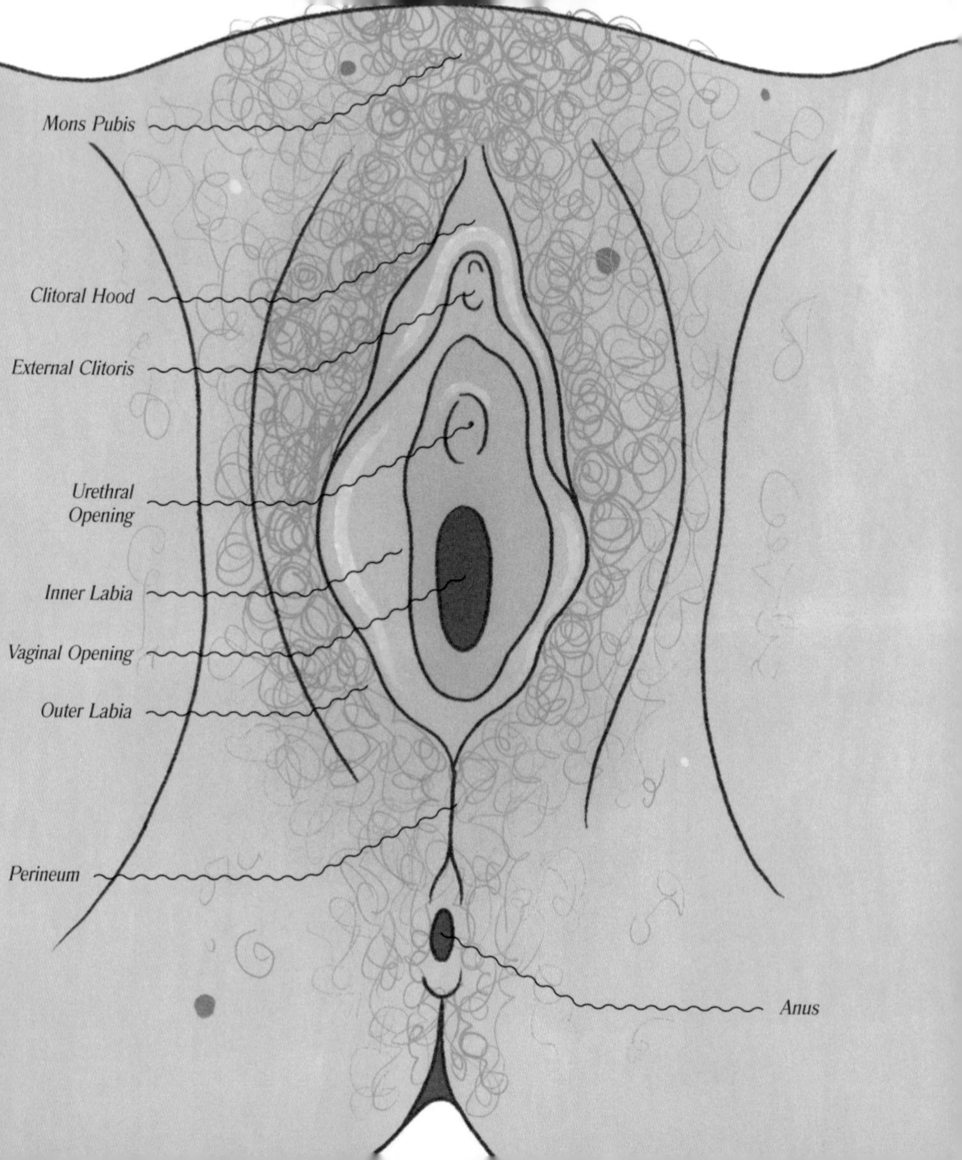

Mons Pubis
Clitoral Hood
External Clitoris
Urethral Opening
Inner Labia
Vaginal Opening
Outer Labia
Perineum
Anus

Anatomy

The Vulva

This is everything you see on the outside. The vulva consists of the labia minora and majora, the clitoral hood, the external clitoris and the urethral and vaginal entrances: quite the supergroup.

Labia

The labia majora are the outer lips. They can be smooth or a bit ridged, and the inside is usually a pinker hue.

> 66
> *My labia is quite long, and I spent years avoiding sex or only doing it in the dark because I didn't want anyone to see. Sleeping with other women really helped me see that everyone's labia is so different, the variety is unbelievable! It took a while, but I finally feel like I'm 'allowed' to feel sexy just the way I am."*

The labia minora are the inner lips. They're thinner and more flexible than the labia majora, and when aroused, they fill with blood, causing them to get thicker and turn a darker colour. The length of labia minora varies hugely – anything from barely visible to around 10cm is normal and wonderful.

If the length of your labia is causing you pain or discomfort, it's worth going to a doctor. Very occasionally, someone may need to have the length of their labia minora altered for medical reasons, but sadly this procedure is also performed cosmetically.

Clitoral hood

Towards the top of the vulva, the labia minora come together to form the clitoral hood, and underneath this lies the external part of the clitoris. I think this being described as a hood is bloody adorable and often imagine my clitoris as Little Red Riding Hood, tucked up warm, ready to fight off pesky wolves. Again, the size and appearance of the hood varies from person to person.

Clitoris

Ah, the clitoris. The star of the show!

It's the only organ in the human body with the sole purpose of creating pleasure, and boy can it deliver.

The tip of the clitoris varies in size, and is made of spongy erectile tissue that fills with blood during arousal. As the clitoris enlarges, the external part can protrude from the hood, or you can push the hood upwards towards your belly slightly to reveal the clitoris further. That's right, CLITORISES GET ERECTIONS!

What we can see of the clitoris is magnificent, but it's not even half the story. If you're not aware of the anatomy of the clitoris, hold on to your knickers, because I'm about to blow your mind.

The clitoris extends into the body, forming two roots and vestibular bulbs that sit either side of the vagina (I like to think of this as the internal clitoris hugging the vagina). It's around 10cm long when not aroused, and it increases in size when aroused. The internal clitoris is responsible for a lot of the pleasure experienced during penetrative sex, and contrary to popular belief, the G-spot is part of the clitoral network!

The clitoris has been misunderstood, and sometimes straight up ignored, for centuries. Two Italian blokes claimed to have 'discovered' the clitoris in 1559 (although come on lads, I'm fairly sure women were aware of it long before then ...)[7] but it wasn't until 2009 that scientists got a complete picture of what happens to a clitoris when it's stimulated. What. An. Outrage. This just goes to show how undervalued female pleasure has been historically. Fuck you, patriarchy.

7. K. Lister, *A Curious History of Sex* (2020), p. 49

Not Aroused

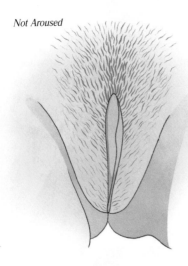

Aroused

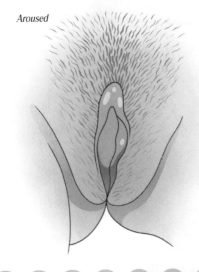

Sidenote: Because so much of the clitoris lies inside the body, there have been great advancements in clitoral reconstructive surgeries for those who have experienced FGM. In many cases it's possible to bring this closer to the surface of the skin, creating a new external tip from tissue which was previously under the surface.[8] Isn't that incredible?!

Also, not to brag, but the clitoris has DOUBLE the nerve endings of a penis. There's a hell of a lot going on in those 10cm.

Put your glands in the air like you just don't care

There are two sets of glands:

- The Bartholin glands sit either side of the vaginal entrance. These glands produce the lubricating fluid during arousal (which we now know isn't the same as desire!), commonly referred to as 'getting wet'.
- The Skene glands, or vestibular glands, are near the urethral opening, and are similar to the male prostate. They produce a milky-white fluid that can be released through the urethra during sex, some of which is believed to make up 'female' ejaculation, or squirting (more about squirting in Chapter 5!).

67

YOUR BODY

8. '5 Years Desert Flower Centre Berlin: The Big Interview', Desert Flower Foundation [charity website], <https://www.desertflowerfoundation.org/en/news-detail/id-5-years-desert-flower-center-berlin-the-big-interview-751.html>

Vagina

The vagina is lined with membrane similar to that in the mouth, and tends to be slightly bumpy to the touch. When not aroused, vaginas are around 7–8cm in length, and when aroused they concertina, which is a process known as tenting. I like to think of my vagina as a happy little accordion that dramatically breaks into song as I get turned on and it expands. The majority of nerve endings are located in the lower third of the vagina, closest to the vaginal opening, which includes the G-spot area (aka the internal clit).

The cervix sits in between the top of the vagina and the bottom of the uterus. It also expands during arousal, and contains loads of nerve endings (far more than the upper parts of the vaginal walls).

> **❝** *It took me until my late twenties to realise unless there's something inside my vagina, the walls are pressed up against each other. Every diagram I've seen shows the vagina as this open tube, so I'd just presumed that's what it looked like!"*

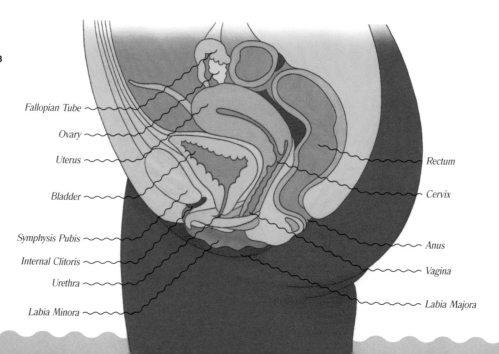

Fallopian Tube

Ovary

Uterus

Bladder

Symphysis Pubis

Internal Clitoris

Urethra

Labia Minora

Rectum

Cervix

Anus

Vagina

Labia Majora

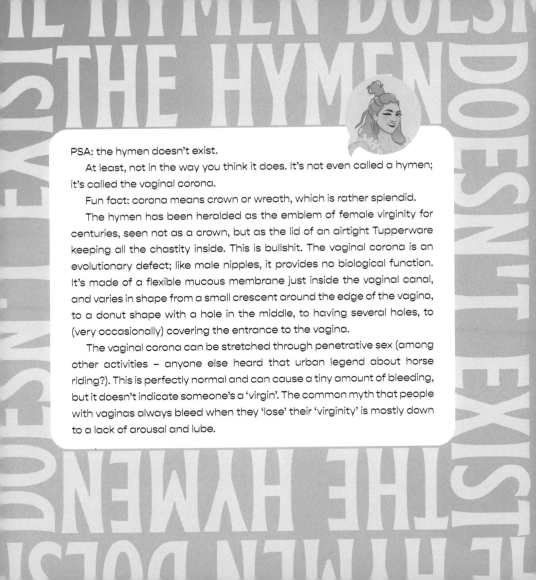

PSA: the hymen doesn't exist.

At least, not in the way you think it does. It's not even called a hymen; it's called the vaginal corona.

Fun fact: corona means crown or wreath, which is rather splendid.

The hymen has been heralded as the emblem of female virginity for centuries, seen not as a crown, but as the lid of an airtight Tupperware keeping all the chastity inside. This is bullshit. The vaginal corona is an evolutionary defect; like male nipples, it provides no biological function. It's made of a flexible mucous membrane just inside the vaginal canal, and varies in shape from a small crescent around the edge of the vagina, to a donut shape with a hole in the middle, to having several holes, to (very occasionally) covering the entrance to the vagina.

The vaginal corona can be stretched through penetrative sex (among other activities – anyone else heard that urban legend about horse riding?). This is perfectly normal and can cause a tiny amount of bleeding, but it doesn't indicate someone's a 'virgin'. The common myth that people with vaginas always bleed when they 'lose' their 'virginity' is mostly down to a lack of arousal and lube.

The Penis

Despite the term 'boner', the penis has no bone in it. The shaft of the penis is made up of two cylinders of spongy erectile tissue. These fill up with blood during arousal, causing an erection. There's a third cylinder on the underside of the shaft, which surrounds the urethra.

At the top of the penis is the glans, known as the head. It's often paler than the shaft of the penis, and is where the urethral opening (known as the meatus) is situated. The underside of the glans is called the frenulum, and contains the largest concentration of nerve endings on the penis.

Shaft

Urethra

Testes (in shaft)

The foreskin is a piece of skin that covers the head of the penis. In some countries and faith groups, it's common for the foreskin to be removed, which is known as circumcision.

The scrotum is located at the base of the penis. It's a fleshy sack containing the testicles, or balls, where sperm is produced. Balls are often used as a symbol of masculinity and toughness, when in reality they are sensitive and delicate. During arousal, the scrotum gets thicker and the testicles move up closer to the body.

Foreskin

Glans

The Perineum

The perineum (commonly referred to as the 'gooch' or 'taint'), lies between the vulva or the scrotum, depending on your genitals, and the anus. Sadly, it can be seen as a bit of a 'no man's land' between two big sexual attractions, but it's a sensitive area and well worth exploring.

The Anus

The reputation of the anus is mixed; it's a very sexy area, but there's no skirting around the fact it's also how poo leaves the body.

The anus is the bit you can see on the outside, and leads to the rectum. There are two sphincter muscles at the entrance of the rectum and learning to relax them is an important part of penetrative anal play. The lining of the rectum is very delicate, and is more prone to tearing or damage than vaginal tissue. The anus itself contains lots of nerve endings, so anal play doesn't have to involve penetration at all – more on this in Chapter 5.

The Prostate

I love love looove the prostate. It's a small gland that produces ejaculatory fluid, and is a source of great pleasure. It sits inside the body of men and amab folks, and can be stimulated externally through the perineum, or internally through the wall of the rectum.

A VERY SILLY FACT: The tubes that connect the testicles with the ejaculatory duct and urethra (called the vas deferens if we're getting technical) have to loop around on their way to the urethra. So when a penis-owner ejaculates, it's like the semen and fluid created in the prostate are on a rollercoaster, doing a little loop-the-loop before they shoot out from the urethral opening! Just imagine the sperm shouting, 'Wooo, look, no hands!' and posing for a photo as they whoosh by a teeny tiny camera flashing in the vas deferens. This is one of my favourite facts about the human body. May it also bring you joy!

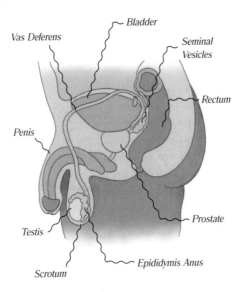

- Bladder
- Vas Deferens
- Seminal Vesicles
- Rectum
- Penis
- Prostate
- Testis
- Epididymis Anus
- Scrotum

Unless you have a penis of your own, it's likely you see erect penises more often than you see them flaccid. While I'm definitely pro-erections, I think we can benefit from consensually seeing flaccid penises a bit more. I find flaccid penises rather adorable: they're gentle and soft and squishy; they curl up among a bed of pubes like a little country mouse. This description might sound like I'm trying to emasculate the penis, and I kind of

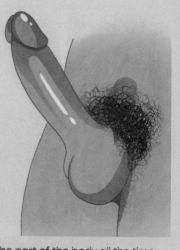

am. I think it's silly that the penis is seen

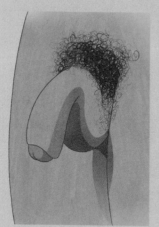

as this tough macho part of the body all the time. Penises are constantly judged by their size and ability to get and stay hard; if I had a penis, I'd find it exhausting. Finding the joy in our genitals in their non-aroused states, and breaking the cycle of them constantly symbolising our stamina or masc/femme energy, is an important part of connecting with them. Focusing on the average size of a penis isn't super helpful either, because it fails to acknowledge the broad range of sizes that go into making that average. Each penis is unique.

Pubes

Surrounding your lovely genitals is pubic hair. It grows on the mons pubis (the happy triangle directly above your genitals), the labia majora or scrotum, and around the anus, and can continue to the tops of the thighs and the belly. It's usually thicker than the hair on your head or the rest of your body, and can be curly or straight.

The current fashion is for people to have little or no pubes. Whatever makes you feel comfortable and happy with your genitals is great, just be wary of making decisions about your body hair based on cultural expectations rather than your genuine preference. I don't think it's a coincidence that I experienced my first orgasm around the time I became more comfortable with my pubic hair – not because pubes possess magical powers (that we know of), but because it symbolised me becoming more confident in my body. I encourage you to try growing it out at least once just so you know what it's like and can make an informed decision about your body.

Pro tip: When you start growing out your hair it can feel stubbly, but if you keep persevering there comes a point where the hair lies flat against your skin rather than sticking out and it starts to feel a lot smoother. Over time, many people find their hair becomes softer.

66 *As a teenager there was a lot of pressure to shave your pubes. Girls at school were bullied for having pubes if they slept with a guy (who btw never got any shit for their own pubes), so the safest thing was to conform. As I got older, I just got sick of the endless waxing and shaving, and partners have cared less about it too. Now I do whatever I want with my pubes. Most of the time there's some hair, I like the way it feels and looks, but when the mood strikes me to shave, I go for that too. It used to be such a big deal, but now I have fun with it."*

Why are we obsessed with BIG dicks?

Why is this considered the most important part of a male sexual partner? A penis is important for some sex acts, but it shouldn't be the only thing we focus on. And while we're here, please can we stop insulting people by saying they have tiny dicks? It's an easy punch to throw, as we've equated penis size with masculinity for centuries, but it's not helping us stop the cycle of body shaming. I see feminist, sex-positive women using the small dick insult online all the time – these are people who would likely be appalled if they saw someone tweet something equally dismissive about someone's vulva/vagina, yet we don't really acknowledge the hypocrisy here. If you do need to insult a man online, my favourite insults to communicate rage without sexualising or shaming someone's body are:

- 'You're a fucking piece of shit' (an absolute classic)
- 'Take my lowest priority and put your agenda beneath it' (ooooh, burn)

It's surprisingly difficult coming up with insults that don't mention sex or bodies – I challenge you to come up with your own!

Love Letter to your genitals[9]

After learning about the genitals, take a moment to send some love to your own. The following activity gives you a moment to reflect and really speak to your genitals, which you may have never done before.

Dear Genitals,

Thank you for...

....

I'm sorry that..

....

In the future I'd like to...

....

....

....

Love, ...

YOUR BODY

9. Developed with Rosy Pendlebaby, as part of Body Love Sketch Club, 2019.

All bodies are beautiful

Let's say bye to our genitals (don't panic, we'll see them again soon) to focus on the rest of the body.

This is not a book about body positivity. But it's impossible to talk about sex without considering our relationship to our bodies.

Bodies are brilliant. I try to spend as much time as possible celebrating the weird and wonderful things bodies, my own and others, are capable of. My path here has not been straightforward, and there continue to be hurdles along the way, but I'm hoping that this book will help you to take a few more steps on your own path to seeing the beauty and power in all bodies.

The impact that a challenging relationship with your body can have on your sex life is huge. In order to connect with someone else's body, I believe you need to be able to connect with your own, and that's rarely a topic we receive guidance on as we're growing up. It's not just about exploring solo sex and generating pleasure for yourself, it's about looking, really looking, at your body, and fostering a sense of love and gratitude for it.

Our economy is based on selling products to improve ourselves, and this can revolve around the idea that your body isn't good enough and therefore needs to be improved. It's an ongoing task to remind yourself that you are in no way lacking, and this is particularly difficult if your body differs from dominant cultural norms. We focus on size a lot, but race is just as much of a factor here, with the bodies of people of colour being othered in mainstream media and large

We often judge ourselves against people whose primary job is to look amazing. They are professionally hot and they have a huge team around them making sure they retain their hotness. I, on the other hand, probably have about 20–60 minutes a day to spend upkeeping my hotness, so comparing myself to them is bloody futile. We must keep reminding ourselves of that.

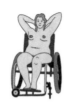

sections of the body positive movement, which is still overwhelmingly white.

I've spoken to countless people who avoid certain sex positions because they are worried about how it will make their body look, who choose only to have sex in the dark because they are scared to be seen by their sexual partners, and who even believe they are not worthy of experiencing pleasure because of their appearance. While it's OK to be in a place where you need less focus on your body in order to tune into your sexuality – I've been there myself – remember that your pleasure is always valid. There's work to be done to shift the perception of bodies, our own and others, so we can all experience an increase in confidence when it comes to the sex we have alone or with others.

I'm a big believer in celebrating nudity in non-sexual ways. In 2018 I co-founded Body Love Sketch Club, a body-positive, clothing-optional life drawing class, with my dear friend Rosy Pendlebaby. During the class, participants pose as well as draw to build a deeper relationship with their bodies. Life-drawing spaces have the power to provide a different perspective on how we connect with the body. We're rarely invited to pause and really look at other people's bodies, or sit still for long enough to feel into our own. The class isn't about being the best at drawing or the most body positive, it's about reconnecting with your body and a reminder to treat it with kindness.

For me, the aim of body positivity is to befriend your body.

Your body is your ally, it's the vessel that carries you through all the incredible and challenging and wondrous moments of human life, and we need to learn to sit with the body, to take time developing a forgiving and empathic friendship with it. Just like a friend, our body is going to piss us off sometimes. We'll feel let down by it, it may not act the way we want it to and will throw us unexpected curveballs; we may sometimes wish it were different. But I hope these feelings pass, and what lies beneath the frustrations is a deep-rooted friendship.

A few tips:

- Unfollow social media accounts that make you feel shitty about your body. Actively follow accounts that celebrate diverse, happy bodies.

- Learn to have a sense of humour about your body. Bodies are weird and hilarious and the more time you spend laughing about that extremely thick chin hair or the way your belly gurgles, the less time you'll have to be so critical.

- If you're having a bad day with your body, fill an A4 page with a stream of consciousness, listing all the things you are unhappy about. As soon as you've finished, turn the paper over and challenge yourself to fill that side with all the ways your body makes you happy. This can be anything from the way your eyelashes curl to the fact that your blood pumps oxygen around your body. The first time I did this it took me a long time to fill the page with nice things, but I felt a huge sense of relief, pride and perspective when I was finished. And after making this a habit, I now find it far more difficult to fill a page with negative thoughts than with positive ones.

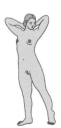

If the relationship you have with your body is impacting your mental health, if it's stopping you from doing the things you'd like to do or is creating a sense of dysmorphia for you, please seek help.

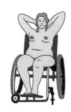

I'm a very naked person: my ideal outfit is naked and over-accessorised. It's absolutely OK if you are not a naked person – whatever makes you feel powerful in your body is great – but if you feel like it, spending time on your own naked can really help you to relax into your body.

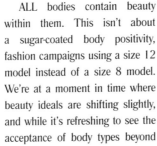

ALL bodies contain beauty within them. This isn't about a sugar-coated body positivity, fashion campaigns using a size 12 model instead of a size 8 model. We're at a moment in time where beauty ideals are shifting slightly, and while it's refreshing to see the acceptance of body types beyond the models I grew up seeing, as a society we still have a hell of a lot of work to do around broadening our ideals of beauty so that no one is excluded.

I encourage you to think hard about how you can reprogramme yourself to genuinely see that every person, every body, contains value and a personal flavour of beauty. A lot of people's appreciation of bodies has a cut-off point, which still perpetuates negativity. It's OK not to be attracted to something/someone, but you still need to appreciate the beauty that others see and experience.

There's no easy answer to feeling confident in your body. It takes patience, dedication and, most importantly, kindness. Try not to be disheartened if you slip back into viewing yourself critically. This is a really challenging thing to face and change, and the path to accepting and loving your body is not a straightforward one. There's no rush, take your time, don't give up – you're doing great.

Boobs, bums and bellies

There's potential for every part of the body to be sexy, but let's focus on these three.

Boobs and bums are simply collections of fat on the body. Lovely fat – and they have important biological functions too, of course (three cheers for breastfeeding!) – but fat nonetheless. Yet from the moment we're born, we're surrounded by the message that boobs and bums are sexy.

Now don't get me wrong, I love boobs – and bums are great too – but try as I might to defend my enthusiasm as a very personal fondness, I have to admit that, like everyone else, my appreciation of these parts of the body is a direct result of advertising and media telling me I should like them. Not only are we constantly told to find boobs and bums sexy, we're told only certain types are sexy. It's a big reason so many of us grow up feeling insecure that our bodies are hideous because they differ from those types, which royally pisses me (and, I hope, you) off.

In reality, the size and shape of boobs and bums varies hugely. Boobs in particular have such different personalities from person to person (even from boob to boob on the same person!).

They may look different at different times in the menstrual cycle and, like the rest of our bodies, they change with age.

Instead of comparing your body to cultural expectations of what it 'should' look like, focus on appreciating its uniqueness. There's no 'should' when it comes to bodies, there is only what we see in front of us.

Most of the time, someone with larger boobs and a larger bum is going to have a beautifully larger stomach too, because that's the way the majority of bodies work. If that's not how they appear (I'm looking at you, Kardashians), it's likely the result of a lot of hard work, and sometimes cosmetic/surgical body modification. Then, of course, there's the media's overuse of photo editing just to create even more unattainable images for us to feel shit about.

So where's the love for bellies? Assuming bellies in all their various glory are undesirable is one of the biggest components of body shaming, and I'd like to see it stopped, please and thank you. With a little reprogramming, you'll see that there's really no reason for them not to be considered an incredibly lovely and sexy part of the body.

Over the last few years I've started to see the beauty and sexual power of bellies – my own and others. This happened through:

- Conversations with friends who felt similarly insecure, making space to unpack all the criticism we've absorbed and seeing just how ridiculous it is.

- Seeing my belly, with its dimples and rolls, drawn as a joyful and integral part of who I am when I life modelled.

- Seeing my belly through the eyes of a partner who relishes it as much as the rest of my body (if not a bit more).

But, ultimately, this acceptance has come from engaging with my stomach a little bit every day. Looking at it from all angles with kindness, feeling how comforting it is to squeeze and squish, enjoying the way it moves and shapes my clothes. If you make a conscious choice to look at any one part of your body as an inherently good thing, you're taking a big step towards loving your whole body.

At the end of the day, it's more about the way you choose to look at bodies than the appearance of the body itself. If you set out feeling critical, you will find things to criticise. If you set out to explore a body, your own or a partner's, with wonder and curiosity, you will find beauty.

In a sexy nutshell:

- The body is so much cooler than you think, and worthy of love. Be your body's most enthusiastic cheerleader.

- The language we use to talk about the body can massively shape our feelings towards it. Use language that makes you feel empowered.

- Regardless of biological sex, genitals are made from the same basic parts and are more similar than you think. The clitoris isn't just what you see on the outside, and it becomes erect just like a penis – spread the word.

- That being said, every part of every body is unique. It's time to celebrate the diversity of our bodies!

So we've got a better understanding of our bodies, but how can we make the most of them? The next chapter is about giving yourself the pleasure you deserve.

SOLO

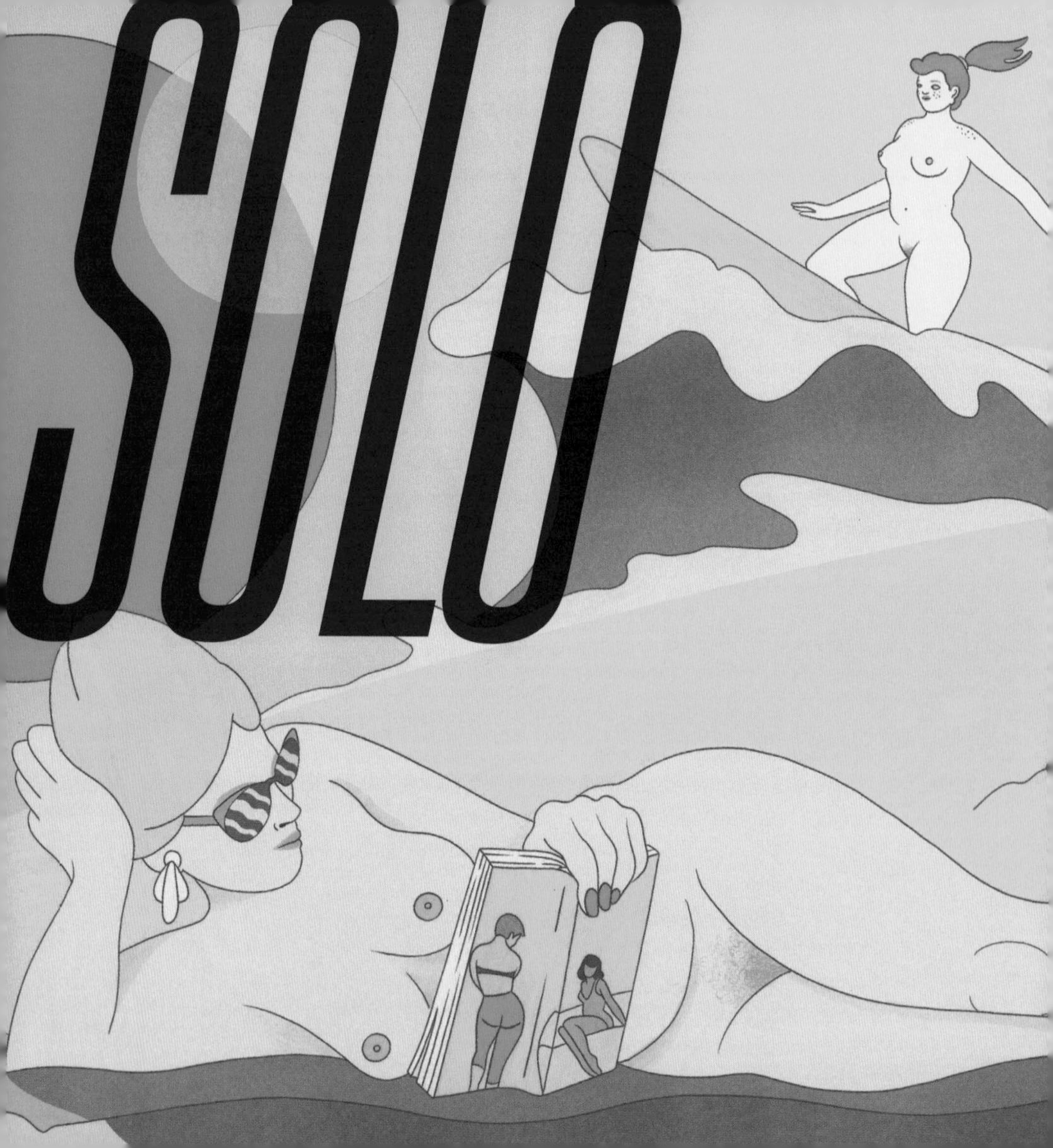

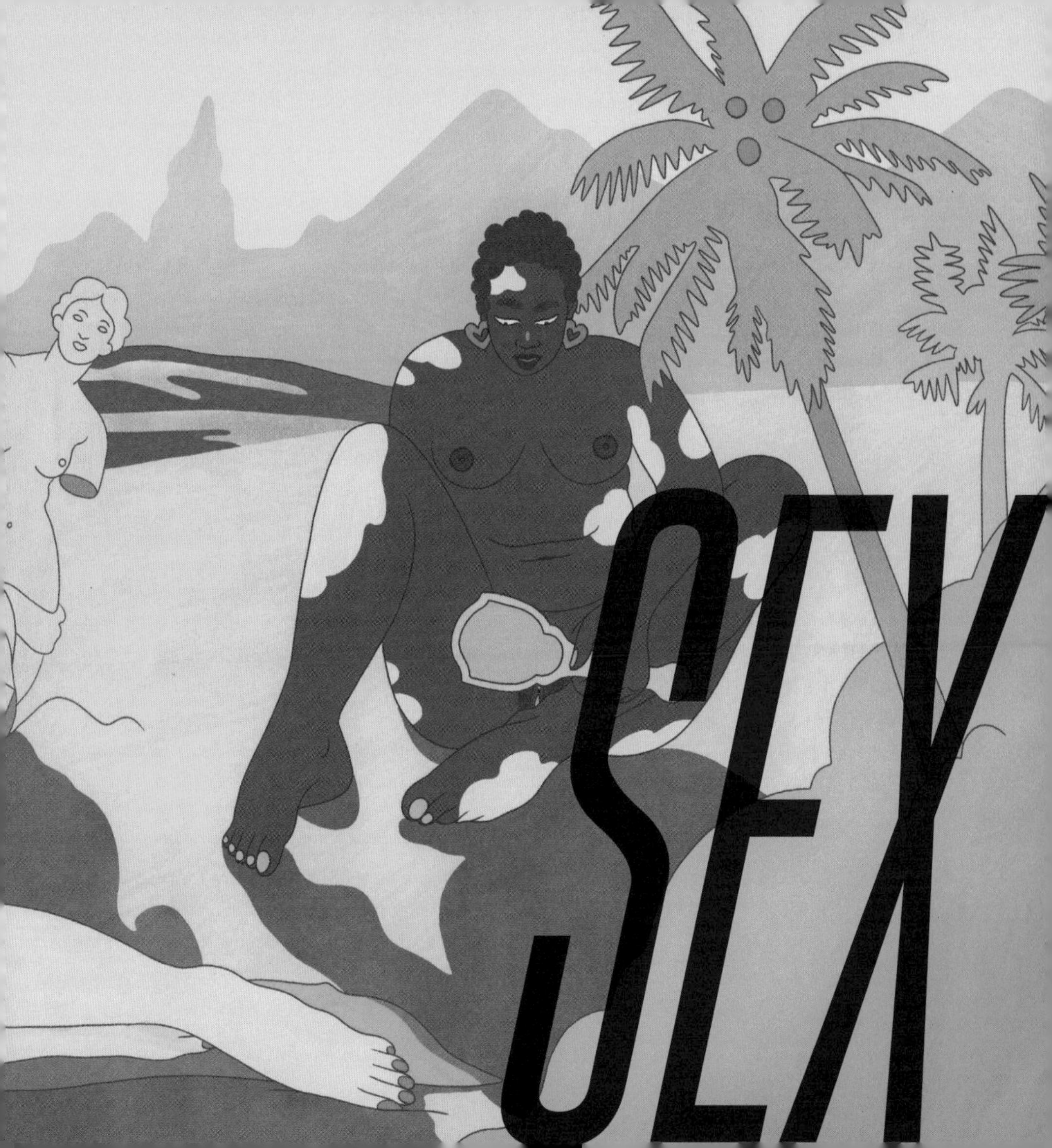
SEX

NOW WE GET TO THE REALLY SEXY STUFF.

Hurrah! Now we get to the really sexy stuff. This chapter is all about how to get the most out of solo sex.

I love solo sex. At its best, it will help you connect with your body; it's a form of stress relief, it gives you space to explore your sexuality without a partner around and helps you get to sleep (we've all been there). Whether it's your first time wanking or you're a seasoned pro, solo sex is valid, safe and very fun.

Solo sex is a brilliant way to figure out the ways you like to touch and be touched in a safe environment. You're able to practise self-consent (more on that later) before moving on to navigating consent and sex with another person (or two, or five – I'm not one to judge).

You can have a valid and fulfilling sex life without anyone else's involvement. A few years ago, a woman in one of my workshops shared that she started exploring solo sex in her late fifties, and that it's hands down the best sex she's had in her life. I loved hearing someone share that the best sex they have is with themselves! (Plus it's also great to know that sex gets better with age. It gives us all something to look forward to.)

There are so many different types of wanks: the really quick one before you go to work, the more leisurely experience when you're bored, shower wanks, the wanks where you decide to make a big thing of it and make luurrvve to yourself, and so much more.

But solo sex isn't for everyone. If you're asexual, or just don't feel like you're ready for solo sex yet, that's absolutely OK. Exploring solo sex isn't a radical act; doing it in your own way is what makes it radical, and that can involve not doing it at all. This isn't about encouraging you to do anything you don't want to; it's about creating a sex-positive space where everyone has the option to engage in solo sex – if, when and how they choose to.

A quick note on language: I love the phrase 'solo sex', and tend to use it instead of masturbation. Masturbation often feels like something secondary to partnered sex, while solo sex elevates the pleasure you experience by yourself so it feels just as important as anything you do with a partner. I also like to use the word 'wanking', because to me it feels silly and joyous.

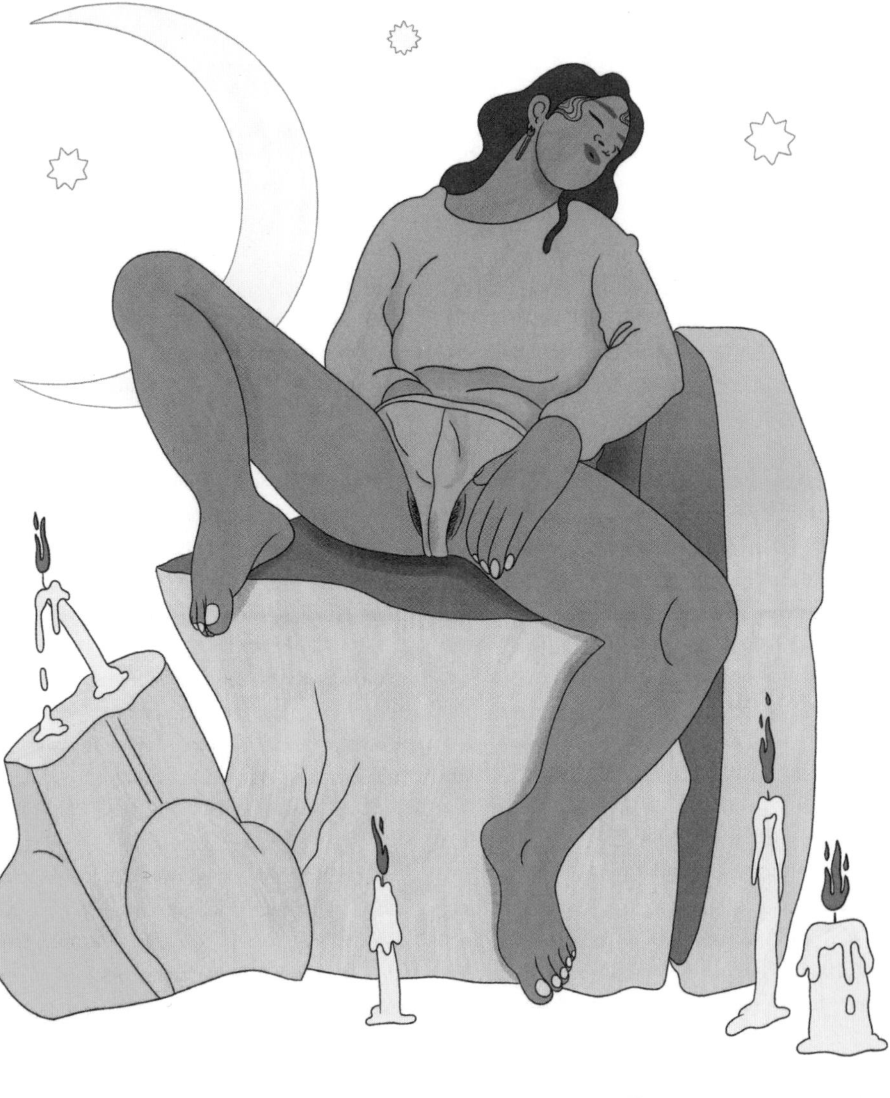

How to get the most out of solo sex: Before

1. Unpacking Shame

Before we get to the fun stuff, it's worth thinking about your relationship with solo sex. Do this thinking well ahead of time – this probably isn't a conversation you want to have right before you dive into your pants, unless reliving early memories of shame is your idea of foreplay (in which case I am so curious, please tell me more).

There's nothing shameful about solo sex. Yet many of us are told there's something wrong about pleasuring ourselves, which may also limit our ability to engage in pleasurable partnered sex of all forms.

It can link back to the messages you received in childhood, and the sex ed you received (or lack thereof). At my all-girls' school, we learnt about masturbation and wet dreams, but only as something that boys did. The pleasure of women and people with vulvas wasn't on the syllabus, and we were raised to deny passionately that it was something any of us were doing. I spent most of my teenage years embarrassed and confused, convinced I was the

> 66 My family's super religious, so all I ever heard about masturbation was that it was evil and anyone who does it goes straight to hell. That, along with the fact I was a closeted queer gal, really fucked up my relationship with sex. I spent years denying myself any pleasure because I thought it was wrong, then I'd 'indulge' and it would haunt me for weeks. It was such a taboo that I couldn't talk to friends about it, I knew I'd be judged.
>
> It's painful to acknowledge how influential this still is on my sex life, but it's important to recognise as I try to move forwards. Therapy's worked wonders, it's allowed me to stop blaming myself for being so destructive. I know in theory I shouldn't feel shame about sex, but it's still not easy putting it into practice."

only person wanking and that there was something inherently wrong with me. Years later, I asked some school friends about it – turns out most of us were wanking, we'd just been too afraid to admit it.

While it's more acknowledged that men and boys engage in solo sex (albeit with the assumption that it's a bit of a sad activity), many women and girls actively deny that they engage in it. And rarely do we discuss what we actually do during solo sex.

While your shame may feel unique, believe me when I say it's something we've all experienced in one form or another. You are not alone.

There is something incredibly empowering about vocalising this stuff. I challenge you to put this book down, head to the nearest mirror, look yourself in the eye and say any (or all!) of the following:

I like wanking

Actually I LOVE wanking

I carry a lot of shame about solo sex

I want to enjoy solo sex more

Socialised shame takes years to eradicate, and for all the work we can do towards that in our private lives, there needs to be a cultural shift alongside it too. More recently we've seen an increase in the visibility of female and vulvic pleasure, but there's still a long way to go.

I encourage you to do your bit to help normalise the topic. Talk to your friends about solo sex.

If a peer had the confidence to do this when I was younger, it would have made a huge difference to the start of my sexual journey. Something as simple as this –

'Can I ask you a personal question about sex?'

Friend gives consent.

'Do you masturbate?'

– can really open up the conversation.

If they say no, it still opens up a conversation. You could ask if there's a reason why and talk about the social pressures around solo sex. (If your friend says no in a way that implies you should feel ashamed, you can challenge that if you feel up for it, or you can end the conversation and try asking another friend.)

And if they say yes – jackpot! This could be one conversation of many where you talk about your experiences and make matching 'we <3 wanking' friendship bracelets.[10]

I know this is a very idealised version of events, but I hope it gives you an idea of how you can approach this topic with friends. If there isn't a confident friend who's going to open Pandora's box and talk about wanking, you may need to be that friend. It will feel scary to admit it at first, but by being honest you're not only shedding shame for yourself, your actions will have a ripple effect and impact others around you too.

10. I'm not saying you have to do this, but it would be really, really cute if you did.

2. Do your Kegels

The pubococcygeal (PC) muscles, also known as pelvic floor muscles, play a big part in our sexual pleasure. Strengthening these muscles through Kegel exercises can create more intense orgasms, an increased control over ejaculation, and has the non-sexual benefit of stopping you weeing a bit when you cough, sneeze or laugh really hard (don't try and pretend this hasn't happened to you).

But – and this is important – Kegels aren't essential for improving your sex life. There's a sense of fear around Kegels because of the stigma that vaginas become 'loose' or 'saggy' over time. As someone who's been in and around several vaginas, I can confirm this is complete bullshit. No matter how many times a finger/toy/penis/fist is inside the vagina, the muscles don't become saggy. If you choose to strengthen the muscles surrounding your genitals to build on your own pleasure, that's wonderful, but this is totally optional.

To locate your PC muscles, try squeezing when you're mid-wee to stop the flow of urine. When you've got the hang of it, there are a few ways to do Kegel exercises:

◆ The classic: squeeze and hold for 10 seconds. Then release and repeat.
◆ Double-time: tense your muscles and release as quickly as you can, squeezing and releasing quickly for about 30 seconds at a time.
◆ Devices like Kegel balls and love eggs can make this exercise easier for people with vaginas, but they aren't necessary. You insert the balls into the vagina and squeeze down on them. These toys come in a variety of different sizes or weights. There are even fancy ones that pair up with your phone so you can track your progress.

Kegel exercises can be done as often as you like, whenever you like – on the bus, in a boring meeting, waiting for the kettle to boil. It's also fun to do them before you have sex as a way of awakening the muscles. For this I recommend doing the faster squeezing and releasing. Sometimes I do this while I'm making out with a partner, which I find really hot.

When you've finished doing Kegel exercises, DON'T FORGET TO RELEASE! Lots of advice fails to mention this, and unless you consciously release, tension can build up in your PC muscles.

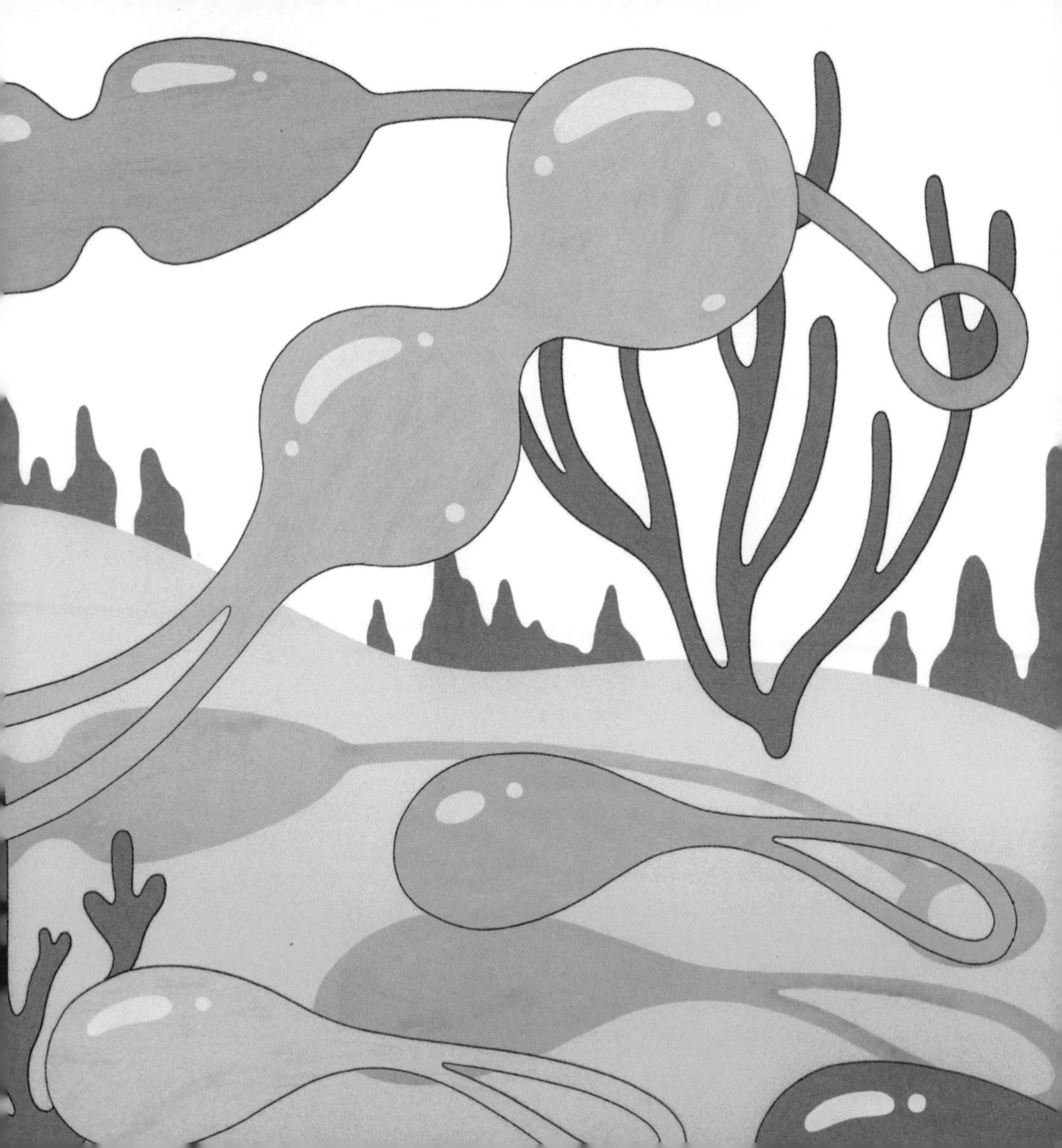

3. Setting the Mood

Once you've given yourself permission to enjoy solo sex, there are some practical things you can do to get into the right mindset:

● Acknowledge what kind of wank you're wanting right now, and match your environment to suit it. A little pre-planning goes a long way: if you want a quickie before you go to sleep, it can be as little as setting your alarm/turning off your phone before you start, so you can go from wanking to snoozing seamlessly. If you feel like treating yourself to an indulgent experience, having a bath before is a classic for a reason as it can really help you to unwind – or find a time when you'll be home alone and have a free afternoon/evening so you can really take things slowly.

● Minimise distractions before you get started. If I have a lot on my mind, I find it helpful to write a to-do list so the tasks exist outside of my own head and I can create some physical distance between them and myself while I'm having sex. And leave your phone in another room. Unless it's to watch porn, screens have no place in solo-sex world.

● Create a space that feels comfortable and safe. If you want to go all out, be my guest and light candles, dim the lights and put on some music.

● Don't rush! Give yourself a warm-up. Start by focusing on the breath, taking a few deep inhalations and exhalations (more on page 133). And before you head for your genitals, touch other areas of your body. If you're in a rush this can be as simple as caressing your belly and hips as you move your hands further down; if you've got a couple of hours to kill, try giving yourself a full massage, from your scalp down to your toes.

● In your head, remind yourself that you deserve to experience the pleasure you're about to create, that there's no reason to feel shame or guilt about it, and that you're doing this to have fun.

Then, you're ready to begin.

SONGS TO GET YOU IN THE MOOD MY ULTIMATE SEXY SONGS

TO GET YOU IN THE MOOD MY ULTIMATE SEXY SONGS TO GET YOU IN THE

MOOD MY ULTIMATE SEXY SONGS TO GET YOU IN THE MOOD

MY ULTIMATE SEXY SONGS TO GET YOU IN THE MOOD MY ULTIMATE SEXY

Love Is a Bitch
–Two Feet

Redbone
–Childish Gambino

Ice
–Alali

Devil I Know
–Allie X

Watercolour Roses
–Ness Nite

Thinkin Bout You
–Laura Jean Anderson

I'm Probably Gonna
Rock Your World
–Logic

Black Cherry
–Goldfrapp

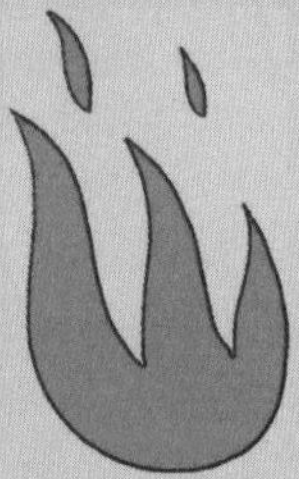

Séduction
–Joanna

Écoute Chérie
–Vendredi sur Mer

Feels Good
–Julia Nunes

Lingerie
–Lizzo

How to get the most out of solo sex: <u>During</u>

1. Finding Out What You Like

The first step of this is learning how to communicate with yourself. I mention this throughout the book, and realise it sounds a bit like I'm having a real heart-to-heart with myself in a mirror. While I'd be up for that – I'm a great date – it's not what I mean.

We spend a lot of time running around being busy people and can forget to connect with what it is we're feeling or what our bodies might be craving at any given moment.

THE FIRST STEP OF SEX IS LEARNING TO COMMUNICATE WITH YOURSELF.

Getting into the habit of pausing to listen to your body is a crucial part of understanding your pleasure. Take a moment to stop, breathe and tune in to what your glorious body is needing right now. Movement? Stillness? Tasty sounds? Warmth? A big cathartic cry? A big cathartic orgasm? There are so many options!

By identifying what it is you're in need of, you're connecting with yourself and making active choices. That doesn't mean you have to act on your wants/needs straight away; I'm not suggesting you have a wank in the middle of your conference call because you've identified that's what your body is in the mood for, but by identifying the feeling, you can acknowledge it and consciously put it to one side until the next convenient time. It's basically mindfulness, but made sexy.

We all need to stop treating these forms of self-care as a luxury; they are necessary for you to feel happy and whole in the body you're in. Give yourself permission to listen to your body and connect.

Exercise: Pleasure Continuums

Figuring out how you enjoy touch is a fun and worthwhile experiment. You won't learn about how your body responds to different types of touch without trying lots of different things. Have a look at the continuums below, and try sliding from one end of the continuum to the other and settling on wherever you enjoy touch the most. I recommend trying this the next time you're engaging with solo sex; and any time you change position, to see what you like.

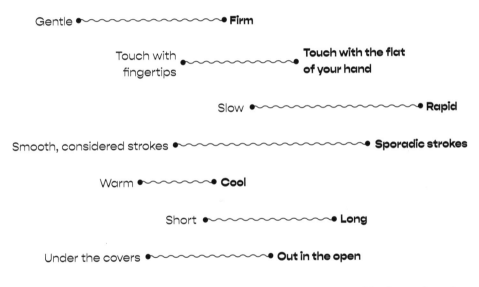

You may find for some you're firmly at one end of the continuum, whereas with others you're curious to experience a variety of sensations. Does your position on any continuum change from time to time, or do you think it would change in partnered sex? During sex, you may find yourself sliding along some of these: starting with gentle touch but gradually building to something firmer.

By reflecting on this, you can enter into sexual situations equipped with more information about how you want to experience pleasure.

Here are some other ideas to get you started:

● Shifting mindsets, from 'I'm touching myself to have a wank' to 'I'm touching myself to give myself a massage, which just happens to be on my genitals' can do interesting things. It invites a broader range of touch, and there's less urgency about the movement.

....
....
....

....
....
....
....
....

● Rather than moving the hand/toy constantly, try holding it in one place and squeezing or pressing.

● Playing with your exposure. If you're entirely under the covers, the weight of your duvet might change the atmosphere. I find that having my head under the covers makes my breath feel more intense – there's something slightly claustrophobic about it which can really turn me on. Alternatively, there's a sense of proud opulence about having a wank on top of the covers, your naked body splayed out with no desire to hide. If the sun shines directly into your bedroom, I highly recommend lying in the suntrap and basking in the rays while you wank.

....
....
....
....
....
....

● Try stimulating yourself hands-free. By squeezing your thighs together, or grinding up on your bed or a pillow, you can create wonderful sensations. For people with vulvas, this is one of the common ways people experience early solo sex, but it's still fun as an adult!

There's some more practical advice for hand stuff on page 140.

Our bodies change over time, so it's worth revisiting this every once in a while as you may find a new appreciation for different types of touch (like how when you were younger you hated olives but now as a grown-up with mature taste buds you fucking love them). And remember the goal isn't an orgasm, it's about having a lovely intimate time exploring your body. Curiosity is key.

95

SOLO SEX

Shout-out to Betty Dodson

Betty Dodson is the queen supreme of wanking. She's 91 years old and has been teaching Bodysex workshops – practical classes held in her apartment, where women learn and masturbate alongside each other – for over four decades.

She's one of the sex-positive pioneers of the women's liberation movement. If you don't know much about her, please set this book aside to do some googling. Then, when you're as in love with her as I am, come back to me.

2. Use Lube

Great sex involves lube. I like to think of it as the ultimate sex toy, because whatever you're doing, a good dollop of lube is guaranteed to change and heighten the sensation.

The notion that you shouldn't need lube to have good sex is outdated and unhelpful. There's still so much stigma around vaginal dryness, and I'm here to tell you it's very common at any age. If you're not wet because you're not turned on, please acknowledge that and pause to figure out how to get to a more relaxed/sexy headspace or if you actually want to be sexual in that moment. Lube shouldn't eradicate the need for foreplay or taking things at a slower pace. But if the juices are flowing in your brain, and that's not translating to your body, fear not, your BFF lube is here to help!

Let's get technical!

There are a few types of lube. There's your classic water-based one, which is condom safe, although some brands dry out quickly and get sticky. Silicone lube is very silky and doesn't dry out as fast. It's condom safe – but avoid using it on toys made of silicone as it can damage the toy. Both can be used internally and externally, and I encourage you to do your research to make sure the lube you're using hasn't got any nasty chemicals in it. (Try to avoid anything that contains parabens, glycerine or glycols. These ingredients can

66 *Even when I'm really turned on I never get that wet, and it's made me feel like an inadequate partner in the past, like my body wasn't working properly. Now I always carry a little bottle of lube in my bag if I'm going on a date, so if it ends well I'm prepared for all sexual adventures – gone are the days of using spit as lube! It feels quite empowering bringing out lube during casual sex, I don't act like it's a big deal and it sets the tone that it's a normal part of sex and nothing to be ashamed of."*

cause skin irritation, bacterial infections and even inhibit the body's moisture production – none of which is going to help your sex life!) Then we get to oil-based lube, which can be great but isn't condom safe! Oil breaks down condoms alarmingly fast, so you'll be at risk of transmitting STIs and unwanted pregnancy.

Only use lube that's designed for sex or is a high-grade oil. I'm wary of flavoured lube. The sugars and chemicals can lead to cystitis, thrush and bacterial vaginosis for vagina-owners. Not what you want.

Use anything from a few drops to get the party started, to experimenting with loads – I'm talking a tidal wave of slippery delight. Notice how this changes the sensation, and be playful with it!

SOLO SEX

3. Embrace the World of Sex Toys

It's a good idea to get to know your body before you incorporate toys into solo play. But if you feel ready, sex toys can expand your sexual play in delicious ways.

There's a whole range of sex toys out there; step into any sex shop and it's like the ultimate 'kid in a candy shop' experience. The industry has boomed in the last few years: we now spend more money on sex toys than microwaves (lol).

A sex toy is basically any object that you use to help aid sex. The first sex toys we encounter tend not to be designed specifically for sex – I spent many nights as a pre-teen humping pillows or stuffed toys, and I've spoken to so many people whose discovery of the shower head/electric toothbrush was their sexual awakening. Be creative with what you use as sex toys, but please be safe! I'd really recommend not using anything internally unless it's been specifically designed for that purpose.

Vibrators. From small battery-operated bullets, to large industrial-sized wands that you plug into the wall, vibrators are available in a variety of sizes, intensities, materials, shapes and prices. There are a number of vibrators designed to be worn during sex, that attach to the vulva/vagina for some hands-free action. While vibrators are primarily used to stimulate the external clitoris, they can be great for perineum/external prostate stimulation. And they have other non-sexual uses: I've used my more intense wand vibrators as a massager on my stomach when I have period cramps, and on my neck/temples if I have a headache (just on the lowest setting, you don't want to give yourself concussion!). Suction toys have become hugely popular in the last few years – they create an air vacuum to stimulate the clit (which means they should really have their own category as they're not technically vibrators).

Anal toys. Dildos designed for anal play must have a flared base. The sphincter tends to tense up and can 'suck up' anything without a base – retrieving toys can be difficult, painful and sometimes impossible without a trip to A&E! Other common anal toys are butt plugs, smaller toys that are inserted into the anus, and anal beads, which provide pleasurable sensations when they are removed as they pass through the sphincter muscles.

Dildos. While they're often phallic-shaped, they offer a whole host of sensations a penis simply cannot. Size, shape, material and weight are the aspects of a dildo that alter sensation, and some dildos vibrate. Curved dildos made of a firmer material will be best for G-spot and internal prostate stimulation. A rookie error I and many others have made is buying a dildo that's too large. The eyes are often hungrier than the genitals, and it doesn't hurt to start slightly smaller than you think.

A harness allows you to wear a dildo, using it to penetrate your partner hands-free. The most popular form of harness goes around the waist and between the legs, so the dildo sits where a penis naturally would, but that's just the tip of the iceberg. There are harnesses that attach dildos to your thigh, arm or face: why keep a dildo where it's 'naturally' meant to be, when you can play around with fucking someone in an infinite number of ways? Again, firmer dildos are easier to use here, and the dildo will need to have a larger base so it doesn't slip out of the harness.

Penile toys. The two main types of toys are insertion toys and cock rings. Insertion toys are designed to have a penis inserted in them. Some toys create a vacuum for an intense pulling sensation, some vibrate and some are made to represent a vulva, anus or mouth, although current trends are moving away from this to more abstract designs. Cock rings are round toys that sit around the base of the penis and scrotum, limiting the blood flow. They provide added pressure on your genitals, which can change the sensations you experience during sex. Some products have a vibrator attached, designed to provide clitoral stimulation for a partner during penis-in-vagina sex (PIV). Cock rings can't 'give you' an erection, but if you have an erection and put a cock ring on, because you're restricting the blood flow it can help to maintain an erection for longer than usual. SAFETY WARNING: Any toy that limits the blood flow shouldn't be used for more than 30 minutes at a time!

SOLO SEX

There's some additional information on BDSM toys in Chapter 7.

Buying the Right Toy

Everybody is different, so it's great that there's such a wide range of products for us to choose from.

Before buying a toy, identify the kind of sensation you're looking for. Do you want something that mimics the way you enjoy being touched (in which case what does that feel like?), or maybe you're looking to experience something totally new?

Sex shops vary widely. I've walked into sex shops and it's felt like entering sex-positive heaven, while others have made me feel like I'm getting creeped on. I prefer visiting sex shops that are femme- or queer-focused, as I'm less likely to feel embarrassed if I know people like me will be working and browsing in the shop. Kink-specific shops also tend to have really knowledgeable and friendly staff. They're the experts, and they can provide amazing advice and help you get the toy that's right for you. Many online sex shops have live chats to discuss products with experts, and they send products discreetly.

If you already own a toy but are looking for more variation, think outside the box with what you already have before jumping straight to new products. Sex toys are just tools; it takes a bit of creative thinking to really get the best out of them.

I encourage you to buy toys from small businesses, whether that be online or by locating the sex-positive shops in your area. And consider the environmental impact of what you're buying.

Products that are made from biodegradable materials will have a kinder impact on our lovely planet, and if you want to dispose of a toy, please take it to an electrical recycling centre instead of throwing it out! And as much as it's liberating to buy sex toys, try to avoid buying them just for the sake of it. Each toy in your collection should have a unique purpose.

Safety

Sex toys that include phthalates (a chemical used to make plastic more flexible) can be harmful for your body and can put your sexual health at risk. Lots of toys are now made of medical grade silicone, but cheaper plastic toys, especially ones with a jelly-like texture, may contain phthalates. It can be hard to tell if this is the case, but if a toy has that plasticky 'shower curtain' smell, there's a good chance it contains phthalates. Using toys made of natural materials like glass, porcelain or metal is generally a safe bet.

Toys and Gender

While toys targeted towards women are more visible in the mainstream than ever, toys marketed towards men have a long way to go. There are some great brands out there echoing the same empowering messages we see with women's toys, but much like solo sex there's still an attitude that men who use sex toys are sad and lonely. This attitude is massively limiting the sexual exploration of men, and this impacts us all. Toys should be accessible for all genders to enjoy.

I have an issue with toys that are marketed in a gendered way, implying toys for clitoral stimulation will be used by super feminine women, and that toys for penises are for super masculine men. The rise in more ambiguous branding is exciting.

Whatever your sex toy preferences, try not to judge others on theirs. There's a trend now for toys to be abstract, moving away from mimicking human body parts or using flesh-coloured tones. There are definite benefits to this – if you're a gay woman who wants to buy a dildo, but everything available to you looks like a penis, that's far from ideal. And these 'realistic' products can lean towards fetishising race, particularly for Black men, and present porn-like ideals for what the 'perfect' genitals should look like. I welcome this new wave of innovative toys, but there are people who may really enjoy more 'realistic' products, and shaming that is shaming a part of their sexuality.

The Future of Sex Toys

As tech industries become more invested in sex toys, we're also seeing a rise in teledildonics, which is basically where fancy tech enables you to communicate touch remotely through toys. It's pretty wild, and we'll continue to see sci-fi-esque advances as the industry grows.

Here are 3 common question I get asked about sex toys:

- ◆ **Can you get addicted to using sex toys?** Addicted is a strong word. You can become desensitised to the feel of sex toys, and may find other types of touch aren't as impactful as they once were. But we're dependent on all sorts of technology in our lives, from phones to contact lenses. I don't see why we should have to be completely 'natural' when it comes to sex. If you feel dependent on a sex toy, see what it's like not using it from the very beginning of a sexual encounter, or try using it in a new way.

- ◆ **I can only have an orgasm with a toy, is that normal?** Again, why the need to achieve sexual pleasure without an aid? Variety, in terms of types of touch or toys used, can be a valuable part of sexual exploration, but it isn't essential. As long as you're having fun, I wouldn't worry about it: give yourself permission to experience the pleasure that works for you.

- ◆ **How do I talk to my partner about using toys together?** I hope by now you feel like there's no shame in using toys in solo sex, and this same attitude should be applied to partnered sex. If you're using toys in partnered sex, think of the toy as a shared tool: involving your partner, or finding toys that can pleasure you both, can be a really bonding experience.

Time to talk about Orgasms!

Orgasms can be surprisingly difficult to describe. Although they are concrete, real, wonderful things, there's also something quite abstract about them because they're a process which is psychological, physical, AND physiological. In a scientific nutshell, an orgasm is a series of muscular contractions and a rush of dopamine and oxytocin. That doesn't sound very poetic, does it? Understanding what's happening to our bodies scientifically is useful, but I think there's great value in celebrating the more romantic notions of orgasms.

There are many different areas you can stimulate in order to feel pleasure: clitoral, internal (which is often still clitoral), penile, prostate, or other erogenous zones (nipples, ears, toes). As part of that pleasure you can experience orgasms.

Orgasms can be frequent or infrequent, from solo or partnered sex, experienced with or without toys, and can range from subtle little hiccups to intensely earth-shattering waves. Orgasms don't need to include the genitals, or touch of any kind. Through breathwork, people can have whole body orgasms. Orgasms can be an effective form of pain management, from the easing of menstrual cramps to longer-term chronic pain. I am constantly in awe of how humans come up with new ways to cum. It's one of our most admirable hobbies.

Orgasms can be categorised by where we feel them in our bodies, or how they are generated. Our sex idol Betty Dodson identifies two different types of orgasm: tension orgasms, which are the result of building tension in your body during arousal and climax, and relaxation orgasms, which come from a longer and slower build-up of stimulation and pleasure. After an orgasm, we all experience a refractory period, a length of time when we're unable to experience another orgasm. This length of time varies greatly – generally, people with vulvas tend to have shorter refractory periods, which can mean multiple orgasms are experienced. By learning to have non-ejaculatory orgasms, people with penises can develop shorter refractory periods and also experience multiple orgasms.

Now, repeat after me: AN ORGASM IS NOT THE GOAL OF HAVING SEX.

AN ORGASM IS NOT THE GOAL OF HAVING SEX.

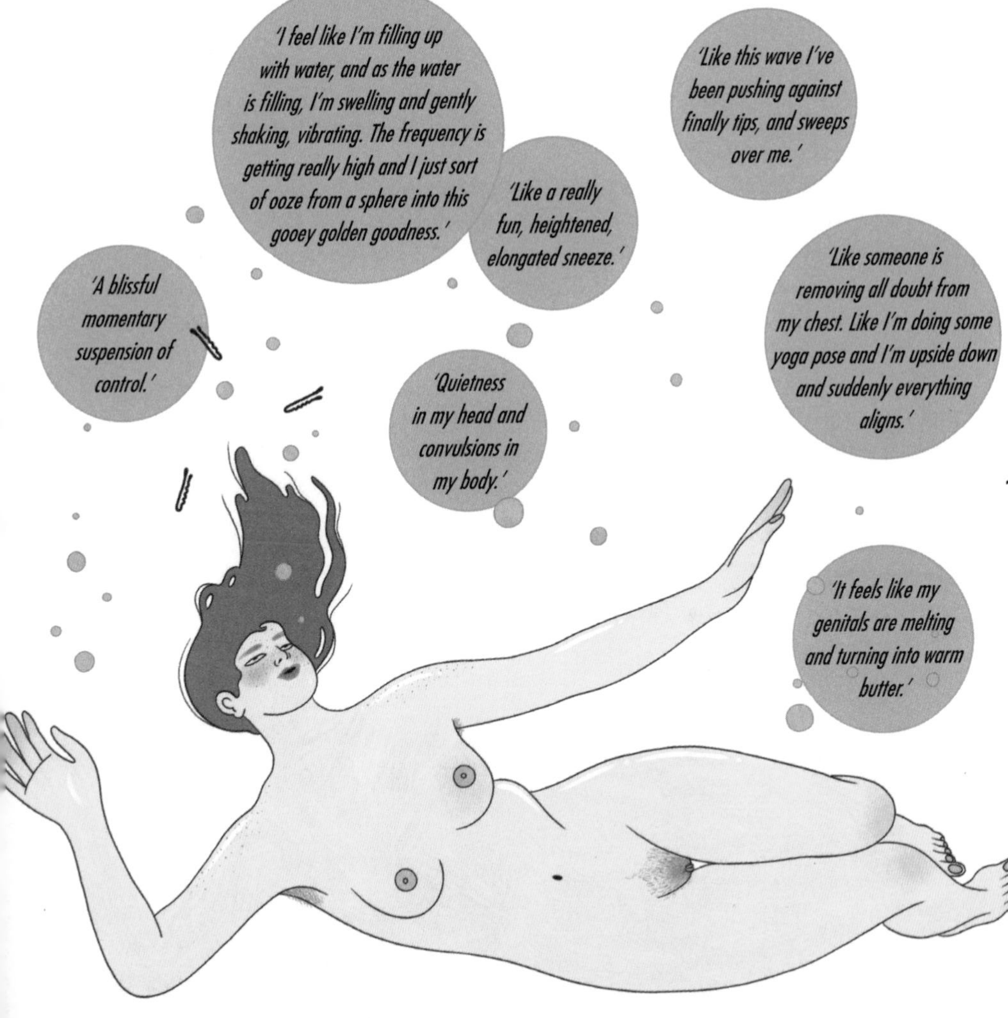
'I feel like I'm filling up with water, and as the water is filling, I'm swelling and gently shaking, vibrating. The frequency is getting really high and I just sort of ooze from a sphere into this gooey golden goodness.'
'Like this wave I've been pushing against finally tips, and sweeps over me.'
'Like a really fun, heightened, elongated sneeze.'
'A blissful momentary suspension of control.'
'Like someone is removing all doubt from my chest. Like I'm doing some yoga pose and I'm upside down and suddenly everything aligns.'
'Quietness in my head and convulsions in my body.'
'It feels like my genitals are melting and turning into warm butter.'

If you've not experienced an orgasm, fear not! While orgasms are a wonderful thing, they don't indicate the success rate of sex. I was unable to orgasm for the first eight years of my sex life, and this is an experience which many people, particularly those with vulvas, have. From when I started exploring solo sex aged around 12, until I was 20, I felt like a massive failure for not being able to have one. It felt like everyone I knew was at an orgasm party and I wasn't invited.

Looking back, a mistake I made was presuming that the harder I worked at having an orgasm, the more I concentrated on it, the more likely it was to happen. Remember the dual control model from Chapter 2? I was so focused on feeding my accelerator when what I really needed was to be in a headspace where my brake wasn't working so hard. When I did experience my first orgasm, it felt good, but it made me realise there was so much pleasure I'd already been experiencing through sex that I'd been taking for granted because I was concentrating so intently on reaching an orgasm.

For me, orgasms tend to appear in my peripheral vision, and if I look at them directly, they often get scared and run away. I've got used to the little dance I do with my orgasms, of acknowledging they're nearby but acting all coy and unaware until they're right in front of me. It's very difficult for me to have an orgasm if someone, myself or others, tells me I should have one; it's like an immediate OFF button lights up inside my brain. And putting the expectation on myself that I 'should' be having an orgasm is the ultimate boner-killer (which is a gender-neutral term btw, given that we can all get erections!).

It can take a while to get mentally and physically in the mindset for orgasms, and become familiar with the pattern of your orgasms. But remember that orgasms do not define your sex life.

Anorgasmia

This is the medical term for not being able to have orgasms. The cause of this can be physical or psychological.

The main advice I like to give is to try and avoid punishing yourself, or making solo sex or any other form of sexual pleasure about getting to an orgasm. Louder for the people at the back: ORGASMS ARE NOT THE ULTIMATE GOAL OF SEX. We've been fed that line for too long, and it's just not true. The sex you experience is unique and valid, and there is plenty of joy and exploration to be found if you take the expectation of trying to have an orgasm off the table.

If you'd like to seek support, your doctor can refer you to a psychosexual therapist, and there's also sexological bodywork, a form of physical sexual therapy.

66

I'm in my mid-thirties and have never had an orgasm. I spent over a decade desperately trying to make it happen – reading all the books, buying every toy – but for whatever reason, I've just never been able to get 'there'. There've been times when I stopped wanting to have sex at all.

I'm still hopeful that I'll be able to have an orgasm one day, but I try not to hang on to that too tight – the expectation is way more damaging than the thing itself. I have to keep reminding myself there's no shame in not being able to have orgasms, I'm not broken and I can, and do, still find sex fun and rewarding."

Creating an Orgasm-Friendly Environment

There's no definitive guide on how to have an orgasm, it takes time and patience, but here are some guidelines that can help:

- Familiarise yourself with your specific anatomy.
- Acknowledge your right to pleasure. Mentally check in with how you're doing, give yourself permission to enjoy whatever sensations you're about to create and remind yourself there's no expectation for this to be anything other than what it is.
- Get in a comfortable position and take a few deep breaths. Some people find being warm helps them relax; figure out what works for you.
- Don't rush, and don't dive straight for your genitals. Take your time easing into each sensation you create, and spend a good solid chunk of time (at least 20 minutes) touching other parts of your body. Not only is this more fun than rushing through everything, but it will help your body acclimatise.
- Try to avoid touching yourself in the way you think you should, instead moving and touching in ways that feel genuinely good in that moment – with your hands or a toy. And see what it's like sticking at it and stimulating yourself for a longer period of time.
- If you're looking for some additional stimulation, my favourite thing to recommend is listening to

an audio masturbation guide. There are trendy apps designed for this, as well as a lot of audio content you can find online. These audio clips are people instructing you on how to touch yourself. Listening to this on headphones feels deeply intimate; it's like having someone right inside your head, and having them guide you through solo sex can take the pressure off you thinking of what to do next.

● Consistency is key. Once you build up to finding a rhythm that works for you, stick to it. Stay focused on your breath, and if you feel the start of a heightened sensation, try to stay relaxed and lean into what you're experiencing. This may lead to an orgasm, but even if it doesn't I hope it'll still result in a lovely, pleasurable experience, which is just as valid.

Thinking outside the orgasm-shaped box

We can really benefit from expanding our idea of climax to beyond orgasms. For example, climax can be reached in different ways if you're participating in a kink scene (which we'll return to in Chapter 7) – there may be no genital stimulation or 'traditional' orgasm, but the feeling of being pushed to a limit can be an incredibly emotional and intense experience, with many describing it as a type of release similar to orgasm.

There's also the release you can experience by being with a partner while they climax. Your body isn't being stimulated, but the connection with the other person's experience can bring about a release for you as well.

And this idea of climax exists outside our sex lives. Having a massive laugh or cry follows a similar pattern to an orgasm: the build-up, the steady or rapid incline, the point at which you feel like you can't control your body anymore – you're laughing so hard your belly aches, you're crying so heavily your breathing is staggered – the sense of release and the slow journey back to earth. These experiences can be hugely rewarding and cathartic.

But if I don't have an orgasm, how will I know the sex is over?

Sex can end any way you like. This can include orgasm, but think of this as one of many options. Sex may end because:

● You have to go to work.
● You get tired, or your hand starts to cramp.
● You simply stop feeling sexual.
● You're laughing too hard about that weird sound your body made.
● You reach a natural end where you're happy with the experience.

By focusing so much on how sex will end, we can limit our enjoyment of everything up until that point.

How to get the most out of solo sex: After

Jumping straight back into 'real life' can feel overwhelming – give yourself time to ease back in. Don't be afraid to give yourself a cuddle afterwards, similar to what you might do with partners after sex.

If you're feeling shame or guilt, take extra time to unpack this. You may find journaling helpful, or anything else that gives your brain time to do a mental cool-down stretch. Remind yourself that what you just experienced was natural and something worth celebrating. If it helps, imagine me giving you two enthusiastic thumbs up as encouragement.

Most importantly, be kind to yourself. Getting comfortable with solo sex is an ongoing process, but don't forget it's meant to be fun.

This chapter in a sexy nutshell:

- Shame is something we all deal with. Half the battle is unpacking shame and learning to feel worthy of generating our own pleasure well before we get into our pants.
- Acknowledging your desire and wanking with consciousness can have a huge effect on your pleasure. Little things done before, during and after can really improve the experience.
- Lube and toys can be absolute gamechangers when it comes to exploring pleasure. Don't be afraid to dive in.
- Orgasms can be lovely, but are not essential components of any form of sex. Enjoy your unique journey; try not to focus so much on the destination.

Partnered Sex

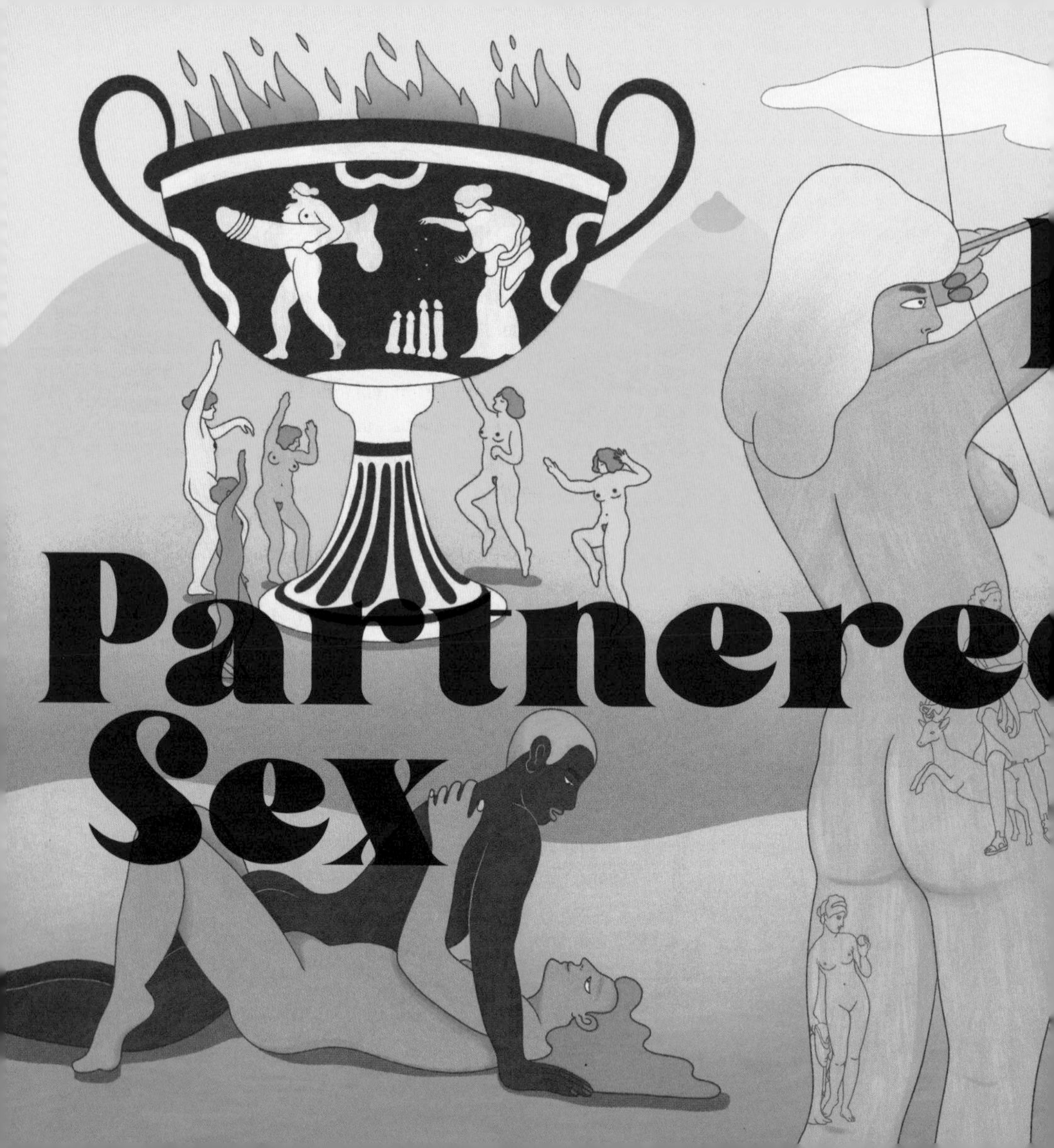

artnered Sex

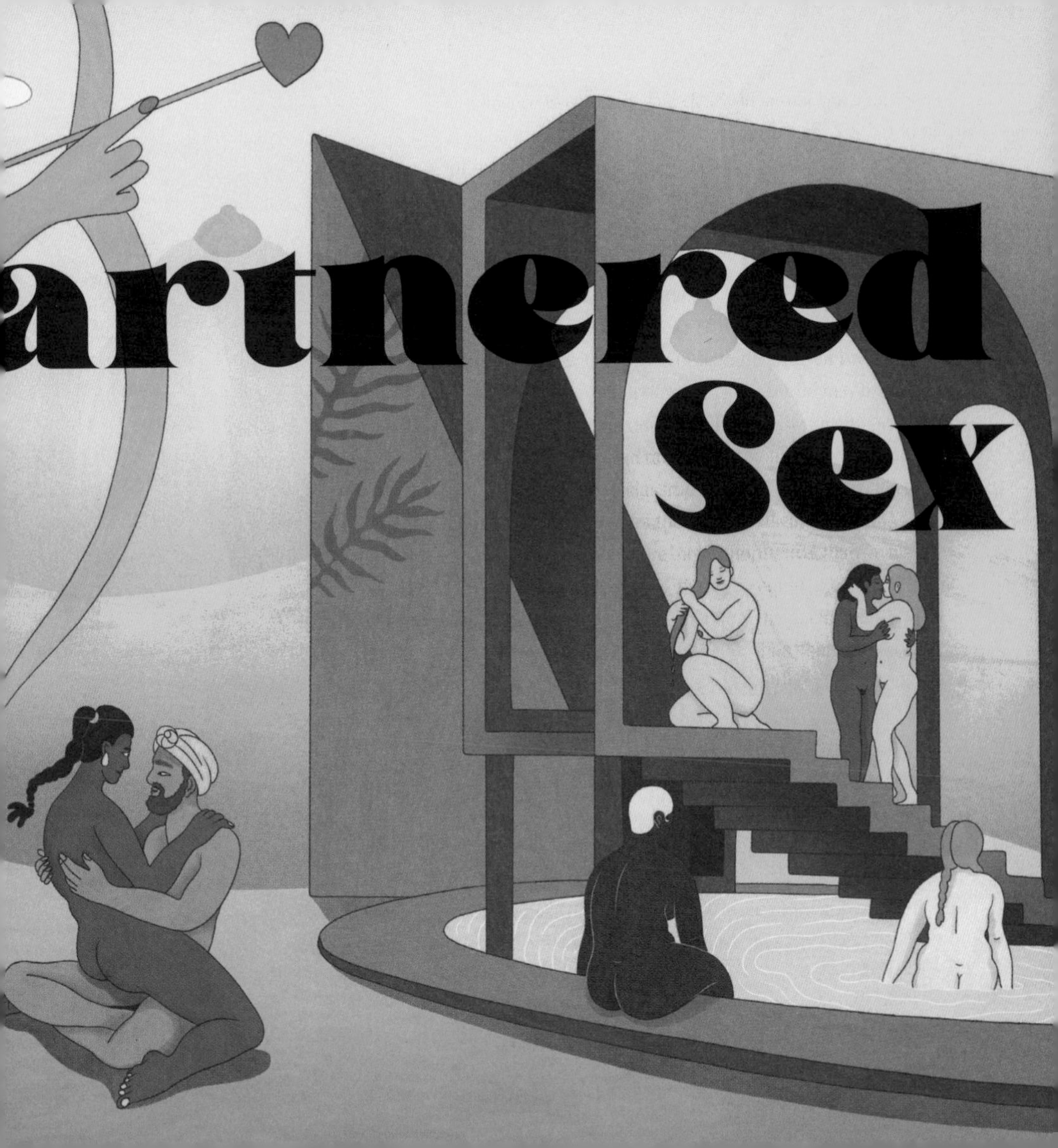

WTF is Partnered Sex?

What even is partnered sex?

To quote a wise woman (me in Chapter 1), the short answer is that it's safe, and it's fun. Exactly the same principles as solo sex, only now there's the added joy of another person to play with! As wonderful as it can be, there's a ridiculous amount of pressure to perform well during partnered sex.

The way partnered sex has been portrayed in TV and film sends the message that we have to be fully prepped love machines with telepathic powers to 'leave our partner speechless', otherwise the experience will be tragic and we'll be ridiculed for it. On top of this, we're handed a formulaic script of what partnered sex 'should' look like, and it can feel like we're doing it wrong if we go off script.

THERE'S A RIDICULOUS AMOUNT OF PRESSURE TO PERFORM WELL.

All of this is bullshit. Sex can be whatever the hell you want it to be.

In this chapter, we'll focus on finding what works for you – and your partner(s) – rather than trying to match up to any ideals of what sex 'should' look like.

Before we dive in, here are my five big takeaways about partnered sex.

1 Understanding your own pleasure, and asking questions about your partners', is the key to great sex.

2 Navigating pleasure-focused consent isn't as scary as you think.

3 Vanilla sex isn't boring! It's actually rather brilliant.

4 Try to avoid having preconceived notions of what's going to happen before you get started, and take the focus away from orgasm. Sex is like meditation – it's best when you're in the moment.

5 It's important to understand the basics, but after that the best quality for great sex is **curiosity**.

Consent

We're starting with the biggie.

Consent exists in all aspects of life, but because sex is so intimate and vulnerable, it's particularly important here. It's crucial to consider what consent means, before looking at when and how you can actively exercise consent:

- Consent is about communication, agency and respect. It's an essential part of sex.
- Consent is pleasure-focused and should be given enthusiastically.
- Consent can be withdrawn, or altered, at any time, and we consent to specific activities: it's not an 'all or nothing' situation.
- Most of the time, we're navigating consent in order to have a fun time, rather than protecting ourselves from danger. There's often more emphasis on communicating what you don't want, when in reality consent is as much about communicating what you do want.

Wouldn't it be great if we were taught how to navigate consensual physical intimacy as children, and were given the option not to hug Great Aunt Mildred, who smelt like cat food? If we all received these messages from childhood, it would be so much easier to understand consent as adults.

Consent is often taught in a way that begins with fear, instead of presenting consent as pleasure-focused. As a rape survivor I know how important it is to discuss this (there's more on being a survivor in Chapter 6). But by ignoring pleasure as a core component to consent, the topic can feel inherently sex negative.

It's great that consent is now included in school sex ed curriculums, but there's still the tendency to massively oversimplify things, and the 'no means no' slogan is at the heart of most education. That's not incorrect: no does mean no. But it fails to recognise the nuance of how we tend to say no to things, or show our discomfort. Very rarely when we're asked to do something we don't want to do (clean the bathroom, call our Nan, go down on our partner or have them go down on us), do we just say 'NO'. We are creative beings, and use language to convey the fact we don't want to in different ways. For example:

- ● Deflection: 'I don't really feel like it right now' / 'I've got a different suggestion'
- ● Excuses: 'I've got a headache' / 'I can't, I'm too busy'
- ● Postponing: 'I'll do it tomorrow' / 'Ask me another time'
- ● Using polite language: 'I'd prefer not to, if you don't mind' / 'That's a lovely offer, but I'm happy doing this instead'

We may also use language to negotiate:

- ● 'I hate cleaning the bathroom. Would you do it, and I'll wash the dishes and hoover?'
- ● 'I can't call Nan right now, but I'll put a reminder in my phone to call her tomorrow.'
- ● 'I don't think I'm feeling sexy right now, could we cuddle instead? Or if you're feeling sexy I could hold you while you touch yourself?'

Negotiation and compromise are important parts of consent, but you should always be OK with the outcome of the compromise.

Sex is all about consent. Every time I say 'ask your partner' or 'talk to your partner' in this book, that is a moment where consent is being exercised. It shouldn't be thought of as one definitive conversation and then you get on

with it: there should be an initial conversation, followed by lots of check-ins, with opportunities to continue enthusiastically consenting, or change/adjust/negotiate or withdraw some or all consent. Communicating consent is something that happens throughout sex, not just before and after.

We also receive messages about consent that are massively gendered: boys are taught to ask for consent, but rarely given opportunities to learn about the value of their own, and girls are taught to give consent, but rarely given the tools to learn how to ask others for theirs.

Alcohol and drugs can limit your ability to consent, so it's really important to discuss your boundaries beforehand. I'd advise not taking a substance you're not familiar with in a setting where you'll need to exercise your consent.

Consent Prompts

We're rarely taught how to exercise consent in the real world, so of course it feels scary when we're suddenly expected to give and receive consent fluently. I hope you find these prompts useful, and can build on them when you communicate consent.

Asking for consent:
- ◆ 'How do you like to be touched?'
- ◆ 'What are you in the mood for?'
- ◆ 'Would you like it if we ...'
- ◆ 'Could you use a bit more pressure?'
- ◆ 'I'd like to go down on you – would you be up for that?'

Giving consent:
- ◆ 'Mhmm, that feels nice.'
- ◆ 'That sounds great, but I've not done that in a while, so I need to go slow.'
- ◆ 'OMG YES PLEASE. THAT SOUNDS SO HOT!'
- ◆ 'Can we start by making out, and then see if we want to build up to you going down on me?'

Withdrawing/refusing consent:
- ◆ 'I don't feel like doing that right now.'
- ◆ 'I'm not into that, sorry.'
- ◆ 'I'd like to stop.'
- ◆ 'This is making me feel uncomfortable.'

Checking in:
- ◆ 'Are you doing OK?'
- ◆ 'How is everyone feeling?'
- ◆ 'Can we pause for a sec?'

I'll tell you what I want, what I really really want

The first step to good communication with someone else is knowing what you want to communicate – which comes from knowing yourself and what you enjoy.

Communication is verbal and non-verbal. When you're establishing initial consent, verbal communication is really important, as it's the least subjective. As you're checking in throughout sex, this can be communicated in other ways.

- Non-verbal noises
- Eye contact
- Body language

I'm sure you've heard about the importance of communication before – but I rarely read any articles that talk about what communicating with your partner actually looks like.

It's good for communication itself to be consensual, meaning everyone involved in the conversation has some awareness that it's going to happen, rather than springing a conversation about your sexual desire on someone. It's also about making sure that you are communicating in ways that you're both able to understand so there are no crossed wires. It's important to let partners know how you tend to communicate, as well as learning about how they like to communicate.

I've seen so much advice (mostly from magazines from the noughties) that suggest surprising partners with new sexual techniques, fantasies or activities. While surprises can be nice, you're denying them their right to consent ahead of time, which is particularly important in a sexual context! Establishing consent beforehand doesn't mean you have to give up altogether on the excitement and anticipation that a surprise brings – you could agree with your partner that, though the activity itself won't be a surprise, the timing will be.

The idea that talking about sex before doing it spoils the mood is a major barrier to navigating consent, and leaves room for miscommunication.

You have a responsibility to communicate with your partners, to get comfortable with your agency and with how you utilise it.

GET COMFORTABLE WITH YOUR AGENCY.

Here are two ways I like to communicate about pleasure during sex:

◆ For all types of touch, use a scale from 1-10 to determine the firmness of touch, with 8 being the ideal. If I ask a partner where they are on the scale and they say '4', not only do I know they want something firmer, but I get quite a good idea of how much firmer. And if they say '9', I know to scale it back a little. Check every so often to see if you need to alter the pressure. This technique also works well for spanking and other forms of impact play.

◆ For internal stimulation, using the numbers on a clock face to identify the placement of pressure works well. 'A bit more to the left' is vague – whose left and how far? But saying 'I like it when you press against 5 o'clock and 7 o'clock' gives clear and specific instructions.

Talk Dirty to Me

Dirty talk is a valid form of communication, and can be instructive as well as really hot. However, if you're not in the right headspace for dirty talk, it can be so cringey you'll want the ground to swallow you up. Let's try to avoid that, shall we?

◆ In my experience, the best kind of dirty talk is simple: describe what you'd like to do or what you're currently doing, and why it turns you on.

◆ We tend to focus on what we can see, but focusing on describing each of your senses gives you more to play with.

◆ If you're looking to familiarise yourself with using sexual language, find an erotic story you like and read it to your partner. It takes the pressure off you having to generate the words/story yourself.

◆ When in doubt, update your partner on your arousal. A simple 'I'm so turned on' works wonders.

There's more advice about phone sex and creating role-play scenes on page 200.

Initiating Sex

If you were raised female, you were probably taught to be passive and docile. But guess what? You don't have to be – fuck that gendered social conditioning! Express your horniness and ask for what you want.

I'm not a big fan of acting coy and playing games, and I tend to be pretty upfront. This doesn't work for everyone, but it does make things a whole lot easier if you just get to the point, and it's empowering as fuck to initiate sex rather than presume your partner will take the lead.

I challenge you to try communicating your desire in the simplest, most direct way possible:

- ◆ 'I'd really like to kiss you.'
- ◆ 'Shall we take our clothes off?'
- ◆ 'Are you feeling sexy?'
- ◆ 'The way you're looking at me is really turning me on.'
- ◆ And most direct of all: 'I'd like to have sex with you right now. Would you like to have sex with me?'

When you use any of these, notice how it makes you feel. If you were nervous beforehand, do you feel any differently on the other side? How did it feel to put your desire out there so confidently – vulnerable, empowering, or a bit of both? Acknowledge these feelings. I promise it stops feeling so scary with time.

Rejection

A common fear is that we'll put ourselves out there, only for our offer to be declined.

I'm actually a big fan of rejection, because it's a clear assertion of boundaries. Someone's communicated their desire, and someone's responded by communicating their boundary – it's far more straightforward than skirting around the issue or avoiding giving an answer.

Rejection is far more scary in theory than it is in practice. Being rejected is a valuable experience much of the time, as it helps you realise it's really not as bad as you thought it would be. Sure, your ego might be a little bruised, but that's nothing you can't shake off.

There's no reason for rejection to be cruel. You can communicate a no firmly without making someone feel shitty about themselves. Again, I like direct statements, communicated with empathy:

- 'No, thank you.'
- 'I appreciate the offer, but I'm not interested.'

Keep it short and sweet, and remember you don't owe an explanation as to why you're saying no. My hope is that anyone hearing that will respect it and back off, but I know this isn't always the case. If someone's being a persistent little twit:

- 'I said no, and that's not up for discussion. Please respect that.'
- 'You're not listening to me, and you're not going to change my mind.'
- 'You're making me feel uncomfortable. I'm ending this conversation now.'

It's good to be prepared for this outcome, and again I recognise it can feel scary being so direct, but it's something you become more confident with in time.

If you're ever in a situation where you fear for your safety, get someone else's attention as soon as possible and ask for support.

Time to talk about Sexual Health

While this book is pleasure-focused, we still need to consider sexual health. So here is a super speedy whistle-stop tour. If you live in a country with access to free and confidential sexual health services (thanks NHS), there's really no excuse to avoid any of this. I've listed where you can find more information on page 220.

Contraception

For the purpose of this section, I'm going to presume that you're having sex for fun, that the sex you're having could result in pregnancy and you'd like to avoid that. Your options are using condoms, a hormonal method of contraception, or the IUD, which contains no hormones. If there's no risk of pregnancy, you should still be using condoms to prevent STIs! But we'll get to that in a bit.

There are many different forms of contraception to choose from. Currently the only hormonal or longer-term contraceptives available are for cis women and people with wombs (there's been talk of contraceptive methods for those who produce sperm for years, but it's still a long way off). You may want something you don't need to worry about for a few years; you may want to have the control to start and stop your method when it suits you. Many people find hormonal contraception has a negative impact on their mental health, which is something to consider before starting one. It's all about finding the method that works for your body and the sex you're having. Head to a certified sexual health website or your local clinic for advice.

Condoms

Condoms don't get the love they deserve, and I'm here to change that. In fact, some would say I am aggressively pro-condoms – I once handed out over 80,000 free condoms in a year (long story).

Condoms come in a variety of sizes and sensations to increase comfort and pleasure. When used correctly, condoms are over 98% effective. Condoms can be external or penile, meaning they go over a penis or toy, or internal, meaning they fit inside the vagina or anus. Internal condoms (also known as Femidoms, but let's not unnecessarily gender vaginas, shall we?) can be put in ahead of time and give whoever's being penetrated the agency to control their contraceptive method – we don't talk about them nearly as much as we should.

Condoms are the only form of contraception that protect against STIs as well as unwanted pregnancy, which is why they're so important to talk about. Some STIs are becoming more difficult to treat with antibiotics, so the key is to prevent them from being transmitted in the first place.

It's OK to slip up and not use a condom – mistakes happen. Don't beat yourself up about it, but try to minimise this as much as you can. And make sure you take precautions afterwards (STI testing, morning after pill if needed).

I'm tired of hearing that condoms 'ruin the moment' or that it doesn't feel as good. It doesn't seem worth it to risk your and your partner's health just to avoid having an awkward conversation or prioritise your short-term pleasure. Penetration is not the only way you can experience pleasure. If condoms reduce some sensation for you during penetration, try using more lube, or focus on other forms of sex for moments of heightened sensation. If it feels uncomfortable to use condoms, it may be because you have a latex allergy. Latex-free condoms are available!

Pressuring your partner to not use a condom is shitty behaviour, and stealthing – where the top (usually a guy) removes the condom during sex without their partner's knowledge or consent – is a form of sexual assault.

Time for a Good Old-Fashioned Condom Demonstration

For external condoms:

1. Check that the outer packaging isn't damaged, that it's in date and has a CE mark or Kitemark, meaning it's a certified product.
2. Push the condom to one side in the packaging, and using the serrated edges, tear open. Avoid doing this with your teeth, as it's more likely to damage the condom!
3. Ensure you have the condom the right way round (it should look like a little hat, with the rolls of the condom going inwards).
4. Pinch the tip of the condom (trapped air can result in the condom breaking), and place it on the head of the penis or toy. If the penis is uncircumcised, gently pull back the foreskin.
5. Roll the condom all the way down to the base of the penis. You're good to go!
6. Check the condom's in place while you're having sex, and if you're having a marathon session, change condoms after 30 mins.
7. When you're finished, hold the condom in place as you 'exit the building'. Tie a knot in the condom so any fluid stays in there, wrap it in some tissue and throw it in the bin. Flushing condoms down the toilet is horrible for the environment and may block your toilet!

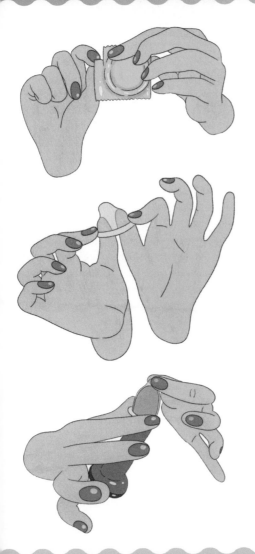

For internal condoms:

Follow step 1 and 2 from the external condoms instructions, and then

3. Squeeze the flexible inner ring (which sits inside the condom), making it longer and narrow, and insert this into the vagina – it's a bit like inserting a menstrual cup. The inner ring should be gently pushed to the top of the vagina, and when it's in place you shouldn't be able to feel it. This can take some practice, but I promise you get the hang of it! If you're using the condom anally, take out the inner ring and insert the condom into the anus with lots of lube on the outside.

4. The large ring at the open end of the condom stays outside of the vagina/anus. Don't worry if the condom feels a bit loose, that's how it's meant to be. And make sure the penis/toy goes inside the condom rather than round the side!

5. When you're finished, twist the outer ring of the condom to keep any fluid inside it. Gently pull the condom out (it helps to keep twisting it as you go), wrap it in tissue and throw it in the bin!

Sidenote: Never use two condoms at the same time – the friction of them rubbing together causes them to break easily! All you need is one condom.

Condoms and Oral Sex

Even though some STIs can be transmitted through oral sex and stored in the throat, and others can be transmitted through skin-to-skin contact, using condoms for oral sex is a hard sell. Technically we should all be using condoms for oral sex until everyone's been tested, but I recognise this isn't something that's particularly appealing.

You have the right to decide how you minimise risk during sex, and you're free to make the decision not to use barrier methods for oral if you so choose. Just make sure that you're getting tested regularly, and try to get a throat swab as part of your testing package.

Other 'Barrier' Methods

You can also use latex gloves for any hand stuff to further limit the risk of transmitting STIs.

Dams are thin sheets of latex or polyurethane which can be placed on the vulva or anus during oral sex. They are available from some sexual health clinics, but there's currently little research to verify how effective they are at preventing STIs.

Sexual Health for Queer Women

STI information for lady-loving ladies, non-binary cuties and afabs is scarce. Even though it's less likely for STIs to be transmitted than during cis-hetero sex, there is still a risk, and it's your responsiblity to minimise it. And odd fact alert: if you and your partner are menstruating at the same time, you're more likely to transmit STIs!

Emergency Contraception:

If you've had unprotected sex or something's gone wrong with the contraception you were using, there are two options to avoid pregnancy:

- **Emergency hormonal contraception (EHC)**: Commonly known as the morning after pill, there are two types you can take, one that's effective for three days after sex and one that's effective for five (but the sooner you take it the better!). It's available in clinics, pharmacies and GPs. The health professional will need to ask you a few questions and may ask you to provide information on where you are in your menstrual cycle to ensure the pill will be effective. While EHC is safe to use, it should only be used for emergencies – please don't use this as your sole form of contraception!

- **Having an IUD fitted**: IUDs are used as regular contraception, but if fitted up to five days after unprotected sex it's also the most effective form of emergency contraception (again, the sooner it's fitted the better!). You need to go to a clinic to have it fitted, but once it's in it lasts for five or ten years.

Abortion

Abortion is more common than you think – one in three women in the UK have had one or more abortions in their lifetime, but many people choose to keep it private. In the UK[11], abortion is legal up to 24 weeks, and is a safe procedure (although like all medical procedures, there is some risk). Between 2008–2018, 90% of all abortions carried out in England and Wales took place before 13 weeks.[12]

It can be a difficult decision to make, but know that you're not alone and there are services out there that can support you. It's a good idea to ask for support from your partner, friends or a family member, but remember the decision is completely up to you.

If you find out you're pregnant and don't wish to be, contact your GP or local clinic as soon as possible. In most cases you'll need to be referred by the NHS to an abortion service. Health professionals are there to provide factual information, and should never try to influence your decision.

> 66 *I was not prepared for how long it took me to decide to have an abortion. I always thought my liberal beliefs would mean that I'd know exactly what to do, but it was still so unclear. It was such a difficult decision to make, and the nature of the process means it takes a while to come to terms with it, but it was the right thing to do for me.*
>
> *I had incredibly meaningful support from my friends, which enabled me to tell my religious mother. Her initial reaction was worse than I thought it could be, but fast forward two days later and she became my rock – people's initial reactions are often out of shock, and not the same as how they'll think long term.*
>
> *The fact that it's such a politicised issue made it emotionally exhausting – I wish I'd been able to process everything on my own, instead of having to deal with religious protesters outside the clinic, and seeing access to abortion debated on the news. I'm not a statistic for politicians to have futile debates over."*

11. As of March 2020, abortion is now legal in Northern Ireland up to 12 weeks, and up to 24 weeks when continuing the pregnancy would risk mental or physical injury to the person in question.

12. 'Abortion Statistics, England and Wales: 2018', Department for Health & Social Care, <https://assets.publishing.service.gov.uk/government/uploads/system/uploads/attachment_data/file/808556/Abortion_Statistics__England_and_Wales_2018__1_.pdf>

STIs

STIs are bacterial or viral infections that can be transmitted through sex. Anyone can get an STI, and they don't always have symptoms, which is why regular STI testing is an essential part of a healthy sex life!

You should be getting tested every six months, but it's a good idea to get tested after each sexual partner, especially if you didn't use a condom. Testing may involve a urine sample, swabs (vaginal, anal, oral or penile) and a blood test. A doctor will only need to look at your genitals if you're showing symptoms of an STI. There's a two-week window after a sexual experience when most STIs don't show up on tests. For HIV and syphilis this goes up to 12 weeks. But if you think you've come into contact with HIV, head to a clinic asap as you can be given PEP, a preventative medication which can stop the virus being transmitted.

~~~~~~~~~~

Sidenote: PrEP is a medication that reduces the risk of getting HIV. If you're interested, ask for more information at your sexual health clinic.

~~~~~~~~~~

If you're feeling nervous about getting tested, ask a good friend to come along with you. It's also worth letting the clinic staff know how you're feeling – they deal with nervous patients every day and will be able to guide you through the process. In some areas you can now access free and discreet self-testing kits sent directly to your door, which makes the process of getting tested even easier.

Talking to partners about testing might feel weird at first, but it's not an indication that someone has had a lot of partners (although why would that be bad?) or that they're 'dirty'. You'll feel so much better for communicating openly – and the fact you're not worrying about your health during sex frees up space to focus on pleasure.

66 *When I was first told I had herpes, I felt so much shame. I lay in the consultation room, jeans around my ankles, thinking my sex life was over."*

Prompts to talk to a partner:
◆ 'When was the last time you were tested?'
◆ 'I haven't been tested for a few months. Should we go to the clinic together?'

Having an STI is not ideal, but it's not the end of the world and certainly isn't the end of your sex life. Most STIs can be cured, and the advancements in treatment for those that can't is amazing. If you're living with an STI, it's best to tell a potential partner before you have sex – partly so they know exactly what they're consenting to, but also in case they lash out at you. If this happens, bin them and walk away.

First Time

The notion of 'losing your virginity' is ridiculous, and possibly the biggest myth that impacts our sex lives. You can't lose sex. It's not the kind of thing that gets stuck down the back of the sofa or falls into a drain. Provided it's consensual and pleasurable, you're gaining a whole new experience, which should be celebrated. And so often virginity means a vagina that hasn't had a penis inside it, or a penis that hasn't entered a vagina, which gives penetration an unjust sense of significance above all the other sexy stuff you can do, as well as excluding the people who are not interested in, or struggle to engage with, PIV sex.

You have the opportunity to redefine what virginity means to you. The first time I had PIV sex, it was spectacularly underwhelming. We were both teenagers, we had no idea what we were doing, and I was having 'real sex' because I wanted to prove something rather than to simply explore my pleasure. I don't want to remember that as my sexual debut, and guess what: I don't have to! Before then, I'd experienced solo sex and had enjoyed long make-out sessions and sexy hand stuff, both of which were far more pleasurable than my first try at PIV.

With this in mind, consider how you'd like to define your first time:

Would your attitude to sex change if you considered every time you had sex with someone new to be a 'first time'? Or even broader, if every time you had sex was thought of as a first? We are constantly changing beings, and every time you enter a sexual space, alone or with others, it's a new experience. This might add unnecessary pressure for some (feel free to ignore this if it makes you panic!), but for me it massively helps.

So how do you know if you're ready to have sex – for the first time ever, or the first time with a new partner? Here are some questions to ask yourself that may indicate you're in a place to be sexual with this person:

Do you want to be sexually intimate with them?

Do you think you're wanting to have sex for similar or compatible reasons?

Do you communicate well? Are you able to give and receive consent?

Do you get the feeling that this person is interested in your own pleasure as well as their own?

And (this is a weird one, bear with me) are you able to laugh with them? Sex is unpredictable, sometimes things go a bit wrong. It really helps to be comfortable enough to laugh with your partner when these things come up, and from experience it's a good indicator of whether the sex will feel safe and joyful. This was the first meaningful piece of sex advice I ever gave; it's what I told my sister before she had sex, and I still feel proud of it.

Have you spoken about boundaries, contraception, and STIs, and do you feel (relatively) comfortable discussing these with that person?

For casual sex this doesn't need to be super in-depth, but you do still need to cover the basics.

Most importantly, when the opportunity to have sex arises with the person in question, ask yourself, **'Do I actually want to do this right now?'** If you like the idea of having sex with them, but are not feeling like acting on it at that moment, that's totally OK!

Simple ways to
make sex better

I'm bored of the notion of 'spicing up your sex life', firstly, because 'spicy' isn't necessarily what makes for good sex, and secondly, because this advice often recommends sticking something novel (a new location or technique, a blindfold, a different lube) on top of the standard formula for sex – kissing, foreplay, penetration, orgasm finale, end scene. It's boring, and it fails to unpack any deeper issues at the core of sex. New activities can be great fun, but unless the foundational work is done on understanding our bodies

I'M BORED OF THE NOTION OF 'SPICING UP YOUR SEX LIFE'

and desires and communicating effectively with partners, it's like rolling a turd in glitter.

When we want to spice things up, we are encouraged to change where we have sex rather than how we have sex. A classic 'spice up your sex life' tip is to take your sexual play 'out of the bedroom'. If this is a kink of yours, go for it, but it's not advice that suits everyone. Most people have sex in their bed because it feels safe, comfy and private. If these are the elements that you need in order to feel sexual, it's absolutely OK to only have sex in places that tick these boxes.

1 Consensual touch given with care and curiosity is always going to contribute something nice to a sexual experience. Not every movement you make needs to blow their mind.

2 If you have a vulva, WEE AFTER SEX! Cystitis is possibly the worst feeling in the entire world, and I wouldn't wish it on my worst enemy. As much as you want to stay in bed and cuddle, get up and wee asap; your urethra will thank you later.

3 Embrace the mess. Lube, cum, discharge, squirting, period blood – there are lots of fluids flying around and that's a part of sex. Fanny farts happen, and you might get so sweaty you drip sweat directly into your partner's eye (true story) – celebrate all of this in its weird and wonderful glory.

4 I don't care what anyone says, sex with socks on is the shit. Keeping your feet warm improves blood flow, and studies have suggested it's easier to orgasm while wearing socks.

5 Ditch the operatic performances, and embrace the *genuine* noises you make during sex. There are times when sex needs to be on the quieter side, but when you're home alone allow yourself to express your pleasure vocally! Embrace the guttural sounds your body wants to create – they're primal and delicious.

6 Try not to worry about looking hot! Nobody looks hot all the time – this doesn't need to be an airbrushed performance. Embracing the fact that 99.9% of the population has a double chin during sex is liberating as fuck.

7 Turn off your phone – there's nothing like the buzz of a WhatsApp message coming through to really snap you out of the zone, and I shudder to think about what could happen if you're in a large group chat.

8 People can look so bloody serious when they're fucking. While I don't want to be accused of telling anyone to smile (oh god, have I become the patriarchy?), reminding yourself to smile and laugh during sex can be transformational. Sex is supposed to be fun, so expressing that through your face and body language makes sense to me.

Kissing

I fucking love kissing. There's so much joy to be had in making out like horny teenagers again. It's the foundation to great sex, but is often overlooked in sex advice.

Some basic guidelines:

KISS WITH CURIOSITY.

Kiss with curiosity. This may be the first time you're getting really intimate with someone – honour that with a curious mind and a playful attitude.

DON'T RUSH.

Don't rush. Going from 0 to 60 is fun on a racetrack, but alarming in your mouth. Even if you want your kissing to lead somewhere rough and passionate, start off gently.

LIPS LOCKED OR OPEN.

You can kiss with your lips locked together, or with your mouths slightly open – this allows you to breathe through your mouth as well as your nose, and the heat of someone's breath while you're kissing can add another sensation.

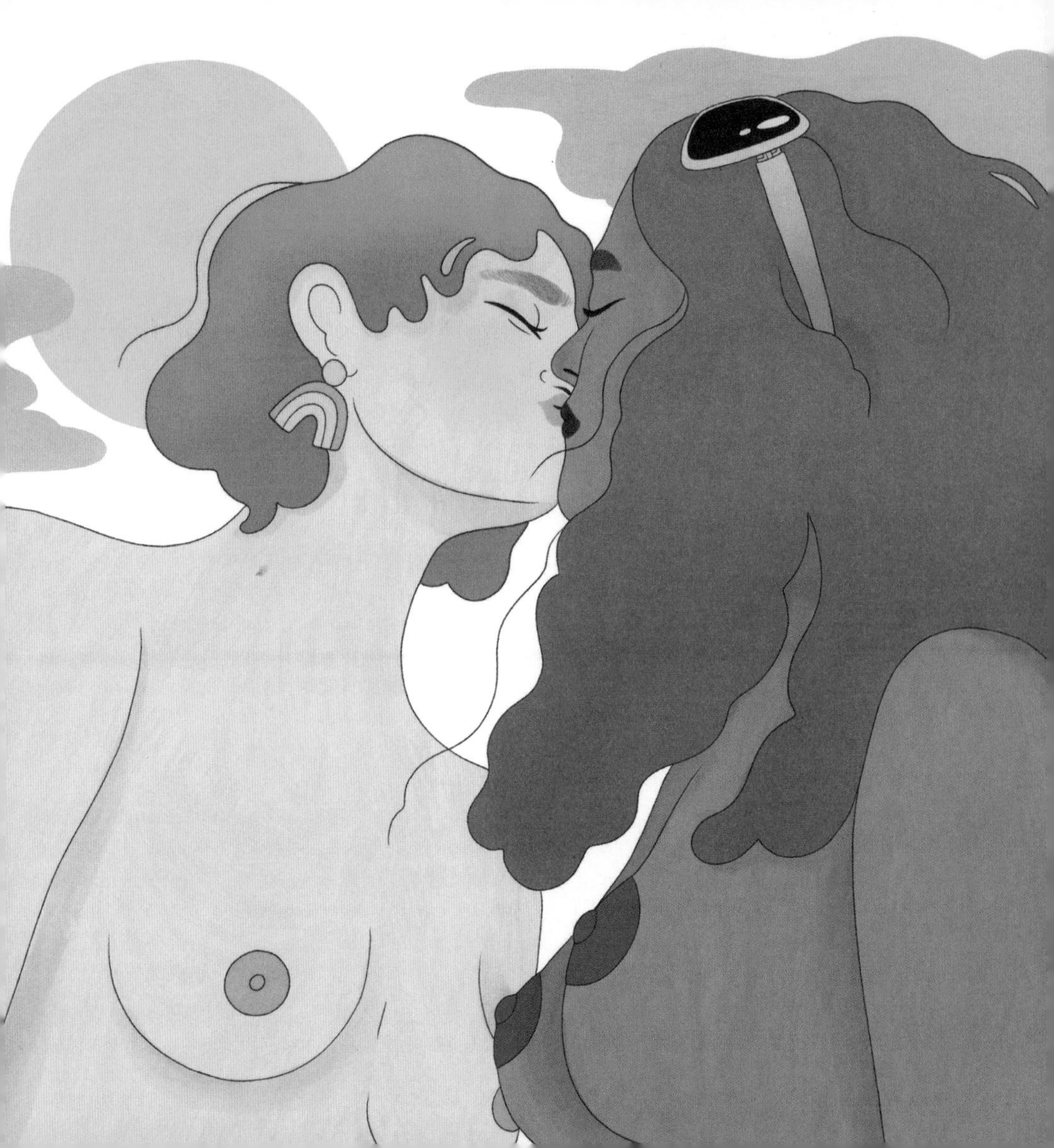

NIBBLING.

Nibbling your partner's lips can be fun. Start softly and gauge their reaction before moving on to anything firmer. If you enjoy more intense biting, either giving or receiving, verbally communicate that to your partner before you dive in.

BEWARE OF TEETH.

Be wary of your teeth. If they mash together, laugh about it and move on. It happens to everyone every once in a while.

NO REPETITIVE MOVEMENTS.

When you're using your tongue, avoid repetitive movements (no 'washing machine' action), and please don't stick your tongue too deep into your partner's mouth – you shouldn't be feeling tonsils. A pointy, jabby tongue is rarely a fun sensation when it's in your mouth, nor is a limp tongue that, upon entry, just kind of sits in your mouth like a sad, lost toy.

A 'bad kiss' can be down to shoddy technique, but I find it's often because someone is kissing in a way that doesn't fit with the current setting. I've had first kisses where they go in with way too much intensity and wild slobberish abandon for me, which felt out of context in a quiet pub on a Wednesday. I love that kind of kissing, but it's far better suited to being at the height of sex, where you're all sweaty and messy and pressed up against each other and your tongues are flying all over the place.

The possibilities of kissing are endless, and like all acts it's subjective – what I like and what you like could vary massively. Often your partner will give you a lot of information about how they'd like to be kissed through the way that they kiss you, and you can do the same in return. Kissing is a form of communication, with both of you contributing to the conversation.

Breath

I don't need to tell you why breathing is important, but it often goes unnoticed when we're being sexual.

We don't all breathe at the same rate, but tuning into our breath and allowing it to be an active part of sex can be really rewarding. Fun breath fact: while inhaling takes muscular effort, exhaling is a result of relaxation. So when you're trying to relax, focus on breathing out.

Here are some ways you can consciously alter the way you breathe during sex:

66 *I dated a guy who was really into breathing together during sex. We'd sync up our breath, and it was like we were absorbing each other's air. It made everything feel primal and intense, and my orgasms were way stronger – give it a try!"*

- ♦ **Extending your exhalation.** Breathe in for a count of 4, hold for a moment, then breathe out for 6. Give this a go right now, and you should feel calmer and more centred. This is a great thing to do before sex, as a way of getting you into a more relaxed and focused headspace.
- ♦ **During partnered sex, try breathing together.** This can be either following the same breath pattern, or doing alternate patterns (one of you exhales as the other inhales). This is basically a bit of tantric breath play, which we'll touch on again in Chapter 7.
- ♦ **Speeding up the breath.** If it's safe for you to do so, you can try consciously breathing at a faster rate, either before or during sex. Focus on pushing out the breath more than sucking it in, as the inhalation comes more naturally with this one, and see how quickly you can move the breath. When I practise this, I try to engage my PC muscles (that's your pelvic floor, remember), squeezing them when I exhale. This is known as 'fire breath' and makes me feel powerful and switched on.

PSA: choking can be really bloody dangerous. It's become more normalised in recent years, but I recommend simulating choking rather than actually limiting someone's breath. More on this in Chapter 7 (page 205).

Erogenous Zones

For many of us, arousal and desire build slowly, so as a general rule try not to dive straight for someone's pants. Erogenous zones are sensitive parts of the body that, when stimulated, can get us feeling sexy. There's no definitive list as we all have personal preferences, but here are some ideas to get you started:

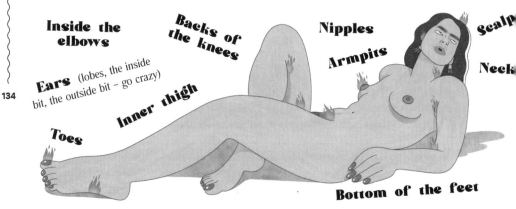

Inside the elbows

Backs of the knees

Nipples

Scalp

Ears (lobes, the inside bit, the outside bit – go crazy)

Armpits

Neck

Inner thigh

Toes

Bottom of the feet

You can always look up the cortical homunculus again for inspiration!

When you're exploring these areas, this can be through kissing, nuzzling and licking, touch (from gentle to firm) and breath. Your partner may already know some of the areas that get them going, and you can make an activity of going on a treasure hunt across their body to find any new spots.

Right, *now* it's time to dive into our pants – woooo! Take the following advice as a jumping-off point more than a list of definitive instructions.

Communicate with your partner regularly, try out different techniques and see what feels good for both of you, and I hope your curiosity leads to developing your own techniques. And remember, lube makes everything better!

External Clitoral Stimulation

It's the return of my anatomical BFF! We're focusing on the external glans here, but remember that's just part of the story. The internal parts of the clitoris are responsible for a whole host of other pleasurable delights.

Don't head straight for the clit. Why rush? Massage the whole vulva, starting gently, but building up to quite a firm pressure.

There are lots of different techniques you can try here. I'd avoid trying all of these in rapid succession – that might feel a little alarming! Take your time with each one:

- ♦ Move your fingers up and down, side to side, or in circles. Play around with varying the pressure of your touch.
- ♦ Keep your hand in one place and use a tapping or pressing motion on the clit.
- ♦ Place two fingers on either side of the clitoris, squeeze gently and move up and down to jerk off the clit. This stimulates the top of the internal clitoris, which isn't always explored.
- ♦ If you're using a toy, play around with the different settings, and try holding the toy in one place as well as moving it around.
- ♦ Ask your partner to show you what they like – they're the experts! I like it when a partner puts their hand on mine and guides me, it feels super intimate to both be following the same rhythm.

Some people find their clitoris is very sensitive, and direct stimulation can feel overwhelming or even painful. For this, try gentle strokes, using the clitoral hood as a barrier between the clitoris and your hand. It's also a good idea to use a wider surface area, like the palm of your hand or several of your fingers lying flat, as using the tips of your fingers can feel too intense.

Of course, for others that direct and intense stimulation is just what they like! You can push up the clitoral hood to expose the clitoris and touch it directly, or stimulate through the hood with increased pressure.

Fingering

If there's anything that's going to persuade the masses that a big dick isn't the most highly prized sexual tool, it's fingering. The variety of touch you can achieve is amazing! As a teenager, fingering consisted of a fairly underwhelming in and out motion, which I think gives it a bad reputation. When you're using your fingers you're not trying to imitate a dick: fingers are so much more dexterous, and you can really utilise that. (We'll focus on vaginal play here, but fingering can also be a wonderful part of anal play.)

Best to have your nails short for this, although I have slept with a few people who manage to pull this off with glamorous long nails.

Note! You're going to be able to reach different angles depending on if you're lying side by side or if you're facing the vulva 'head on'.

Most nerve endings in the vagina are located in the lower third, towards the vaginal opening, so the aim isn't to see how deep you can get. Like all internal stimulation, it's always a good idea to have some sort of foreplay before you venture in.

- Start with one finger at a slow pace and gradually build up the pace and fingers.

- Fingering can involve moving your fingers in and out of the vagina, but it doesn't have to. Try keeping your fingers inside and moving them round in a swirling motion.
- Don't forget the external clit. Depending on your position, you can stimulate the clit using the palm of your hand while your fingers are inside, or use the other hand to do this. For a gradual build-up, alternate between fingering and external clit stimulation.

The G-Spot

Fingering isn't all about G-spot stimulation, but it can be part of the fun. Keep in mind that the G-spot is not a holy grail which guarantees pleasure, orgasms or ejaculation. It's just another part of the body that may or may not feel good when it's stimulated.

- Start with fingers in order to feel what's going on inside the vagina. If you want to use a toy, try one that has a curve in it and is firm enough that it will hold its shape while it's being used.
- Insert fingers or a toy inside the vagina, and

feel the top part of the vaginal wall, like you're pressing up towards the belly. The G-spot is usually around two inches inside the vagina; it's an area that can feel slightly more bumpy than the rest of the vagina.

- ◆ I'm a fan of using my middle finger and ring finger inside the vagina, with the forefinger and little finger pressed on either side along the labia. The pressure from the two fingers outside 'anchors' those on the inside. The two common G-spot 'moves' are:
  - × With your fingers curved, move them up and down across the G-spot (the classic 'come hither' motion). I find it more effective to move from the arm rather than the fingers with this.
  - × Keep your hand in the same place, pulsing your fingers up and down, putting pressure on the G-spot area.

If you're a fucking maverick, you could try both of these at the same time. Some people enjoy quite a firm pressure, but ease into it, and keep checking in with your partner.

When doing this during solo sex, the 'curved fingers' angle can be tricky on yourself. Try out different positions that work for you (I find lying on my side in a foetal position, and using the arm that's not pressed against the bed works well for G-spot stimulation). But this is an area where toys can really help. The extra length from a toy gives you more freedom to position yourself comfortably but still have full access to internal stimulation.

If you feel like you need to wee during G-spot stimulation, don't panic! Rather than draw away from the feeling, bearing down on it and engaging your PC muscles can intensify G-spot stimulation and can result in ejaculation (squirting).

There's still controversy and varying opinions about squirting as we know so little about it. In an age when we have smart fridges and Alexa, this baffles me, but it just goes to show how underfunded scientific studies about pleasure are.

But I can assure you, squirting's no myth (see next page).

Squirting FAQs

Is it wee?

NO! There's so much panic around this. From studies, we know that some of the same compounds (urea, creatinine) are found in both wee and squirt, but that doesn't mean it's the same thing. PSA (prostate-specific antigen) produced by the Skene glands is also found in squirt. I promise you, wee and squirt look and smell different, and the sensation of expelling them out of your body feels very different too.

But most importantly, if it was urine, would that be such a bad thing? A bit of wee is really quite harmless when you think about it. Plus, some people are really into piss play, which is lovely! This is one of those areas where I think we're taking the social norm, that wee + sex = icky, rather than really considering it from our own perspective.

Can everyone do it?

There's still some debate about this, but it's thought most people with vulvas are able to learn how to squirt. Developing a knack might come quickly or be more of an ongoing project, but like most things it gets easier the more you do it. Having a strong PC muscle really helps, as does being well hydrated. While many people find internal G-spot stimulation helps them to squirt, it's not necessary. It's possible to squirt through external stimulation and engaging the PC muscles alone. Repeat after me: ALL OUR BODIES ARE DIFFERENT AND ENDLESSLY COOL!

Do I need to be doing it?

NO! Ejaculation of any kind is fun, it can be a pleasurable part of your sex life, but it is by no means essential to having a wonderful time. The abundance of squirting ladies in porn has put pressure on many to feel like it's something they should be doing in their own sex life. You're no less of a glorious sexual being if squirting is not in your sexual repertoire.

My pal Lola Jean is the world record holder for the largest volume of ejaculate produced (1250ml if you're wondering), and talks about her relationship with squirting brilliantly.

" *I have a complicated relationship with squirting. It's something my body does (quite a lot) and it's taught me SO much about my body. I wouldn't change it for the world, but I do think it's overrated. I began squirting in my mid-twenties and promptly taught myself how to do so on my own. Squirting came very easily to me, while orgasming did not. I began to lean on squirting, so much so that I began to lose sight of my orgasm. It became something I was equally shamed and fetishised for – neither a place I wanted to be.*

That doesn't even take into account the mess. Even though there are many blankets, pads and products to alleviate this, you can't get away from the mess. Masturbation became a nuisance and many a lover disengaged from me sexually or romantically because of this.

Squirting can be wonderful, but it's not all it's cracked up to be. At the end of the day, all of our bodies do things another person may be envious of. It's time to stop focusing on what our bodies can't do and start enjoying what they can do. And if you don't enjoy what someone else's body happens to do … mind your own god damn business."

Handjobs

Handjobs are underrated. I get the most out of giving handjobs when I think of it like giving a massage – it's an opportunity to be more sensual, and touch the whole genital area.

- If you want to feel really close, lay next to each other and press your body against your partner's. For the best access to the whole area, have your partner lying down and sit between their legs, next to them, or straddle them. Sometimes when I'm straddling a partner I like to pretend it's my own dick I'm touching. It's hot, you should try it.

- Whether your partner is circumcised or not plays a big part in how you approach handjobs. Think of the foreskin in a similar way to the clitoral hood, where you have the option of stimulating the glans through the foreskin. If a penis is circumcised, using lube is essential, and you may find the glans are less sensitive.

- Some people like the whole penis to be touched,

others will want most of the focus to be on the head of the penis. You can position your hand so your thumb runs over the frenulum as you move up and down, which allows you to increase the pressure in this area specifically.

- With your hand wrapped around the penis, move it up and down in a straight action, or twist your wrist slightly while you move to add another layer of sensation.

- Try using both hands. You can wrap both hands around the shaft and move them as one, or try holding on to the shaft and applying pressure with one hand while the other stimulates the head.

- It's not all about the dick! You can stimulate the balls, perineum or anus at the same time – more on page 145.

Again, ask your partner how they like to be touched, and invite them to show or guide you. Learning from them is never a failure on your part.

Oral Sex

In some ways oral sex is the most intimate sex act, and putting care and attention into it, making your partner feel like you're really engaging with their genitals, is as important as any fancy tongue technique. The best abstract advice I can give for great oral sex is to think of it like you're making out with someone's genitals. Think of the various ways we can change our kisses – the tempo, depth, intensity – and apply that inquisitive nature to oral.

THINK OF IT LIKE YOU'RE MAKING OUT WITH SOMEONE'S GENITALS

Think about what you're doing with your hands. Engaging other parts of the body – thighs, hips, belly, breasts – can layer new sensations on top of what's going on with their genitals. Holding their hand can also build connection.

Some positions for oral sex:

- Classic. Partner lying down on their back, with you lying on your front between their legs. For oral sex on a penis, you could do this on your knees instead of lying down for greater access.
- From the side. Partner lying down, you kneeling next to them to one side.
- Partner lying with their legs off the bed, you on the floor on your knees.
- Face-sitting. Damn, this is a hot one. If you're sexually into vulvas, having someone sit on your face is the most intense way of experiencing a vulva and I highly recommend it.
- Standing up. This position makes oral sex feel like a you're worshipping a deity. Just make sure to protect those knees!
- From behind. You may not have the same access doing this, so there might be less direct stimulation, but it's hot to play around with. And this is perfect for rimming.

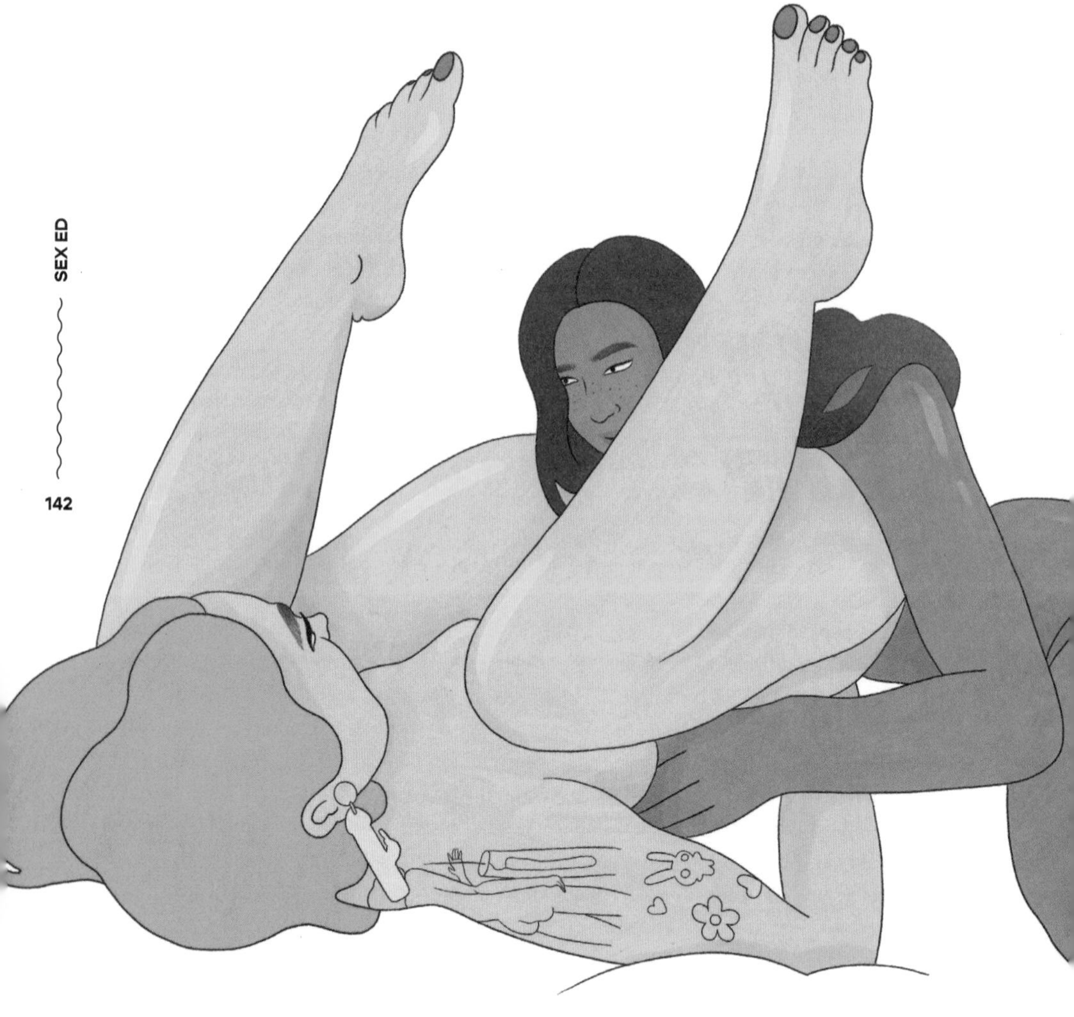

Finding your rhythm is key to good oral sex. If someone is going to have an orgasm, it's usually as the result of finding a steady rhythm that works for them and sticking to it. Many have made the mistake of speeding up/increasing the pressure when they recognise a partner's about to cum, thus 'killing' the orgasm. It's a sexual tragedy.

There are many ways to read your partner's pleasure during oral sex – changes in their breath, in their moans or what they're saying, if they're rocking their hips – but it's not your responsibility to read their mind, so ask for prompts or directions if it's useful.

Eye contact during oral divides a room even more than marmite. Some people love the intensity of it, and for others there's nothing more cringey. I personally enjoy occasional eye contact. I'm not interested in your eyes laser-beaming into my soul while your tongue's inside me, but it's nice to lock eyes every once in a while to connect. You may also want to close your eyes to focus on your pleasure. And if you're giving, closing your eyes can change the experience for you too and heighten your other senses.

> 66 I find it difficult to fully 'let go' when someone's going down on me, even if it's someone I really trust. When I get into it I love the way it feels, but there's this sense of shame that prevents me enjoying myself a lot of the time. It helps to tell my partner beforehand so they know to go at my pace and give me time to unwind afterwards."

Genitals smell and taste like genitals. They're not the fresh ocean breeze, they're not a garden of roses, they're genitals. In *How To Be a Woman*, Caitlin Moran describes a partner telling her her vulva tastes like 'a lovely pie'[13], and I think this is quite an accurate comparison. There's something earthy about genitals. If oral sex is really not for you, that's absolutely OK. You're responsible for communicating that to your partners, and for making them feel like it's not because of them specifically. But often people's reservations about giving or receiving oral sex can melt away once they try it with someone they feel connected to.

13. C. Moran, *How to be a Woman* Ebury Publishing, London; (2011), p. 303

PARTNERED SEX

Blowjobs

As my first boyfriend so lovingly said: 'If you put it in your mouth, it's probably going to feel good.' What a charmer. Blowjobs can be fun for everyone involved ... here are my guidelines:

- Try to avoid giving blowjobs with the sole aim of providing an orgasm – be playful and curious.
- Don't dive straight for the dick. Run along the inner thighs, nuzzling and kissing the base of the penis and the mons pubis.
- While the head of the penis is in your mouth, use your tongue to stimulate the frenulum while your hand holds the shaft. Using your tongue to flick the frenulum can feel different if you're doing this inside or outside the mouth.
- Move your mouth up and down the shaft. You can let their dick slip all the way out of your mouth and back in, or keep it in your mouth for longer without taking it out.
- If you're feeling like an absolute legend, you can use both hands on the shaft, or one hand on the shaft and the other on the balls/perineum. A bit of balance is required

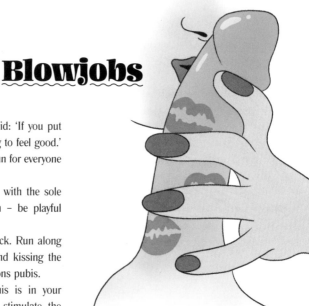

for this, I recommend having your knees at a slightly wider distance to steady yourself.

- Your hand can stay still, or you can move your head and hands at the same time.
- Don't rely on one motion only, or focus on only one part of the penis – there's something playful about moving around a bit and trying new things, particularly at the start. If things are building up to a climax, find that consistent rhythm and stick to it.

Let's talk about gag reflex

For most people, the gag reflex is pretty far down the throat, and there's a lot you can do without engaging it. Some people can train themselves to get past their gag reflex so they can take a whole dick quite far down their throat. This can feel great, but it's certainly not the most important aspect of a blowjob. The vast majority of the nerve endings on the penis are on the frenulum, so stimulating that should be more of a focus – deep-throating is not the be-all and end-all.

Balls glorious balls

Balls are really fun to play with during oral. You can take the balls into your mouth, together or one at a time; you can lick or suck them. Some people enjoy the sensation of having their scrotum pulled down gently: using your thumb and middle finger, make a ring around the top of the scrotum (above the balls, not directly on them!), and gently pull down away from their dick.

You may notice I'm using the word gently a lot – and for good reason! Ball play can drive people wild, but there's a fine line between pleasure and the not-so-fun kind of pain here, so be careful.

Perineum love

Place a finger on the perineum and apply firm and steady pressure on there while you're stimulating other areas. I do this with my thumb as it's stronger, and lets me put a little pressure on the balls with my other fingers if my partner is into it.

Don't forget about the anus!

Stimulating the anus during a blowjob can also feel amazing (so I'm told), but doing it can be a bit like rubbing your tummy and patting your head – it needs coordination. You can either circle your finger around the anus, or gently insert a lubed finger.

It goes without saying – but I'm going to say it anyway – a finger in the arse should never be a surprise. Consent is key.

The whole spit or swallow debate

I'm a bit bored that this is still seen as an issue, when there are far more interesting sexual debates!

If you're not into swallowing for whatever reason, that's absolutely OK. You can avoid coming into contact with cum by switching to using your hands before your partner reaches climax, or by asking your partner to wear a condom while you go down on them, or you can spit it out after they cum. Often when someone cums in your mouth, the head of their penis will be further into your mouth than most of your taste buds, so by swallowing you're actually engaging with the semen less than if you spit it out, if you're not keen on the taste.

Cunnilingus

There's no great phrase for going down on a vulva. 'Cunnilingus' feels so serious, but I'm also not a fan of 'eating out' or 'eating pussy' – please do not eat my genitals. I quite like 'going down on' and 'giving head', but am open to suggestions.

The clit's your main focus here, but that doesn't mean you can't wander off and explore other areas – there are nerve endings across the vulva. And remember, think of this like you're making out with your partner's genitals. Like with hand stuff, keep in mind the sensitivity of your partner's clit.

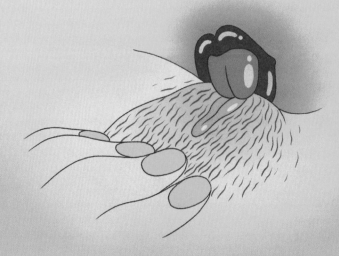

66 *I'm always amazed at how different people enjoy such different techniques. My girlfriend likes a lot of pressure and fast movement when I go down on her, while I enjoy really slow gentle strokes. We're polar opposites, but we make it work."*

- Using the flat part of your tongue, lick from the perineum all the way up to the clit in one long, slow stroke.
- Push up the mons pubis to lift up the clitoral hood. I like to apply some pressure on the mons as I do this, as it can stimulate the internal clitoris.
- You can move your tongue up and down, left to right, or in circles. You may find one of these is easier to do over a longer period of time.
- Tense your tongue so it's pointed and firm, and flick it over the clitoris for more intense stimulation.
- Create a bit of a vacuum with your lips over the clit, and then try sucking or using your tongue – gently or firmly.

You can also incorporate penetration during oral sex, using fingers or a toy. It can be tricky to use fingers at the same time as your tongue, mostly because of the angles (you can end up with your hand mashing into your chin), and because of the angle you're not able to engage the muscles in your arm, so your hand can get tired. There are ways to figure this out – toys can be easier to use, or keeping your fingers inside your partner but moving them up and down or in circular motions instead of in and out.

Sex and Periods

Period sex is a hot topic right now. I'm glad people are talking about it, because for so long the default assumption was that sex while you're bleeding was disgusting. There's already so much shame associated with bleeding and the menstrual cycle, so adding further sexual shame on top of this feels bloody unfair.

You don't need to want to have sex while you or your partner is bleeding, nothing's mandatory here. It's totally down to personal preference. While some people find they get more turned on than usual in the run-up to their period or while they're bleeding, for others it's a total no go, especially if they have health conditions linked to their periods, or bleeding makes them feel dysphoric.

But there are health benefits to sex while you're menstruating. Studies suggest sexual pleasure can reduce cramps, so the next time you're stuck in bed with a hot-water bottle, a cheeky wank can really do the trick!

The first worry tends to be about mess. Bleeding involves blood, which is famously unkind to our bed sheets. Why are we so concerned with mess? Sex is squelchy regardless of your period, and for me a little extra fluid really doesn't change things. People tend to build up a fear about leaking/staining sheets which looks way more dramatic in their heads than in real life. But fear not, there's an easy solution to this – a dark-coloured towel is your BFF. The times when it has got messy for me, I've laughed about it with my partner and we've hopped into the shower afterwards. Neither of us have felt awkward, it's just a part of life. Or if you're really after a seamless experience, multitask and have sex in the shower.

> 66 *My partner came while sitting on my face. She got off and lay down next to me, both of us panting our asses off after really great sex. After a little while she looked at me and screamed. Terrified, I asked her what's wrong and then she started howling with laughter. She'd just come on her period and my face was covered in blood, and so was hers from making out with me afterwards (we must have had our eyes closed). We didn't stop laughing for about 15 minutes, and ended up taking a load of selfies before getting in the shower."*

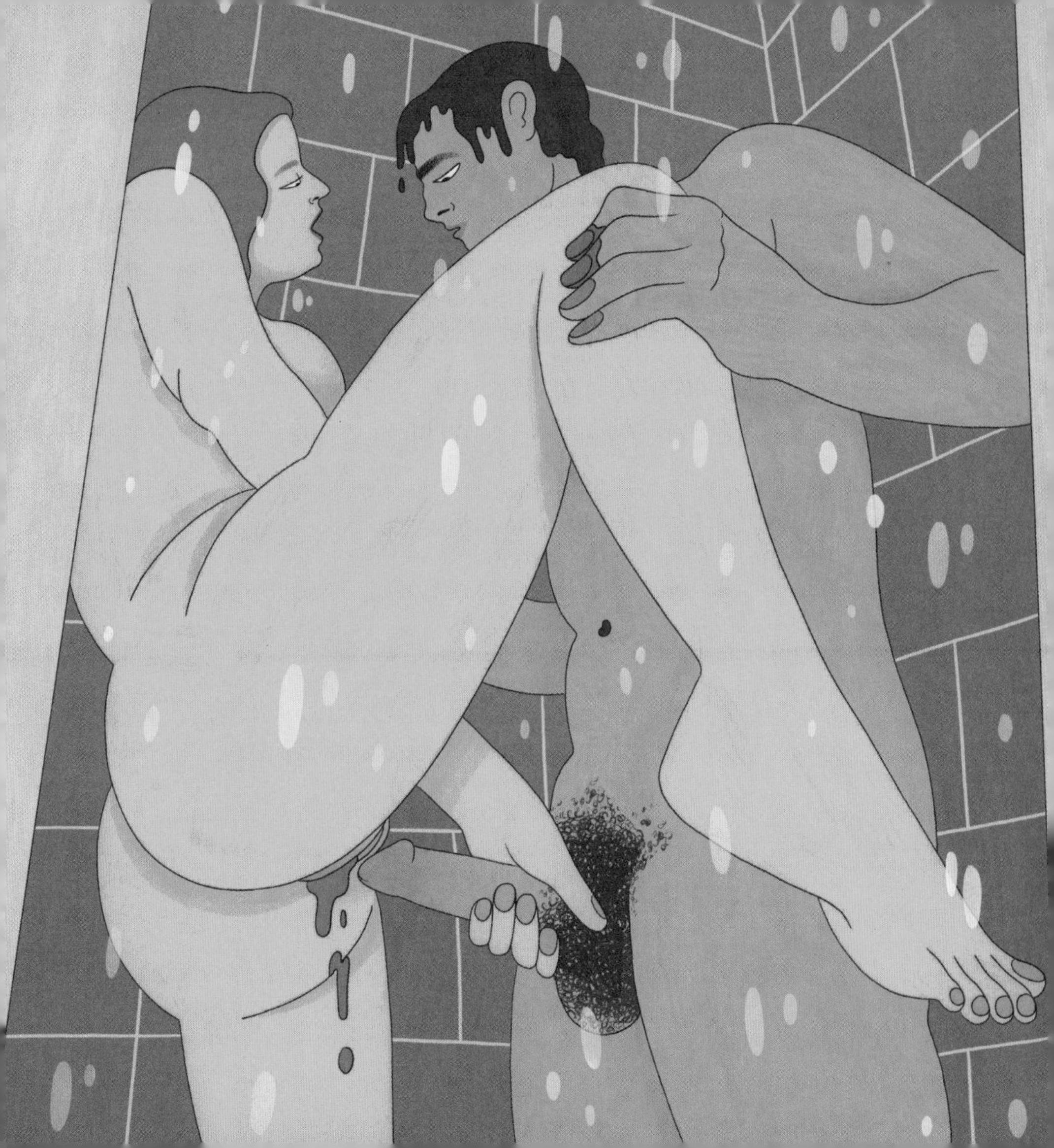

Exploring sex on your period through solo sex can help to address and process any shame you may have associated with your bleeding body before you engage in partnered period sex.

Consider whether you fancy some acts more than others, and communicate this to partners. Many people find the cervix sits lower in the vagina when they bleed, which may cause deeper penetration to feel painful. For me, I'm less interested in PIV while I'm bleeding, but that doesn't mean I don't want to experience other types of sexual touch. My preferred period product is a menstrual cup, and these beauties can be great for having sex on your period. Because the Bartholin glands are located at the entrance of the vagina, you still get wet while a menstrual cup is inserted. The contents of the cup stay inside it, but the vaginal lubrication flows forth beneath! So I can do everything other than vaginal penetration with ease.

In my experience, most of my partners have been chilled about periods and happy to engage in all forms of sex while I'm bleeding. There can be something lovely and empowering about a partner going down on me while I'm bleeding. Obviously this depends on the individual, and if someone is genuinely not into period sex and communicates that in a respectful way, that's OK. You may be able to work around that and find compromises that work for you both, or you may decide you're just not compatible.

When people jump to being grossed out by periods, it often comes from a place of ignorance. Most men and people with penises won't have had any education about periods – it's a big, unknown topic and can get built up in their heads. Having open conversations about your menstrual cycle can help to shift this, with partners as well as other people in your life. Personal preference is valid, but no one in your life should make you feel like a natural function of your body is gross.

Endometriosis is a condition where tissue similar to the lining of the womb grows in other areas of the body. This can cause pain during and after sex, as well as severe period pain and lower back/belly pain. It's a long-term condition, but medical treatments are available. The main worry is that people are diagnosed so late – on average it takes someone with endometriosis 7.5 years to receive a diagnosis in the UK. If you're experiencing pain, seek medical advice. It helps to have someone else come along who can vouch for you if your pain is not being taken seriously.

Penis in Vagina

Penetrative sex, whether that's vaginal or anal, allows for a lot of physical contact between your bodies, which is one of my favourite aspects of partnered sex.

But the emphasis on penetration is a little old hat. Don't get me wrong, it can be a fantastic part of your sex life, but it's far more exciting to see it as one option of many.

It's also not as pleasurable for everyone. Around 70% of women and people with vulvas report they need direct clitoral stimulation in order to experience an orgasm. This has a lot to do with individual anatomy and how close the clitoris is to the entrance of the vagina.

❝ *Watching porn as a teenager gave me the impression you should change positions every five minutes, jumping from one impossible position to the next. Whenever I've tried this it's been exhausting, and I've never stayed in one position for long enough to even think about cumming. I had to learn that there's nothing boring about knowing what I like and sticking to it."*

If penetration is on the cards there's no need to rush! Listen to your body and your partner's, and take the time you need to build up to it. There are so many sexual journeys we can go on with our minds and bodies, and while penetration might be a welcome part of this adventure, it's nice to take a moment to think about what it is you're in the mood for rather than going through the motions when it comes to sexual play.

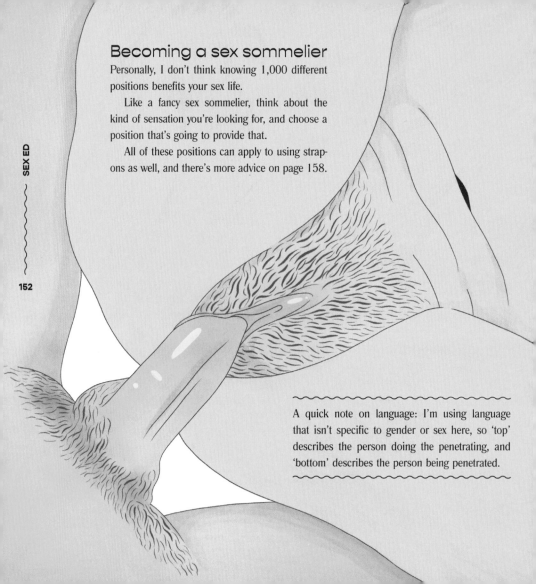

Becoming a sex sommelier

Personally, I don't think knowing 1,000 different positions benefits your sex life.

Like a fancy sex sommelier, think about the kind of sensation you're looking for, and choose a position that's going to provide that.

All of these positions can apply to using strapons as well, and there's more advice on page 158.

A quick note on language: I'm using language that isn't specific to gender or sex here, so 'top' describes the person doing the penetrating, and 'bottom' describes the person being penetrated.

If you're looking for ...

- ♦ **Lots of body contact:** missionary is the absolute classic. You can put a pillow underneath the bottom[14], which will press your bodies together even more (and increase clitoral stimulation). Alternatively, try the bottom lying on their belly with the top lying on top, penetrating from behind. In both of these positions your faces are right next to each other, so you can make out, have some really intense eye contact or nuzzle your head into your partner's neck.

- ♦ **Clit stimulation:** positions where the vulva-owner (or whoever's being penetrated, if you both have vulvas) is on top often work best – that way you have more control over the movement.

  My favourites are:

  × Cowgirl, or the gender-neutral cowperson, which allows you or your partner to stimulate the clit with fingers or a toy during penetration (plus I find the name hilarious – yee-ha!).

  × A variation of cowperson where both of you are sat up, with the bottom straddling the top. This presses your bodies together and creates friction against the clit. I'm not sure why, but this position always works particularly well

14. Cheeky double meaning there!

for me when I'm on a sofa – something about my partner's legs being bent down instead of horizontal changes the angle.

- ♦ **Deeper penetration:** doggy style is your BFF. In this position it's much easier for the top to thrust their hips, so you get a greater range of movement. A modified missionary is also great here: the bottom lifts their legs up, or presses their knees against their chest, creating a better angle for deeper penetration.

- ♦ **Something that requires very little physical effort:** try sex while you're spooning. This is perfect for sleepy morning sex, or when you're both royally hung-over. Alternatively, you can see if your partner fancies doing 90% of the work, but bear in mind this can create an IOU situation and you may be asked to return the favour in the near future.

This isn't a comprehensive list, but it's a starting point. A quick google will show you hundreds of ideas for new positions to try, and if you feel like exploring something new be my guest, but most people find they return to the same few positions time and time again, and there's nothing wrong with that.

And remember, while penetration can be wonderful, it's one of many ways to enjoy sex. You can have a fulfilling sex life without ever penetrating someone or being penetrated.

Vaginismus

Vaginismus is a condition where the vaginal muscles tighten and spasm, and if penetration is attempted (which could be as small as trying to insert a tampon), it can be incredibly painful. Please don't push through anything that's painful; pain is your body telling you to stop. If your partner has vaginismus, listen carefully to their needs and be extra attentive to how they're feeling during and after sex.

It can be treated by therapy and learning techniques to relax your muscles. But it's absolutely not the end of your sex life! As we've already explored, there are plenty of lovely non-penetrative ways to experience pleasure.

66 *I'd always been a very sexual person, but when it came to any form of penetration – fingers, penis, it was like I clamped shut. I didn't have full penetrative sex until I was 20. I was too embarrassed to tell my partner that I was in pain, so I just allowed sex to happen to me, I didn't feel it was something I was participating in.*

When I finally discovered what vaginismus was, it was a relief. It helped to know it was an actual 'thing', to learn that I wasn't broken, and gave me the opportunity to research and understand what was going on with me.

When I was 24 I met someone who I felt I could open up to, and we worked through it together, with lots of encouragement and open dialogue. Having that level of intimacy with someone completely changed my sex life, I finally felt free to experiment and enjoy sex.

Now at 30, vaginismus is still a part of my life. I don't think it's something that will ever really go away, but I've learnt how to handle it. Understanding that penetration isn't the pinnacle of sex has been an important lesson for both myself and my partner, and is important to remember whether you are dealing with vaginismus or not. Sex without penetration is VALID."

Anal Play

Anal play can be the main event, or it can be incorporated into other fun activities. It ranges from external play using your hands or mouth (rimming), to using fingers and smaller toys internally, to deeper penetration with a penis or toy (or fist, if you're feeling adventurous). If you have a prostate, internal anal play will put pressure on the prostate, which you may find highly pleasurable. And if you don't have a prostate, anal play can actually stimulate internal areas of the clitoris!

EVERYONE CAN ENJOY ANAL PLAY, REGARDLESS OF GENDER OR SEXUALITY

Not a week goes by when I don't feel a little bit sad that I don't have a prostate, and it makes me sad too that so many cis straight men deny themselves prostate stimulation because of the nonsensical homophobic beliefs that exist in the world. Repeat after me: everyone can enjoy anal play, regardless of gender or sexuality.

The lining of the anus is more sensitive than the vaginal walls, so it's important to be extra careful:

- ♦ Make sure nails are short and hands are clean, and remove any jewellery.
- ♦ You can use latex gloves to smooth out the surface of the skin, and this is particularly important if you have any cuts or snags on your hands/nails.

And remember, only use toys with a flared base! Also, don't put anything – fingers, toys, penises – into the vagina, around the vulva or in the mouth if it's been in the anus. To keep things clean and minimise the risk of infection, use a new condom and wash your hands or toys before changing to any other type of play.

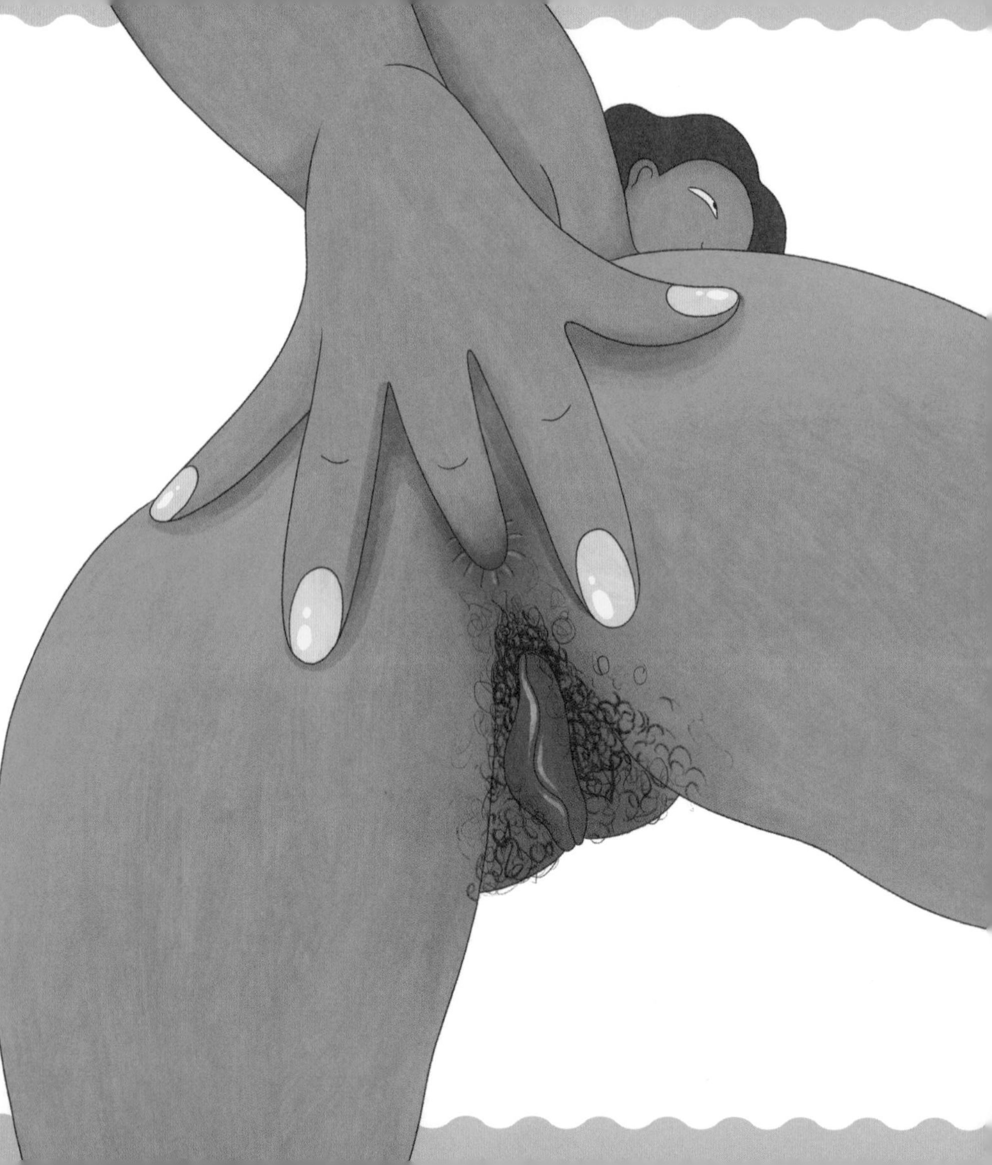

Rimming

The techniques for going down on vulvas on page 146 can also be applied to rimming – moving your tongue in circles around the anus works particularly well, and play around with the pressure here, as the anus is more sensitive than you think.

Fingering

Unlike the vagina, the anus doesn't produce lubrication when aroused, so lube is essential for any anal play. You need more than you think – like a lot more.

Like all internal play, stimulate the outside before you venture in. You can do this by massaging the area. Forming a fist and using your knuckles to massage works well, or circling your fingers around the anus.

When it comes to penetration, TAKE YOUR TIME. There's no rush, and it can take a few sessions to build up to internal stimulation. If there's any pain or discomfort, stop – or ask your partner to stop. Anal play should not cause pain – it may be that you're moving too fast, your partner's body isn't relaxed or you're not using enough lube. If you feel pain, pause what you're doing and focus on your breathing to relax, and start again when/if you feel like it.

If your partner has a prostate, it can be felt by gently pressing your finger against the upper wall of the rectum (like you're pressing up towards the stomach). Move your fingers from side to side to locate the prostate – it should feel a little firmer than the rest of the rectum. You can hold your finger there with some pressure, gently pulsing on the prostate, or slide your finger side to side or up and down. Or, keep your hand still and get your partner to move around: they can try arching their back or tilting their hips to see how it changes the sensation.

Pegging

Pegging is a type of anal play where a person (usually someone without a penis) dons a strap-on and penetrates their partner. Typically pegging is where a woman fucks a man, but like everything in this book, all gender identities and combinations are welcome here.

If you don't have a penis, wearing one is SO MUCH FUN! It's such an interesting experience to get a new perspective on sex.

Many cis women have been taught that sex = being passive, receptive and penetrated. I have found it hugely rewarding to take ownership of my sexuality and subvert these ideals, and pegging is an excellent way of exploring this. Obviously this needs to be consensual. While it's hilarious to jump into a room wearing a strap-on to make a partner laugh (trust me, it works every time), ambushing or pressuring a partner into any sexual acts is not OK. If this isn't your cup of tea that's totally fine, and if it is your cup of tea, talk about it beforehand.

My teenage years were spent sleeping with guys who were more interested in watching their dick go in and out of me than in engaging with me as a person, and I thought it was pretty pathetic.

Cut to the first time I used a strap-on: I became just as obsessed with watching my dick going in and out of someone's body as my horny teenage boyfriends. I owe them an apology. I was overwhelmed by how fun it was, and without fail I still feel like this every time I penetrate someone with my strap-on. I invite you to experience it for yourself and relish in the feeling, but don't let how much fun you're having stop you from treating your partner like an active participant in the action. I love telling my partner just how hot it looks and how exciting I'm finding the whole thing – it's another way we can bond through sex.

Some advice for how to peg successfully (which can be applied to other forms of strap-on sex as well):

♦ When you're wearing a strap-on, you can't feel what's going on internally, so communication with your partner is really important.

♦ It's hard work if you're not used to thrusting, but over time you'll get the hang of how to move your hips. Positioning the strap-on so it sits slightly higher on your mons pubis helps.

♦ I like to start with the bottom on top (cowperson) – that way they can control the depth and movement. Plus, it's really fucking hot watching someone ride you. Another popular position is doggy. You can start off with the top staying still, allowing the bottom to control the movement, and if you feel like it you can move on to the top thrusting. This doesn't need to be a full 'in-out' motion; try staying mostly inside and rocking your hips.

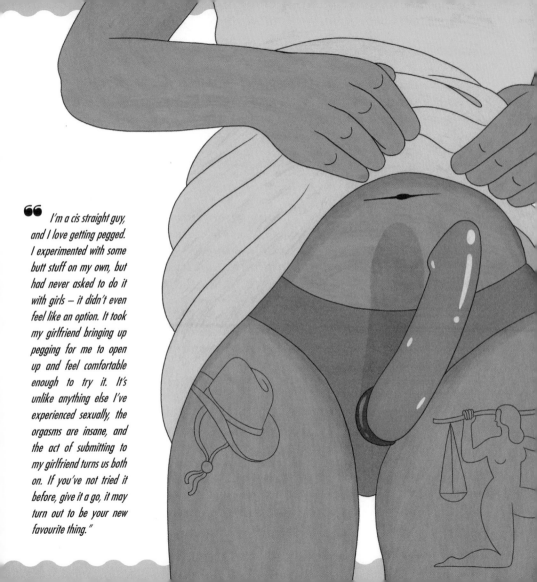

" I'm a cis straight guy, and I love getting pegged. I experimented with some butt stuff on my own, but had never asked to do it with girls – it didn't even feel like an option. It took my girlfriend bringing up pegging for me to open up and feel comfortable enough to try it. It's unlike anything else I've experienced sexually, the orgasms are insane, and the act of submitting to my girlfriend turns us both on. If you've not tried it before, give it a go, it may turn out to be your new favourite thing. "

To douche, or not to douche?

A big concern about anal is poo. The anxiety of this happening is often far worse than the reality, because unless you are actually about to do a poo, the rectum is pretty empty. Granted, pretty empty doesn't mean completely spotless, so there are a few ways to help minimise mess and put your mind at ease. I like using latex gloves/condoms on anything going inside the anus, and it's a good idea to have some wipes handy.

Douching, where the rectum is flushed out with water, isn't always necessary. Another way to clear out anything that may be lurking in there is to insert a finger into the anus while you're in the shower to give it a quick clean. But if you're feeling particularly anxious, or if you're going to engage in some more intense anal play (for a longer stretch of time, using a larger toy, or with deeper penetration), douching can be helpful.

Please don't douche your vagina; it disrupts the microbial balance of the vagina and can increase the chance of you getting bacterial vaginosis (BV)!

66 *Douching is a bit trial and error. It was definitely a process that used to scare me, but over time I developed my own technique.*

Using a handheld douche:

- *Fill your douche with lukewarm water, insert the nozzle and set on the side.*
- *Sit on the toilet, lube up a finger and massage your hole. Insert a finger and just open yourself up a little so you feel comfortable.*
- *Lube up the nozzle, and gently insert it. When as much of the nozzle is in as comfortable, squeeze the bulb with your hand until the water has squirted up into your ass.*
- *Remove the douche and lay to the side for now. Give a little push and let the water flow out. This may come in a few squirts, don't worry, it's all good.*
- *Refill the douche with water and repeat once or twice.*
- *Wipe up, flush, and have a quick shower if you feel necessary. Make sure you wash the douche well after use, let it air-dry and store.*

I usually set aside 20–30 mins to douche, and douche well before I think I will be having sex. Most people are fine having sex immediately after douching, but I prefer to leave my body to 'settle' so I feel more comfortable during sex."

Stamina

My Jesus-loving sex ed teacher was right: sex can be knackering. This tends to happen most often when I'm using my hands, tongue or a strap-on. Try not to beat yourself up for feeling tired – it happens to everyone! There are a few techniques you can use to manage this:

- When we're using hands, we often focus on generating movement from the muscles in the fingers, hand or wrist only. These are relatively small muscles, and therefore likely to get tired quite quickly. Try focusing on using the movement from more of your body: your forearm, biceps, shoulder and even back/hips, in order to relieve the pressure on your hand.

- Alternate between using different body parts (hand to mouth, switching hands) to reduce the pressure on one part of the body.

- Match your breath with your movement, exhaling with each thrust or stroke. It helps you feel more centred and focused.

- When my body's feeling really tired, I find I can usually power on that bit further by focusing on my partner's pleasure. Sitting with that, basking in the glory of their pleasure which you're helping to create, can change the focus in your mind. But don't go on for longer than you can just for your partner. If your body is in pain, it's time to stop. That doesn't mean stopping entirely; you could move on to something else that puts less pressure on that part of your body, suggest using a toy or having a pause to rest before you dive back in!

Orgasm with a Partner

We explored our varying relationships with orgasms in Chapter 4, but this gets even more complicated when we add a partner to the mix. Having another person there while you orgasm can feel intimate and bonding, or just really hot, but it can also add pressure for us to reach that orgasm.

It can take a while to figure out the patterns of someone else's body, and how your patterns mesh with theirs. It usually takes me a while for my brain/body to feel comfortable enough around a new partner to orgasm, and I like to communicate that with my partners instead of keeping it to myself.

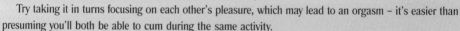

Hopefully, you'll be aware of how to make yourself feel good, which may result in an orgasm, and so during partnered sex you can either guide your partner so they know exactly what to do, or you can do it yourself.

Try taking it in turns focusing on each other's pleasure, which may lead to an orgasm – it's easier than presuming you'll both be able to cum during the same activity.

PSA: you can't 'make' someone else have an orgasm! This is a great example of porn influencing our sexual language and expectations. 'Make me cum'/'I'm going to make you cum' is a line we are so familiar with, and many of us, myself included, echo this in our real-life sex. It's language we can use in sex which can be hot in the moment, but it's important to retain agency around your orgasms. Your partner might play a fairly large role, providing thrusting, rubbing, flicking motions with any number of sexy equipment while you lie back and enjoy like a sexy starfish, but ultimately your orgasm comes from within you. **It's your property, it belongs to you.**

Some people can take great pride in someone else's orgasm. When I was 19 I slept with a ~~dickhead~~ guy who was deeply wounded by the

fact that I wasn't able to have an orgasm. He used every trick in his book, and when none of them resulted in fireworks he made me feel guilty that my body wasn't programmed in the right way. My orgasm was more about validating his masculinity and prowess than it was about me. Please don't treat other people's pleasure as your property – it's theirs, and you're simply lucky to be there and lend a helping hand.

And a penile orgasm doesn't signal the end of sex, OK?

The Orgasm Gap

There's a shocking level of orgasm inequality when it comes to cis hetero sex: a study carried out in 2017 showed that 3 in 4 women don't regularly orgasm through partnered sex, while for men it's only 1 in 4.[15] What the actual fuck?!

This isn't because the female body is more complicated, or because orgasms are so elusive for women: studies looking at solo sex and queer sex between women indicate far higher orgasm rates (I'm trying not to be smug as I type that, but I can confirm queer ladies know how to FUCK).

So why is this happening? I have a few theories:

- There's an emphasis on penetration, despite the fact so many women struggle to have an orgasm through penetration alone.
- The bullshit archaic presumption that female pleasure is less important than male pleasure means most of us are raised to not even consider female pleasure as an essential part of sex. Cheers, patriarchy, you utter fuckwit.

66 *I've always found it really difficult to orgasm with a partner. I only experienced my first solo-sex orgasm once I had already started having sex with other people, so for a long time partnered sex was about helping a partner orgasm.*

Even once I realised how to make myself cum, it stayed very separate to having sex with other people. Because I felt like I couldn't cum from partnered sex, it felt like a waste to devote a lot of time to my pleasure, and I felt like I was letting my partner down or not holding up my side of the sex-bargain by not being able to cum. I know this sounds stupid, but it's how I felt for a long time.

I'm slowly learning that I deserve to take up space in partnered sex, and using toys helps massively. But it's a weird road, and as much as I can be in the mindset for it and be with a great partner who doesn't make my orgasm feel like a burden, it's still something that happens rarely. This doesn't mean I don't have fun – I get a lot out of sex with other people, but at least for now, cumming is something I tend to do on my own."

15. 'The Orgasm Gap', Durex [company website], <https://www.durex.co.uk/blogs/explore-sex/the-orgasm-gap>

The expectation that women should be passive receivers means women feel less confident to communicate what they want, or ask for more. Rather than being a standard part of sex, this is often seen as a radical and surprising act. A woman? Asking for what she wants? The horror! Again, shout-out to the patriarchy for this absolute gem.

And there's one more thing that contributes to this ...

Faking Orgasms

Hands up if you've faked an orgasm (you can't see this, but my hand is raised). I'd say the majority of us have, regardless of gender, although this is something more often associated with cis women.

I totally see the appeal here. If you know you're just not going to get there, faking an orgasm to signal you're done with the sex portion of the evening makes sense. It gives your partner a cue that it's OK for them to cum, and it's easier than explaining that you're just not going to get there, which runs the risk of hurting their feelings or could change the mood of a special moment. Maybe they've tried so hard to make it happen, you can see the concentration in their face and you want to give them a little pat on the back.

This is patronising and counterproductive. I don't know about you, but I'd be mortified if I found out a partner had faked an orgasm while we were having sex. I'd feel worried that I made them feel uncomfortable in some way, or like it wasn't safe to communicate if they wanted a different kind of stimulation, or that I gave off the vibes that them orgasming was an expected part of sex. In faking orgasms, you're denying yourself the possibility of a more pleasurable experience, and withholding information from your partner about your pleasure.

I get that if you're in the habit of faking orgasms, it's difficult to go cold turkey. But please can everyone promise to reduce the number of faked orgasms out in the world? We owe it to each other, and to ourselves.

Winding Down

With the right partner, I enjoy the intimacy after sex just as much as the sex itself.

Cuddling, pillow talk, discussing what just went down and sharing tips on how to improve for next time – all of this is so bonding (people with vulvas, just remember to go for a wee before the cuddling begins). But if this isn't for you, if you'd rather avoid the smooshy stuff and get on with the rest of your day, that's also OK.

Whatever your style, try to make your partner feel validated, and ask them to do the same for you. Sex is intimate and vulnerable: we're opening up a part of ourselves (sometimes quite literally) for someone else to see, and it's nice to recognise the beauty in that.

Keeping it Casual

Casual sex is sex that happens outside of more traditional romantic relationships. It can be anything from random one-night stands to something more ongoing. Apps now dominate the casual sex and dating world, which is a blessing and a curse.

Casual sex ≠ bad sex!

Some of the loveliest sexual experiences I've had have been casual. You can be intimate with someone and it still be casual: it's all about communicating boundaries clearly. Often the notion of casual sex is that it should be 'just sex' – none of the sensual touch or affection we might associate with relationship sex. I think this is bullshit! Cuddling afterwards doesn't mean I'm going to fall in love with you. Although there are some people who might be freaked out by this, particularly if they have an avoidant attachment style, so it's worth checking in before you reach over for a massive spoon sesh.

My style of dating and casual sex is fairly upfront, and I know that's not for everyone, but I do think that most people could benefit from being a bit more direct when it comes to casual sex. Playing games is essentially a lack of communication. If everyone's honest about what they're looking for and is on the same page, the real fun can begin! You'll know where you stand, and will be able to appreciate the moment for what it is.

Just because the sex is casual, doesn't mean we should treat the other people involved like they're disposable, nor should we be treated badly ourselves.

It may be less likely that you have an orgasm with a partner who isn't familiar with your body, but by touching yourself or using a toy, you can still experience the stimulation you enjoy while in the company of this new person.

A big reason I love casual sex is because of the stories. Yes, being in the moment is important, but there's nothing like a wild one-night-stand story to liven up a dinner party.

Years ago I picked up a guy while life modelling. Our eyes kept meeting while he drew me, and the tension built throughout the class without us saying a word to each other. The sex was ok, but that initial connection is what stays with me.

I once rocked my hips so enthusiastically that I bruised the upper lip of the woman who was going down on me – it looked like my vulva had punched her in the face. I apologised profusely, but she seemed quite proud and wore it like a badge of honour.

I bumped into a hunk in the middle of a Vietnamese War Museum (sexy) who I'd met weeks before, we had a whirlwind 12-hour sexual adventure before running to catch flights to different countries.

The foursome I had with my best friend and a queer couple in their grandparents' living room. Don't panic, the grandparents were away for the weekend, but the combination of wild hedonistic sex in an OAP setting (plastic sofa covers and everything) was hilarious.

Sex in Long-Term Relationships

We evolve both as individuals and as a partnership throughout a long-term relationship (LTR), and so does the sex we have. Embracing change is essential to getting the most out of LTR sex.

There's a particular joy in getting really familiar with someone's body and desire. It can make for incredibly intense and bonding sex, becoming a dance that you flow through without thinking, but we don't want to get to the point where we're taking our partner's body or the sex we have for granted. Trying new things, or varying our standard sex patterns can really help, but only if we're also having honest conversations about how we feel and why we want to try something new.

THERE'S A PARTICULAR JOY IN GETTING REALLY FAMILIAR WITH SOMEONE'S BODY AND DESIRE

If you haven't had sex with your partner in a while, putting pressure on yourself to kick-start your sex life is probably not going to help. There may be underlying reasons why you've got out of the habit that need to be addressed before you return to anything sexual. Many sex therapists recommend consensually deciding to take sex off the agenda for a while, because it means there's no looming expectation that you should jump into bed whenever things are going well between you.

If one of you feels sexual when the other doesn't, solo sex is a useful tool. Either in private, or consensually involving the partner who's not feeling so sexual. It can be lovely and intimate to hold and kiss a partner while they're engaging in solo play.

But remember, no one has the right to make you feel guilty for wanting more or less sex.

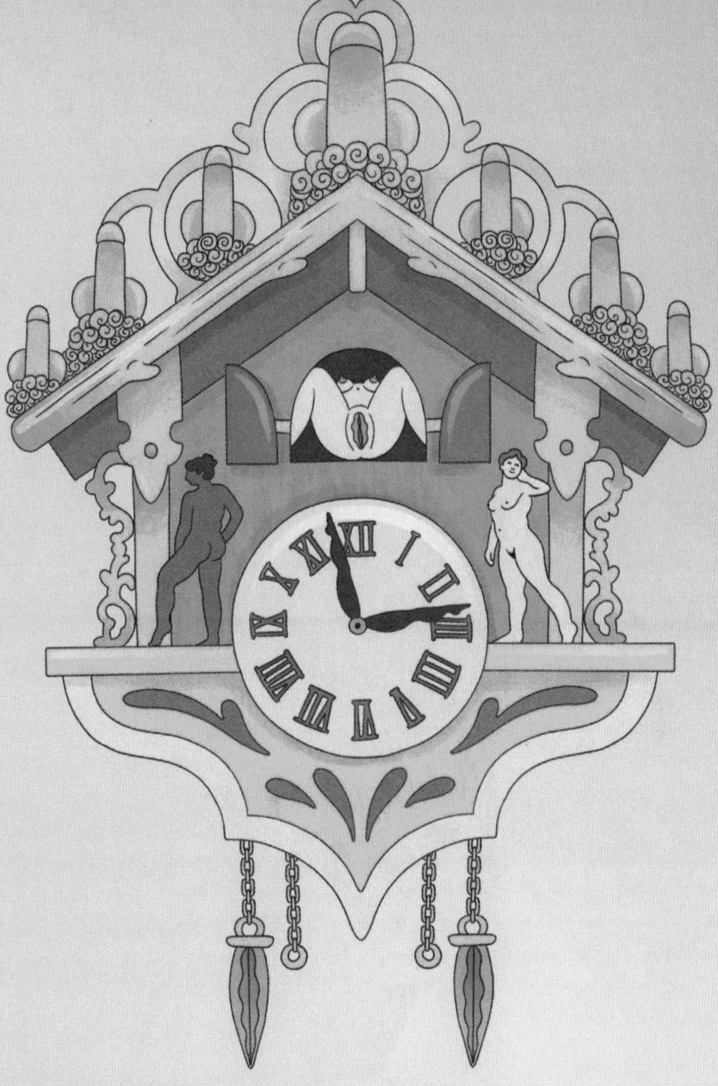

Ways to improve your LTR sex life:

- Schedule time for sex. That doesn't mean that just because you've got it in the diary you're obliged to have sex (as always, only have sex if you want to). But by carving out some time just for yourselves, you're giving your brain some prior warning to engage your accelerator and minimise things that set off your brake.
- If you're having a date night, don't leave the sex to the end! You may be tired by the time you get home and having sex may feel like a chore. Try having sex before your date, and I recommend having evenings where sex is the main event you have planned, rather than something you stick on the end of another activity.
- Giving your partner a heads-up about if you're feeling sexy or not helps to limit

66 *Opening up my relationship has helped build a stronger sexual bond with my existing partner. It's allowed us both to appreciate each other more, and often when one of us goes on a date we'll end up having really intense sex the next day. I know it doesn't work for everyone, but it's really helped put the fun back into our sex life."*

differing expectations. It can feel so frustrating if you've been waiting all day to jump into bed with your partner and tear their clothes off, while they've been feeling fragile and all they want is a cuddle. No

66 *I've been with my husband for 11 years, and find that our sex life goes in waves. There have been times where we're fucking like rabbits, and times when one or both of us have just felt uninterested in sex. It's good to remind ourselves sex isn't the only thing that makes us feel connected, and know that wherever we're at right now is likely to change, and we'll ride it out together."*

one's in the wrong here, but because you've not communicated ahead of time, there's the risk that both of you can feel resentful for not being on the same page and getting what you want.

- Try to treat each other with kindness and patience and, if something's bothering you, talk about it.
- And don't forget about solo sex! You may be in a couple, but your sexualities still exist as individuals. Maintaining a relationship with the sex you have on your own is just as important as the sex you have with a partner.

Woah, what a chapter! Here she is in a sexy nutshell:

♦ Partnered sex is lovely, but more complicated than when you're on your own. Communicating consent is essential, and isn't as complicated as you may think.

♦ If you're having sex, it's your responsibility to make active choices about your sexual health.

♦ Virginity is a social construct – you get to define what first-time sex means to you.

♦ There are a million different ways to get off. I've provided guidelines on the basics, but it's up to you to be curious while you're fucking, and adapt these to suit you. Take your time, be playful, and remember there's no default 'right' way to do anything.

♦ Orgasm is not the ultimate goal of sex. Focus on the journey, not the destination, and please let's stop faking orgasms.

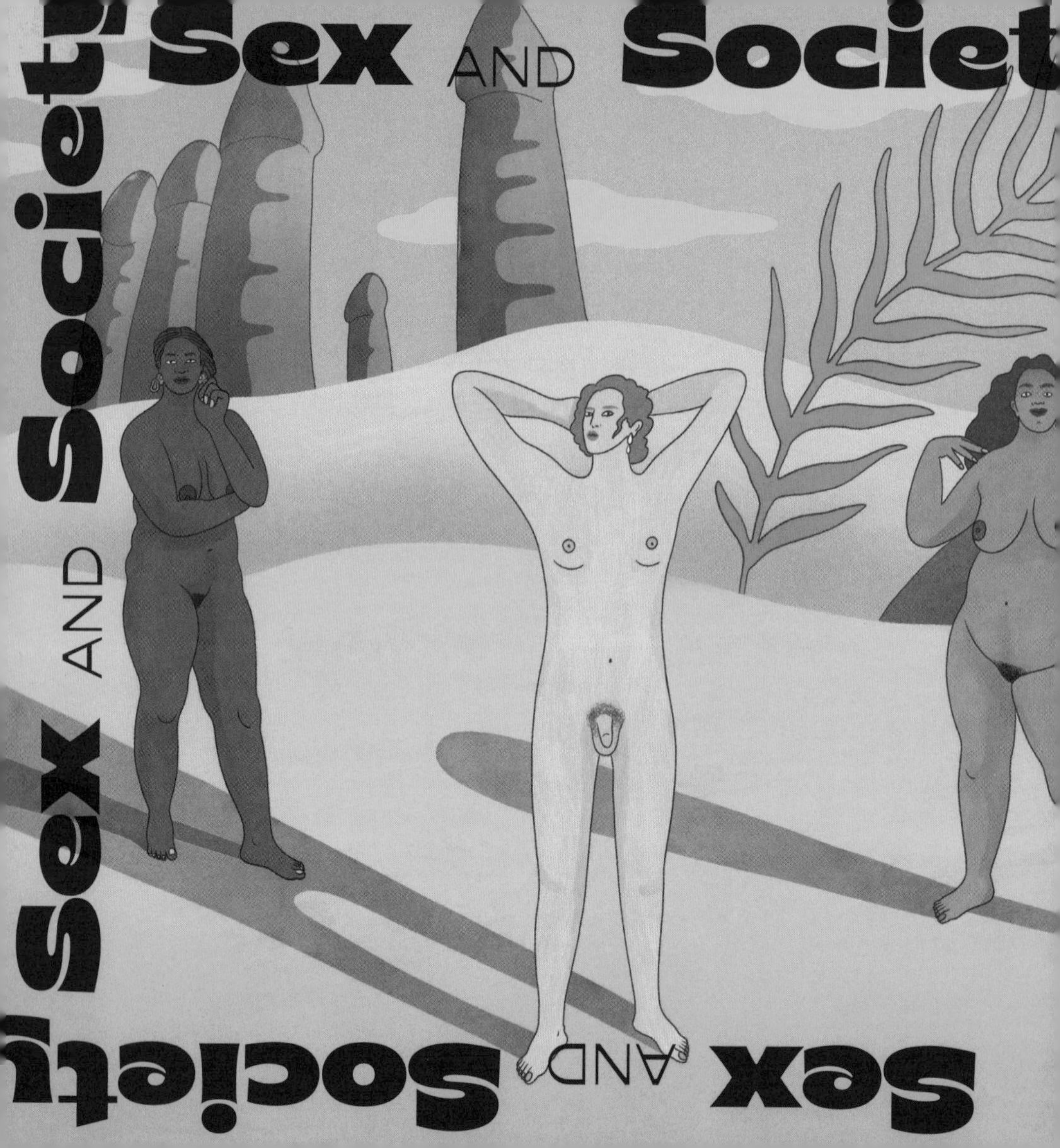
Sex AND Society
Sex AND Society
Sex AND Society

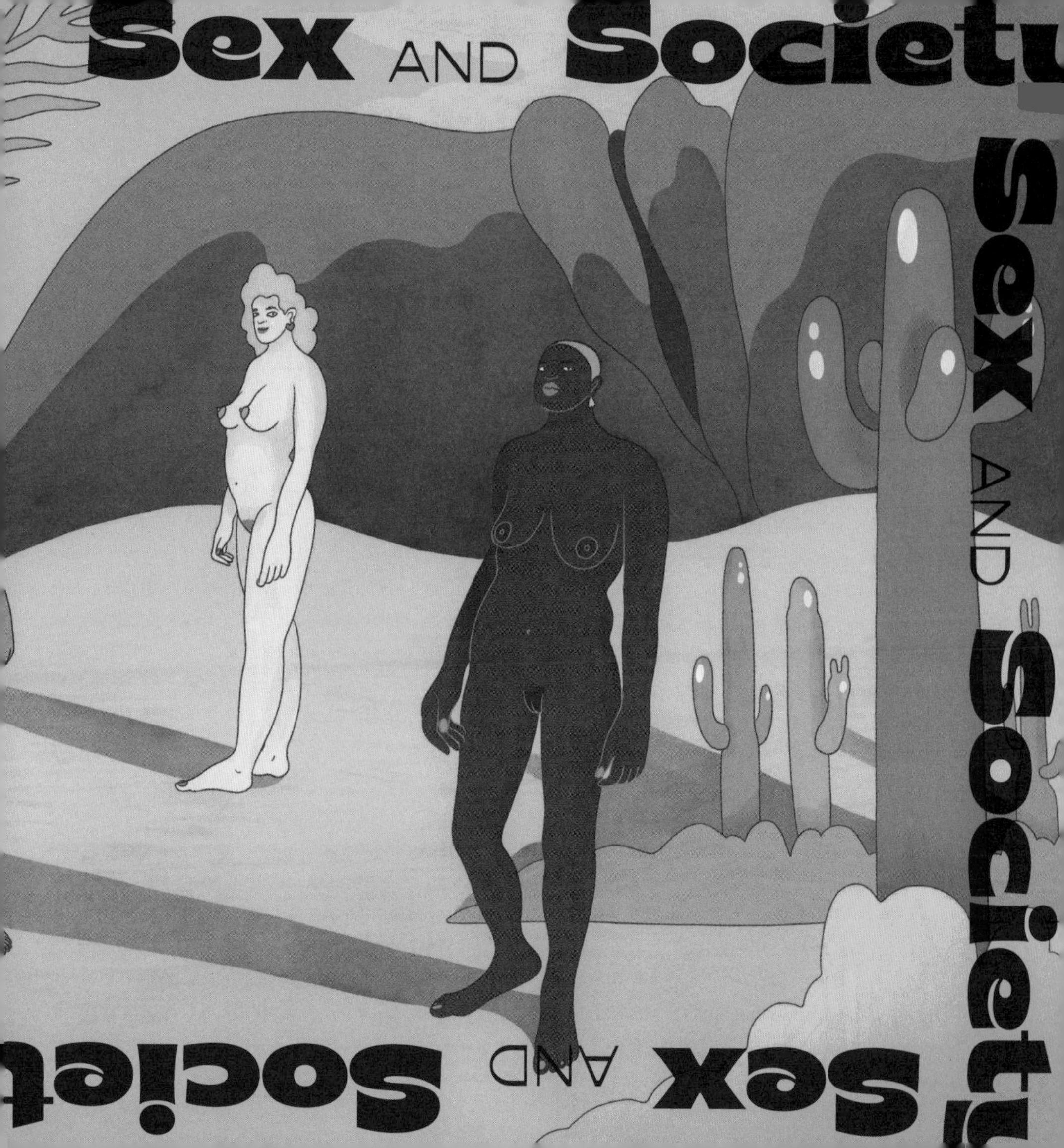
Sex AND Societ
Sex AND Societ
Sex AND Societ

The Politics of Sex

Everything is political. By that I mean all our actions are governed by and viewed through invisible agreements created by wider society. Who holds power in situations – between individuals, or between an individual and a larger system – is at the root of politics. And because sex is an area of life that's particularly taboo, it's important to investigate the way power and politics play into sex.

If you sit within 'normative values', you might not consider sex as a political act. But anyone whose identity sits outside these norms will have some experience of their actions being politicised – just living your life in a way that makes you happy can be challenging to convention. Our personal (and often quite private) choices rub up against societal systems of what is and what isn't acceptable to society.

That shame you might feel after a one-night stand? Political.

When you get catcalled and wonder if it's because your skirt really is too short? Political.

That shame you might feel for wanking (which hopefully you're working through with the aim of feeling empowered)? Political.

Understanding that your sexual desires are unique, while acknowledging the part that society plays in shaping them? That's political too.

There are so many issues I care about – and subsequently rant about a lot. Here are a few:

- ◆ The policing and censorship of bodies, particularly the bodies of women, people of colour, queer and trans folks, and those with disabilities.
- ◆ Access to sex education, contraception, STI testing and safe abortion. This is incredibly inconsistent. These services are not typically valued by governments, and when they're underfunded it costs lives.
- ◆ The prevalence of sexual assault, and the fact that it's still prosecuted at a shockingly low rate.
- ◆ Trans-Exclusionary Radical Feminists (TERFs) and Sex Worker-Exclusionary Radical Feminists (SWERFs). These people believe trans women aren't real women, and discriminate against sex workers. They fucking enrage me. If you're limiting the rights of others, you're not a feminist.
- ◆ The choices we make as consumers about sex-related products: are your toys made in factories that treat their employees fairly? Do you pay for the porn you consume? Do you buy biodegradable products where possible? If we have the privilege of choice, it's important to be ethical consumers.

Write down some of the issues that matter most to you:

....

....

♦ The fact that there are still MILLIONS of people who try to force their religious beliefs on others. Do whatever makes you happy, but don't tell me how I should live, love and fuck.

Sexual injustice is something that affects us all, so it's important to speak up about it, the louder the better. We need as many impassioned voices as possible to shift cultural norms, to demand that our sexual rights are upheld by law and society.

Sex doesn't have to be a radical norm-defying act, but it can be; it can be a space to subvert all this political bullshit. (I'm picturing a femdom scene where I dominate a gang of slimy bankers, politicians and oil moguls. It's hot.) It can also be a nurturing space, an opportunity to heal from normative expectations. However you choose to engage with the political aspects of your sex life, know that you are not alone.

Sex-Positive Divide

If you're reading this book, there's a good chance you're already into sex positivity and happy to geek out about all this stuff. Hurray! I'm so glad you've joined the party. But this can be tricky if the people in your life, particularly those who you're sleeping with, aren't aware of any of this, or don't feel like the sex-positive movement benefits them.

Not wanting to engage in this conversation isn't necessarily a bad thing. There may be any number of reasons for it: they feel excluded from the conversation; they're worried that admitting they want to learn will imply they're not good in bed; they're not comfortable talking about sex; it may be linked to trauma they've experienced; they're not that interested in thinking about sex outside of when they're having sex.

And all of these are OK! It's important to respect any personal reasons why someone may prefer not to engage with this stuff; you can't make them do anything they don't want to do. You can lead a horse to water, but you can't make it drink up the inclusive pleasure-focused sex-positive goodness. Give them space to come to this in their own time.

But if it's something you're really interested in and there's no understanding from those close to you, you can end up feeling resentful. I see this happen in hetero couples a lot, where the woman is broadening her horizons about pleasure and sex, and the man isn't as interested. Straight sex isn't going to get much better without men being part of the conversation!

Here are some ways to invite your loved ones into the conversation:

- ♦ First off, actually invite them to talk about it (and ask your partners to read this book!).
- ♦ Ask them questions and give space to really listen to their response – it may surprise you.
- ♦ Be patient; embracing sex positivity is a gradual process, and it might take them a while to warm up to this if it's new territory.

And remember, if you're in different places and that's unlikely to change, it's OK to acknowledge that you may not be compatible. We all grow at different paces, and not everyone is going to have the same levels of enthusiasm for sex-positivity as you. It's better to be honest about that and do something about it.

Being a Slut

I'm a massive slut. So much so that I run workshops called 'How to be a Slut', and my housemates and I have matching T-shirts that read 'MASSIVE FUCKING SLUT'. Traditionally a slut is seen as a promiscuous woman, and I definitely fit the bill. But rather than seeing that as an insult, I embrace it as a positive – I'm making my own choices about who and how I fuck, and I think that's something worth celebrating. Taking ownership of the word was an important step in my sex-positive journey, and it's a label I now wear with pride.

That being said, you don't need to embrace the word: it still holds a lot of weight and if you don't fancy using it, that's absolutely OK. Calling yourself a slut can feel powerful, and you may have friends who feel the same and are happy for you to call them sluts, but being called a slut by others who are weaponising the word? Not so fun. I've been maliciously called a slut since I was a teenager. Back then, it felt like a curse: somehow I'd crossed the line from sexy to slutty, and was being shamed for trying to express my sexuality. As a grown-up lady, this can make me feel rageful or insecure or paranoid, but I've developed an armour for this kind of stuff, and on most days I have the capacity to rise above it and not let it affect my self-image. Claiming the word for myself is a big part of this.

Being a slut is less about how many people you've had sex with or the outrageous places/positions you've done it in. It's a state of mind. You can be a slut and not be having sex, you can be a slut and be in a long-term monogamous relationship. Regardless of what you're doing, the spirit of the slut can live inside you if you so choose. And that can feel powerful as fuck.

Porn

I really like porn. I enjoy consuming it, and because I'm a sex nerd I'm also fascinated by the industry itself. It influences our real-life sex in so many ways, but this is rarely examined because we've been taught to keep our porn habits top secret. It's time for that to change!

The way porn is made can be broken down into three categories:

- **Mainstream porn** is made and distributed by larger companies, and is designed to appeal to a broad audience. If you picture a typical 'porny' porn scene, what you're thinking of is mainstream porn. Most of what you see on free tube sites (Pornhub and pals) is content made by mainstream companies but uploaded without their consent.

- **Ethical porn** respects the rights of the performers. It's less about the themes and practices of the porn being deemed 'ethical', but rather ensuring the environment in which it's shot and distributed is safe and consensual. It's often made and distributed by smaller independent companies, although a company can be both mainstream and ethical. It tends to celebrate the diversity of bodies and sexual practices more than mainstream porn, and focuses on the pleasure of performers.

- **Amateur porn** is what it says on the tin: it's created by amateurs rather than professionals, so it's got more of a DIY feel to it. Because it feels closer to real-life sex, some people prefer it. There are sites that show verified amateur porn, but unlike the porn made by mainstream and ethical companies, lots of it is unregulated, so you can't be 100% sure that what you're watching is consensual, or that everyone involved is over 18. Because of this, I'm wary of recommending it – please tread carefully.

There's also audio porn and erotic fiction, both of which are HIGHLY underrated in my humble horny opinion. They're just as explicit as visual porn, but by taking away the visuals you're able to exercise your own imagination. I discovered the community site Literotica in my teens, where amateur smut writers upload their work for free, and it's been a constant in my solo sex life ever since. And a few years ago I discovered the wonders of erotic audio and my porn habit experienced a glorious renaissance.

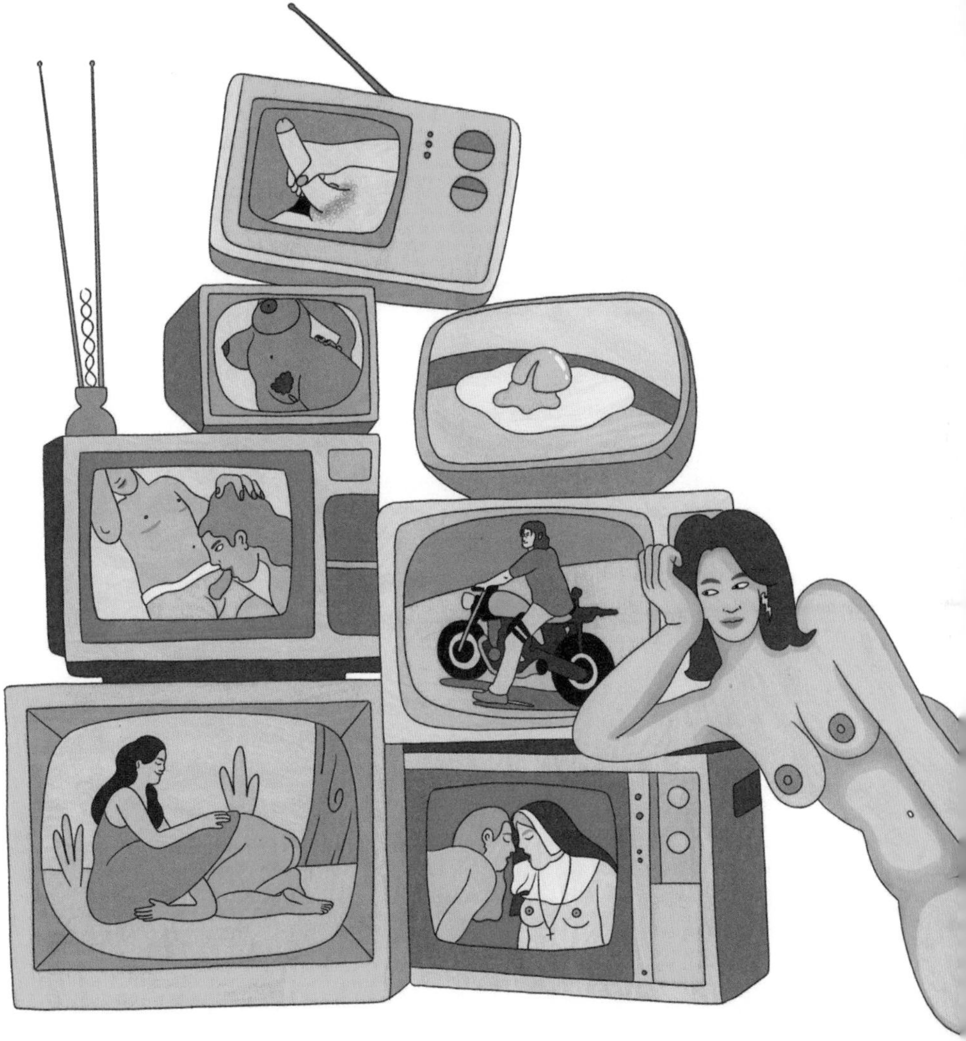

Things I love about ethical porn:

- It can be really fucking hot! Porn at its best pushes all my buttons and is such a joy to watch.
- It provides a safe space to learn new things, explore fantasies, and have parts of your identity validated. Watching ethical porn created by and for the queer community has helped me feel more connected to my sexuality.
- The diversity! Porn allows you to dive into the broadest variety of sexual fantasies imaginable.
- There can be something beautiful about watching porn with others – it really helps to unpack shame. I once organised a viewing party with my friends to watch the most expensive porn film ever made (it's called *Pirates* – you're welcome), and watching porn with a partner can be bonding as well as sexy.
- Porn can be political. It can be funny, or abstract, or convey broader social messages. Sure, a lot of porn out there is just designed to get you off, and I like that porn too, but that's just the tip of the sexy iceberg.

Things that annoy me about porn:

♦ Very rarely is there visible condom/contraception use, or on-camera discussions about consent. That doesn't mean it's not happening on set, but the choice to cut that out of the end product massively warps people's expectations of sex IRL.

♦ Mainstream porn tends to depict a limited range of people and practices, and lots of the content contains hardcore and objectifying activity without showing visible consent.

♦ The way porn fetishises certain identities can be really problematic. We hear a lot about the way women's bodies are objectified in mainstream porn, but the racism embedded in the porn industry is less acknowledged and equally important. Racial typecasting in porn – the submissive Asian schoolgirl, the aggressive BBC (big Black cock) – is one of many examples of systemic racism prevalent in all creative industries. The longer this goes unacknowledged, the greater impact it has on the ways we view ourselves and those around us.

♦ The majority of porn is uninspired. Scenes lack imagination and feel repetitive and formulaic (we all know the order of a typical porn scene: crap acting, brief making out/foreplay, blowjob, PIV, maybe PIA, then the cum shot). We're a horny species, and many of us don't need something super high quality in order to get off, but is it too much to ask for some decent lighting and a slightly creative plot?

♦ Genitals in mainstream porn are so predictable: giant veiny cocks and teeny tiny vulvas and assholes. All hairless, obvs. Promoting such a narrow ideal is unrealistic and can damage our self-esteem. In other news, I think pubes are sexy as fuck and it would personally turn me on to see more of them in porn-world. Who's with me?

♦ Endless scrolling through tube sites, and overconsumption of porn, can change our attitude to sex, and mainstream porn is so influential it has the power to dictate our fantasies and desires rather than reflect them.

♦ The hypocrisy of many consumers: the majority of people benefit from consuming porn but look down on the performers who create the very content they consume.

♦ The fear surrounding porn means it's rarely spoken about. Consequently, we're all living secret undercover porn lives, which continues to internalise shame and makes it harder to distinguish between fantasy and reality. I'm less pissed off about porn itself than the current lack of education about porn.

Finding Porn You Like

If you enjoy watching porn, you owe it to the performers in the industry to pay for what you're consuming.

Free tube sites have dominated the internet and how we consume porn since 2007. I know it's so easy to watch porn for free – trust me, I've been there – but the people who run those tube sites, the people who are profiting from you going to their site, are bleeding the creatives in the industry dry. The majority of the content on tube sites is stolen and uploaded on to the site without the creators' consent. Creators spend all this time (and lube) making sexy content, only for it to be viewed on a platform where they see none of the profit.

YOU OWE IT TO THE PERFORMERS IN THE INDUSTRY TO PAY FOR WHAT YOU'RE CONSUMING

Try to find ethical performers and production companies you love and feel proud to financially support. If paying for porn is not an option for you (or if you're under 18, in which case it's illegal for you to be sold porn in the UK), I recommend searching for community sites like Literotica, where the content is created by users and published for free. We owe it to the industry and to ourselves to be proud, mindful and supportive consumers of porn.

Fun fact: A lot of people watch porn that isn't designed for their sexuality. I've spoken to countless straight or queer women who love watching gay male porn, and many gay men enjoy watching straight porn. Watching a different kind of porn doesn't 'turn you' gay/straight, although it can be useful to investigate if there's anything underlying (you're welcome to join me in the bisexual soup anytime). It's a space to exercise our fantasies and curiosity without having to question ourselves or rationalise our desires.

How much porn is too much porn?

It's tricky to say, as what's too much porn for me might be just the right amount for you. Try not to judge yourself against anyone else, but be mindful of when your porn consumption stops being fun. If it's getting in the way of you living your life – socialising, working, having sex IRL – then it's time to evaluate your relationship with it and seek some professional help.

66 *I've had a complicated relationship to porn. As a closeted lesbian, watching straight porn allowed me to develop deep attractions to the woman performing. I used to masturbate three times a day and couldn't go to sleep without watching new content. When I entered my first relationship with a woman at 19, I realised that porn had had an adverse effect on my mental health. I had huge expectations on myself and deeply struggled not to watch it; especially when my partner didn't feel like having sex."*

My thoughts on hardcore porn.

I don't think hardcore porn is bad. It certainly has a place in the porn world, and it does a great job of getting a hell of a lot of people off, myself included. Some feminists argue that porn depicting rough sex leads to an increase in sexual assault and warps young men's attitudes towards women, but this is something of an oversimplification and fails to recognise the nuance of the topic, such as the many other places people might receive these messages in their everyday lives. It feels like the blame is being put on the existence of porn and people's sexual tastes rather than the way in which porn is made and consumed.

The issue I have is the conversations we're having – or rather, not having – about these attitudes. It's pretty much impossible to censor someone's fantasies. What we can do is provide education for people to healthily distinguish between fantasy and reality, and spaces for open discussion. It's often the shame associated with these fantasies, and the fact they're locked up in people's minds, that causes the most damage.

With proper communication and consent, 'un-feminist' sex acts can be carried out in empowering, feminist ways. Lots of people enjoy rough sex, or being objectified during sexual play; you can ask to be called 'cumslut' during sex and still feel respected, because you've created a consensual context to play in. I want better communication about scenes to be visible in hardcore porn. Many ethical hardcore sites include debrief footage, where performers discuss how they navigated the scene, demonstrating the connection between performers and a sense of genuine enjoyment. By watching content that breaks the fourth wall, you can see performers as real people with agency and desire, which allows the consumer to engage in fantasies in a healthier way.

Supporting Sex Workers

Being sex positive means supporting sex workers' rights.

Sex work is anything that falls under the exchange of material goods for sexual services. It takes many forms: full-service sex work, porn performers, strippers, webcam performers, proDoms or subs, sugarbabies, and so on. While the majority of sex workers are women, people of all genders engage in the industry as service providers and customers.

Media portrayals of sex work fall into two categories: the glamorous high-class escort and the impoverished street worker. The reality is that most sex workers sit somewhere in between these two extremes. Sex workers are regular, multifaceted humans who happen to make some or all of their living through sex. Yet the stigma attached to anyone involved in the industry is still so huge.

Campaigns against sex work often fail to distinguish between people working by choice,

BEING SEX POSITIVE MEANS SUPPORTING SEX WORKERS' RIGHTS

those who are exploited and trafficked into the sex trade against their will (a form of modern-day slavery) and those forced into sex work because there are few other options available to them (known as 'survival sex work', which is driven by poverty). A sex worker doesn't have to love every moment of their job in order for it to be an acceptable career – do you love every part of your job? Sex workers deserve the same rights as everybody else: to work in an environment that's safe, to feel supported by the law, and to be able to access services they might need.

My views on sex work have been shaped by engaging in sex-worker-led conversations (look up the SWARM collective – they're brilliant) and listening to the needs of those within the industry. As a result, I believe in the decriminalisation of sex work, which the World Health Organisation recommends all countries should be working towards. I encourage you to consider your own stance on the issue.

Despite the WHO recommendations, governments are still so reluctant to support sex workers in meaningful ways. Legislation, like the USA's anti-trafficking bills SESTA/FOSTA, can be made under the guise of reducing exploitation, but often ends up doing far more harm than good. These bills double down on online censorship (they're the reason why explicit content is now banned on Tumblr and the personal ads on Craigslist are no more), but there's no evidence they're doing anything to reduce sex trafficking. Instead, they've forced sex workers further underground, which has a massive impact on sex worker safety both online and IRL.

Whether you agree with sex work or not, it's an industry that has always existed, is currently happening, and will continue to happen for as long as people choose to exchange goods for services. I believe that allowing people to make their own choices safely is a fundamental aspect of sex positivity.

66 *One of the biggest benefits of sex work is experiencing the wide buffet of bodies and tastes; people aren't afraid to voice their kinks because they're paying not to be. It gives me a broad insight into men's varied tastes.*

It's also taught me to be more forthcoming with what I want when I'm having sex for fun, as when I'm having sex for work it isn't so much about my wants and needs. If I'm having to fake it four times a week, I make damn sure I get what I want when it comes to personal life hook-ups."

Sexual Trauma

Before you read this, pause for a moment and take a few deep breaths.

This was hard to write, but it felt really important to include in the book, because it's something that's rarely discussed. Be kind to yourself as you read: take breaks, be gentle, and if you're not in a place to read this right now please skip to the next section.

A bit of background information:

According to Rape Crisis, 12% of adults in the UK have experienced sexual assault, and around 97,000 people in the UK experience rape or attempted rape every year, but it's likely figures are higher than that. Many people don't disclose their experiences for a variety of reasons, so be aware of how you speak about trauma around others because they may have direct experience of what you're discussing without you knowing.

There's no way of telling from appearance or behaviour who an abuser is going to be. While most abusers are men, people of all genders can be perpetrators of sexual abuse, as well as survivors. Boys and men who are abused often feel unable to disclose their abuse because of the damaging misconception that men want to have sex all the time, so they can't be forced into anything sexual. Another misconception is that most often sexual violence is perpetrated by strangers. In fact, the vast majority of survivors know their abuser beforehand. Sexual abuse can occur within 'romantic' relationships – giving consent once, or even thousands of times, does not mean that you have consented to sex in the future.

I've taught lessons about sexual assault in schools, but I'm mostly writing this from a personal perspective, as I'm a survivor. From my early teens onwards, I've experienced various forms of sexual assault and harassment, and in 2016 I was raped. It was fucking horrible. Unless you're a survivor as well, it's hard to understand what that loss of agency feels like. And I find it additionally complicated because sex is such a defining part of my life: talking confidently about sex is literally how I earn a living. I resent having to carry around this identity for the rest of my life, but it doesn't define me; I try not to see myself as a victim.

There's this cultural idea of what a 'typical' rape looks like, when in reality sexual abuse takes so many forms. I spent years convincing myself it was all in my head, that my experience wasn't 'enough' of a rape to warrant my reaction, which had a huge impact on my mental health. I found it difficult to shake the feeling that I was partly responsible for what happened, which brought with it feelings of shame, isolation, blame, guilt, and a disconnection from my body. Sometimes my sexual pleasure reminded me of the abuse, which would cause me to dissociate or crumble during happy, consensual sex.

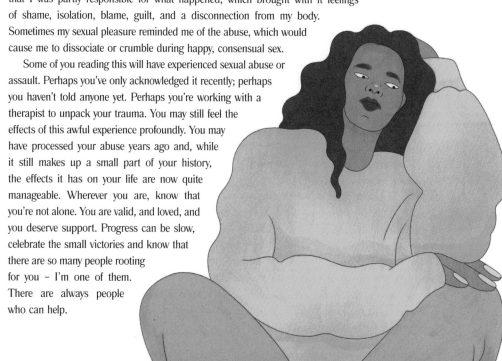

Some of you reading this will have experienced sexual abuse or assault. Perhaps you've only acknowledged it recently; perhaps you haven't told anyone yet. Perhaps you're working with a therapist to unpack your trauma. You may still feel the effects of this awful experience profoundly. You may have processed your abuse years ago and, while it still makes up a small part of your history, the effects it has on your life are now quite manageable. Wherever you are, know that you're not alone. You are valid, and loved, and you deserve support. Progress can be slow, celebrate the small victories and know that there are so many people rooting for you – I'm one of them. There are always people who can help.

Healing

Healing takes place in many different ways. First of all, you must remember that what you experienced was not your fault. It was not your choice. You deserve to heal.

Recovering has been challenging – some days are harder than others – but it's possible. It's involved going to therapy, support groups, and accepting the support of friends and family. I still get flashbacks, but as time passes this tends to happen less often. Recovery from sexual trauma isn't linear, which I've found frustrating. I'll have done all this work and feel strong, and then out of nowhere something will come along that triggers me, and I'll feel like I'm back at square one. But the more this happens, the better I get at rebuilding – it doesn't become so taxing, and each time I become a little more resilient because I know I've done it before.

Everyone experiences trauma differently, and being aware of your personal triggers is an important step in healing from abuse. Thoughts and flashbacks can be triggered by particular types of touch, smell, sounds or scenarios. You may find you're more likely to experience trauma at particular times of day, or during particular seasons. I am always very gentle with myself around the time of year when I was raped, because I know I'm likely to experience more trauma then. Spotting a trigger early may not stop it from happening, but the sooner you shift into a protective role and ask for support, the less impact that trigger is likely to have.

Whether you choose to report abuse or not, I recommend talking to someone in your life about your experiences. I kept my rape private for two years, and it made me feel even more alienated and isolated. It's a very heavy burden to carry alone. This doesn't need to involve going over the abuse in detail; someone can support you without knowing all the details. You also don't need to publically out yourself as a survivor. I made the decision to talk about my experiences online a few years ago, and while I'm glad to have provided support and comfort for others, it can be tricky to navigate.

An important part of healing for me was learning to remove myself from triggering conversations and spaces. While the #MeToo movement was a pivotal moment in addressing sexual assault and power dynamics, I really struggled when it was all everyone could talk about. I was made to confront my own experiences of rape multiple times a day: through the news, casual conversations with colleagues and scrolling through social media. It caused me a tremendous amount of pain, and it took a lot of strength to recognise that and give myself permission to check out of those spaces.

Sex as a Survivor

Trauma of any kind impacts our sex life, but especially when it's linked to sex. It feels so unfair that it's a burden you have to take on, but it is something that you can overcome. You can build a path to feeling sexual again after experiencing trauma. Whether the trauma is historic or more recent, you need to acknowledge that this will shape your sex, but also that you are in control of how you rebuild your relationship to sex.

I've taken breaks from sex in the past to focus on emotional healing, but when I've begun to have sex again I've found it to be a great comfort and an important part of my recovery. There's no rush with feeling sexual again; even now if my trauma is feeling particularly close to the surface, I'll make the decision to stop engaging in sex for a while.

When I feel ready to start rebuilding, I begin with solo sex. In solo sex everything is in your control, you are the only person touching yourself, and this can be a wonderful way of healing from past experiences. I'm able to take things as slowly as I need to, and put a lot of emphasis on aftercare – taking time to hold myself, using journaling to reflect on the experience and anything it may have brought up, and possibly reaching out to someone in my support system.

When I feel ready to engage with a partner again, we start with exploring sensuality before sexuality. Intimate gentle touch, the feeling of skin on skin, holding them or being held – all of these non-sexual activities help to build a sense of calm and closeness which I need in order to feel safe. And when I'm ready to be sexual again, it follows a similar pattern to my solo sex: gentle, slow and lots of aftercare.

You don't necessarily need to disclose abuse to partners if you feel that you are able to manage it yourself, but I recommend it's something that you bring up. This doesn't need to be immediate. I tend to talk about my abuse after I've hung out with someone a couple of times, but before then I may have alluded to it when we discuss boundaries and consent. It can be a good idea to share any information about your triggers and how to support you if you dissociate or experience flashbacks.

Supporting a survivor

The key to this is clear communication, patience, and taking things one step at a time. You can do everything in your power to help your partner feel safe and secure, but it's good to acknowledge you may not always be able to provide the right support for them. You can't take their pain away, but you can stand next to them and hold their hand while they navigate it.

Do what you can to become familiar with their triggers, and how they tend to react when trauma rises to the surface. This can be through direct communication, observing behaviour, and talking things through when they're in a better place.

> " *A few of my partners have experienced sexual trauma. Up until a few years ago there was always a level of nervousness when learning this about someone I loved. A sense that the violence and trauma would be close to the surface, and a sense of shock at how absolute the experience would have been for them.* "

> " *I thought that trauma resurfaced if I did something wrong: if I was overly physical, wasn't mindful with language, or didn't actively reaffirm consent. These considerations can all be triggering, but in my experience partners have been just as affected by their own behaviour.* "

> " *What I've begun to learn is that sometimes it's not about you at all. Sometimes you are a part of someone else's experience of old trauma only inasmuch as you are there with them. Not a direct reminder of their experience, but rather an opportunity for company and comfort; analysis if it would be cathartic, or just hugs when they're up for touching people again.* "

If you're sexual partners, recognise that building intimacy and a sexual connection may need to happen at a slower pace, or be more tailored to where your partner's at. It goes without saying that consent is essential – it can be helpful to consciously build consent into all the activities you do together.

How are you feeling after reading this session? Exhale, check in with yourself, and give yourself a big hug if you need one. I'm right here with you.

Finding Your Community

Carrying all the stuff in this chapter is a heavy burden, and can be hard and lonely work. But you don't have to do it alone. You'll find communities out there who can relate closely to your experiences, and connecting with them might help to lighten the load.

It could be to do with a specific aspect of your gender or sexual identity – I've benefitted hugely from building friendships with other bi people, where we've tackled 'queer imposter syndrome' together – and groups like the Vaginismus Network and 100 Women I Know help bring people together who've experienced similar health conditions and trauma. There are countless online communities and IRL events to explore. Knowing there are other people similar to you (believe me, there always are) helps to quieten down the 'omg, am I normal?' panic we all experience.

> 66 *Through attending sex-positive events, I found myself building connections with like-minded people. Having friends in your life who date and fuck in similar ways to you is a joy. Even if other people in my life don't get it, I know there's a group of people who understand where I'm coming from and are there to offer advice and support. Feeling seen by my community is so rewarding."*

Different chapter, same sexy nutshell:

♦ Sexual injustices exist everywhere. It's not your responsibility to tackle them single-handedly, but adding your voice to the crowd is impactful. Learn about and support causes that don't just benefit you – no one is equal until all of us are equal.

♦ PAY FOR YOUR PORN! Please and thank you.

♦ Sexual trauma is fucking horrible, but it doesn't define you. Healing is an ongoing process, but it does get better: you can be a survivor and have a joyful sex life.

♦ Above all, be kind. We don't all have to be on exactly the same page to empathise with one another. Respect other people's choices in the way you'd expect others to respect yours.

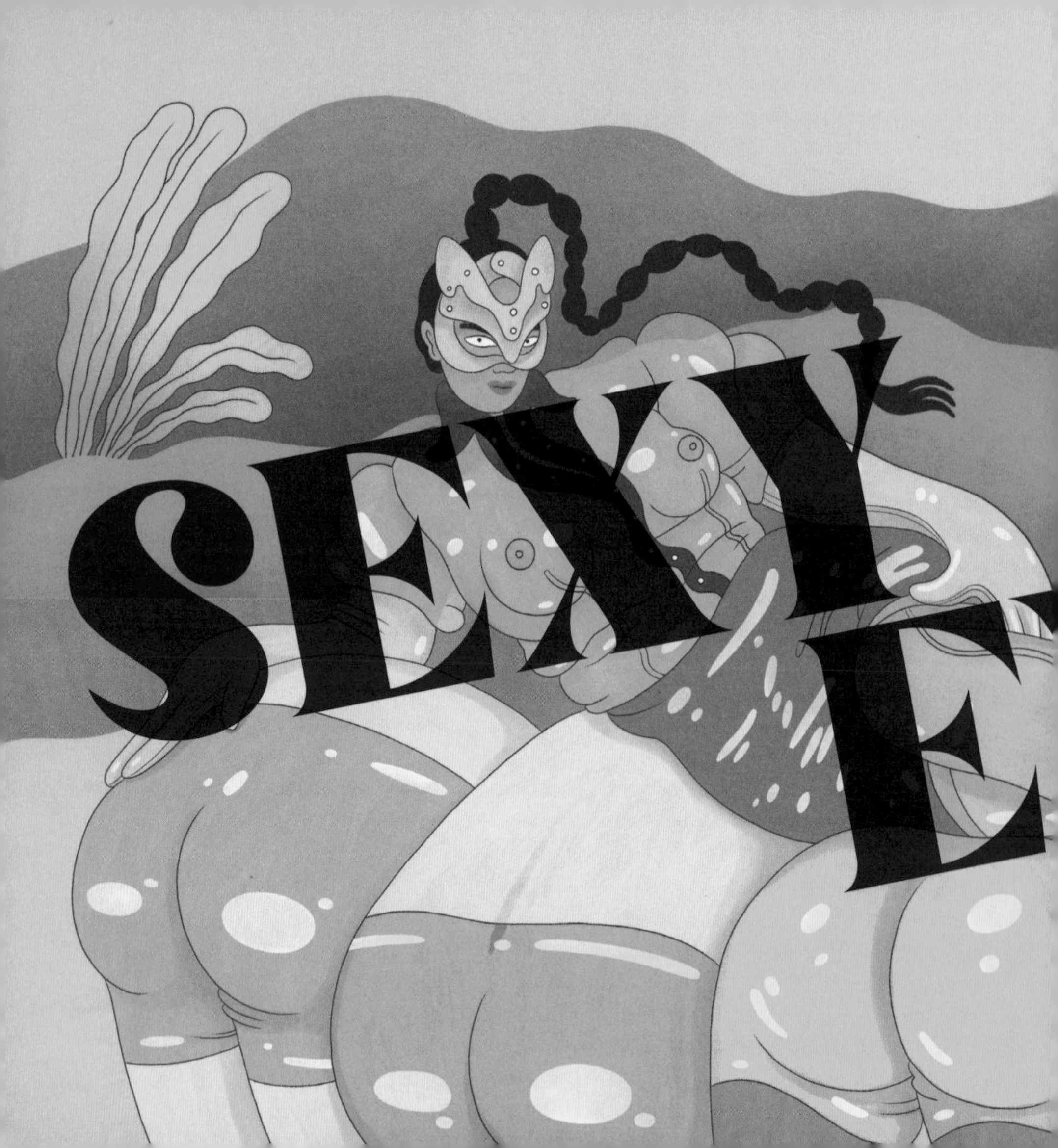
SEXY
E

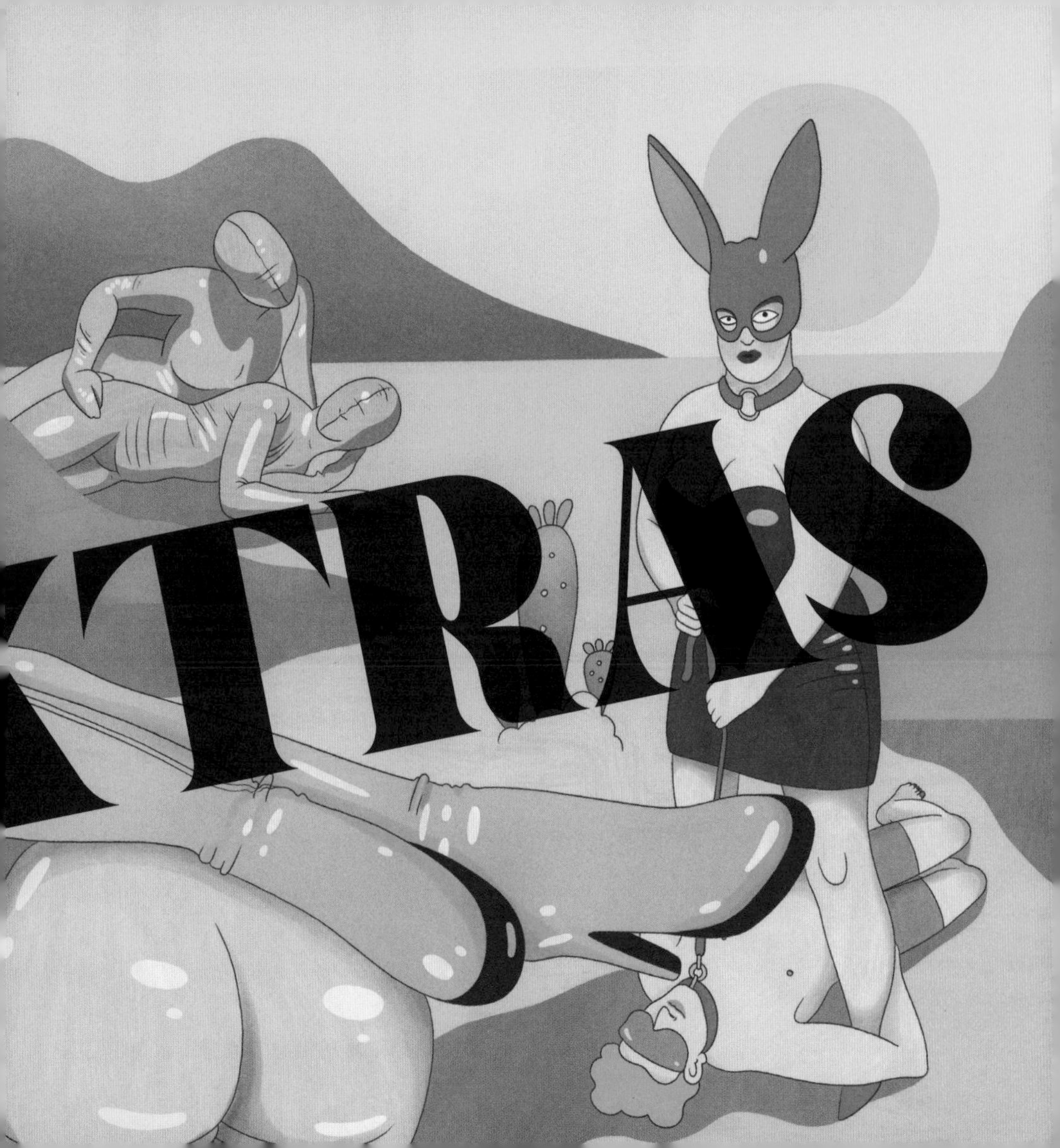
TRAS

I've put these juicy topics in a chapter together not because I consider them less important, but because for many of us these practices and communities are built up to rather than incorporated into our sex life from the very beginning. They can become an integral part of your sex life or be something you occasionally dip your toe into. Either way, they're no less valid than everything else we've discussed.

There's a lot of vulnerability in admitting you're curious to explore something new. Perhaps you're at a place where you're ready to try something different, or maybe these practices are already embedded in your sex life, or you may have no interest in exploring them – it's all OK! Wherever you're at, it's useful to have some foundational knowledge so you're more informed about the world around you.

Sex Online

The internet's primary purpose is to facilitate ways we communicate with each other. So of course one of the types of communicating we'll be using it for is sex! And as our definitions of sex become broader and more abstract, and there's less of a gap between our online and offline lives, online sex is becoming a more important part of the wider conversation. The possibilities are endless, but we're rarely taught about how to practically do this in a way that feels safe and fun.

There's a lot of fun to be had here, but it's not without its risks. Remember to set your own boundaries and only do what you feel comfortable with.

Nudes

The most popular form of online sex is the humble nude – sharing explicit images is a quick and easy way to sexually connect with someone from afar. Whether you and your significant other are doing long distance, or you're bored and horny on your lunch break – nudes are more common than ever. But we have a very singular idea of what a nude is, which I think can be expanded (let's move away from blurry close-ups of genitals please), and there are risks attached to sharing nudes, so it's worth thinking about before you press send.

The Health and Safety Bit

As an adult, there are still risks attached to sending nudes. If you're in a position where your friends, family or professional contacts seeing a nude would cause irreversible damage, think twice before sending anything. This is particularly important if your job involves working with young people. You can still have a wonderful sex life, on and offline, without sending nudes. And one way of minimising risk is by sending nudes that hide your face and any other identifying features. As a heavily tattooed lady with a big birthmark next to my genitals, this is easier said than done ...

IF YOU'RE UNDER 18, PLEASE DON'T SEND NUDES!

If you're under 18, PLEASE DON'T SEND NUDES! Any explicit image of anyone under 18 is legally considered an indecent image of a child, and you can face prosecution for the possession or distribution of these, even if you've consented to taking and sending the image. There's also a higher chance of the images being sent around to loads of people than there is in adult life. So many of the schools I've taught sex ed at have had incidents of nudes being sent around the school. It's a form of sexual bullying, and can massively impact a young person's self-esteem and mental health. I know I sound like a boring parent right now, but honestly it's not worth it.

So if you want to, here's how to take a banging nude:

1 Think about how you want to feel. Playful? Silly? Sexy? Gentle? Badass? Playing some music to match the feeling is the easiest way to get into that frame of mind.

2 Find a way to celebrate yourself while you get ready. This can be a relaxing shower or bath, giving yourself a gentle massage while you moisturise your body, or putting on some make-up. Whatever works for you.

3 Once you're ready, find a spot with good lighting (natural light is best). You can always take selfies, but propping up your phone somewhere allows you to move around and try different angles.

4 Before you begin taking photos, take a deep breath, and remind yourself you're doing this to have fun and celebrate your body, not to criticise it.

5 Self timer is your BFF here. Play around with angles to showcase different parts of your body, and don't forget to smile/make silly faces in some, even if it's just to make you laugh when you look through them. Take a lot of pictures. I mean A LOT! This gives you plenty of options to look through, to ensure there are a few at the end you feel great about.

6 Now it's time to curl up and look through all your photos! Remember that we all look weird in some photos/from certain angles, and that's ok! I take 30+ photos to get one I'm happy with, but I still enjoy looking through the weird ones. They are all a celebration of my body, and if I start to think about my body in a negative way I take a breath and remind myself that I choose to be beautiful and powerful. Pick a few that make you feel great, keep an outtake or two for the lols, and delete the rest. You can edit them if you want, but fuck the apps where you can photoshop your body and morph it into something unrecognisable.

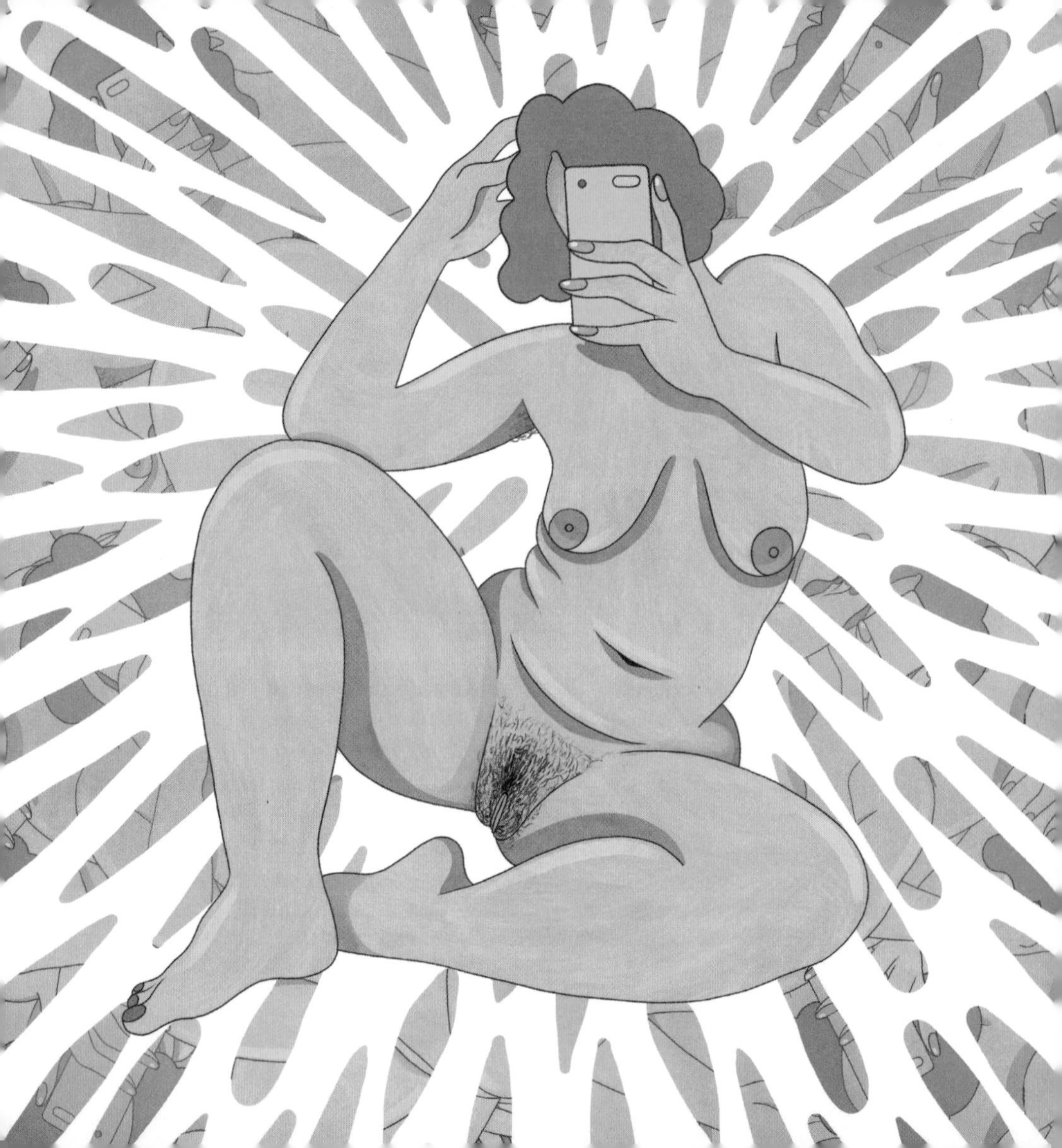

ASK FOR CONSENT BEFORE SENDING NUDES!

I imagine the people who send unsolicited nudes (mostly dick pics, but I have been sent unsolicited boob/vulva pics too) wouldn't flash me their genitals if we passed each other in the street. From my perspective, sending pictures isn't that different – I'm still being greeted with some genitals I didn't ask to see in the middle of my day. At best it can be annoying, at worst it's a trigger and can ruin my day. No one has the right to make you feel shitty like that.

Don't assume that just because you've sent a nude to someone once, they're up for being sent them anytime. What if they're at work, or with their kids, or their nan is using their phone to look something up? It's ALWAYS worth checking before sending nudes. And just like any other sexual act, sending a nude does not guarantee you anything in return.

Asking to send nudes:

- 'I just took some ridiculous nudes, care to see them?'
- 'I'm feeling really sexy today, could I send you a photo?'

Giving enthusiastic consent:

- 'Ummm YES PLEASE! Can't wait to see xx'
- 'You've just made my day. That would be lovely! If I'm in the mood for it later, would you like me to send something back?'

Saying no:

- 'Thanks for checking. Now's not a great time, but I'd love you to send them over this evening when I'm in a more relaxed headspace?'
- 'It made me smile to get your lovely message, but I'm struggling with my mental health today and I don't think seeing your beautiful nudes will help with that. Maybe another time xx'

(These can also be adapted for saying no if you're asked to send a nude.)

Sexting and Phone Sex

This is essentially sexy improv. You're telling a story together, either by describing what you're doing to yourself, what you'd be doing to your partner if you were together, or talking through a more elaborate fantasy.

The guiding principle of improvisation is 'yes, and ...', which basically means rather than simply agreeing to a suggestion, you make a conscious effort to add to it, building on the idea. If you and your partner keep doing this, you'll both be contributing to the escalation of your steamy sexting session.

Try not to shut down suggestions from your partner (obviously this doesn't apply if you're feeling uncomfortable and need to change/stop the conversation), provide specific descriptions and instructions, and be imaginative with the way you phrase things and how you develop the story. If your partner's a little more quiet, asking them a question invites them to relax and express themselves a little more.

'I reach for my favourite dildo, and taking your hand in mine, help you guide it inside me ...'

'Your velvety cunt welcomes it, and ever so slowly I start twirling it round, hitting every angle inside you. I watch as your breath shifts, your chest rising and falling with each inner rotation. My free hand slides down your torso, and landing on your clit I start to massage you with the palm of my hand ...'

'As the pressure intensifies, I reach down and turn on my toy. The vibrations surprise us both, strong enough to echo through my body. My thighs start to softly shake ...'

Hot, right? Use your newly found improv skills to keep the scene going ...

Don't forget to have fun! Phone sex is playful and imaginative – you don't have to take it seriously. If something funny or weird happens, don't be afraid to laugh.

Voice Notes

I **LOVE** a sexy voice note – they're so intimate. You can leave your phone recording and have a glorious wank, narrate what you're doing or throw in a bit of dirty talk for good measure. And unlike phone sex, you have the joy of listening to the audio whenever it suits you (perfect if you're on different schedules/time zones), as well as being able to play it back over again. Just remember that once you've sent it, you don't have total control over the content.

I'm also a big fan of recording the audio while I'm having partnered sex. I've only done this a few times, but it's been so fun to listen back to – I find it more stimulating than videos. I've been known to replay them when I'm out and about, so if you see me with my headphones on looking particularly flushed, you know what's going on ...

Cam sex

I define this as anything sexy happening on screen in real time. Could be a quick cheeky FaceTime, or a steamy Zoom date you planned days in advance.

In my experience, this works best if you take it in turns being the 'performer' and the audience member. I find it too complicated to do both at the same time, but maybe I'm just bad at multitasking.

Throwing yourself into the performative aspect of this can be fun; think about it like you're putting on a show for your partner. If you need inspiration, why not spend some time (and money) on a cam site – they're the experts, so watching how they do things might inspire you.

It can feel weird seeing yourself in the corner of the screen. I've definitely been put off by that before and realised I was checking how I looked more than I was focusing on my partner. An easy fix is sticking a Post-it note or piece of tape over the part of your screen where you pop up.

Remember, just because lots of people are engaging in forms of online sex, doesn't mean you have to. Make sure you're only doing what you want to, and in ways that work for you.

BDSM, Kink and Fetish

What even is 'kink'?

Kink is defined as 'non-conventional' sex practices, but once you realise the notion of 'conventional' sex is socially constructed bullshit, this definition is suddenly very vague. Simply put, kinky sex is anything that falls outside cultural perceptions of more vanilla sex.

This makes kink incredibly subjective, and once we begin to explore different ways to enjoy sex, our personal attitudes to what is considered kinky evolves.

You might start off using a blindfold during sex, which feels wild ... but as time passes and your sex life changes, whipping out a blindfold may feel normal to you. But a WHIP, now that's kinky ...

If you so choose, you can explore different areas of kink until you find the stuff that feels juuust right. A bit like Goldilocks, but in fetish gear.

BDSM

BDSM is the umbrella term for sexual play involving:

- ♦ Bondage: restraining or being restrained.
- ♦ Discipline: a dominant role ('Dom') training the more submissive role ('sub'), which can involve physical and/or mental punishment.
- ♦ Sadism: pleasure through inflicting pain or humiliation.
- ♦ Masochism: pleasure through experiencing pain or humiliation.

Power play is at the heart of BDSM. It's a space to exaggerate or subvert the power dynamics we experience in everyday life. There's typically someone in a position of authority, and someone submitting to that authority. However, though it might appear that the Dom is the figure with all the power in a BDSM scene, in reality it's a collaborative space where the sub retains a great deal of the control.

Yes, BDSM does often involve one person inflicting pain on another.

If you're not into inflicting or experiencing pain, you may find it hard to understand why others are. But pain is just another sensation; it produces a dopamine release fairly similar to the release we experience during pleasure. When practised in a consensual kink space, pain can be exciting, cathartic and pleasurable for the giver and receiver.

Consent, communication and trust is at the heart of all ethical BDSM, even if what you're acting out appears to be contradicting this.

BDSM isn't all leather and dark dungeons. It can be that, and that's wonderful if that's your thing, but let's broaden our idea of what it can look like. You don't have to dominate someone in the typical way you might see in porn, all mean and tough: you can Dom as a caring, loving partner, you can Dom dressed up as a camp fairy (trust me, I've seen it and it works). Try not to stick to the prescribed rules of what BDSM 'should' look like – it's all about finding things that work for you. Fantasy and role play can play a big part in BDSM, but don't have to. It can be just as hot experiencing the same sensations outside of a role-play scenario.

66

Before I found the kink scene, I'd been so ashamed of my desires, and hadn't felt able to express them with lovers. It really helps to meet people who've been in the scene for a while and who can show you the ropes (pun intended). I experience an overwhelming sense of calm during BDSM scenes, to me it's a form of meditation. It might look violent and extreme to others, but for me it's my happy place."

Safewords

Safewords are used to communicate consent during kink scenes. They're often (you guessed it) words, but they can also be non-verbal sounds, actions or types of touch – dependent on the participants' abilities and how they might be restricted in a scene (you're not going to be able to say your safeword when you're wearing a ball gag, are you?).

Safewords need to be agreed before any of the action starts. You may also want to incorporate ways of checking in throughout the scene. Some people do this by using a traffic light system: green means they're loving life, amber means they're getting close to their limit or need some adjustments, and red signals they need to stop right away. And remember the 1–10 system from Chapter 5? This works brilliantly in kink scenes. Find a system that works for you.

BDSM Toys

These toys are designed to heighten or restrict the senses rather than providing specific genital stimulation:

◆ Impact toys: feathers, floggers, paddles, canes. These toys provide anything from a delicate tickle, to a stinging pain, to a heavy thud. Look up how to use them ahead of time to learn how to build up sensation, and become familiar with the areas of the body to avoid (gotta protect those kidneys).

◆ Bondage: restraints, ropes, collars, ball gags, blindfolds. When you are restraining someone, make sure you're not cutting off circulation or cutting into the skin. If using a collar, make sure it's not so tight that it restricts breathing, and never pull someone's collar sharply!

◆ Clamps: nipple clamps, clothes pegs, bulldog clips. These are most commonly used on nipples, but they can be attached almost anywhere. The most intense sensation is felt once they're taken off and the blood rushes back to that area of the body.

There are great resources on how to use these toys safely, and it's really worth doing your homework before you dive into using anything. You must be aware of your partner's boundaries and preferences, and check in with them before, during and after a scene.

Please don't fuck around with choking

One of the most common aspects of BDSM that's brought into vanilla sex is choking. There's so much of it in mainstream porn that it's become normalised, but choking can be incredibly dangerous. People die from choking. It's really not something to fuck around with. Instead, gently holding the sides of the neck will have a similar psychological effect without actually limiting someone's breathing.

Aftercare

Kink scenes can be mentally and physically intense. I've burst into tears during scenes, and have tapped into emotions buried deep in my subconscious. Because of this intensity, the way you come out of scenes is very important. Aftercare provides a soft landing back into the real world, and can take many forms:

- Curling up in the foetal position and crying
- Being spooned
- Talking to a partner or friend about what the scene brought up
- Journaling to unpack the experience
- Asking your partner to check how you're doing the next day

Be mindful of your own aftercare as well as that of your partner's. For me, aftercare makes the bond developed through kink play even stronger.

Fetish

A fetish object is something that elicits a strong sexual response from someone, and it can be an object or body part that isn't culturally considered to be sexual (again, very vague!). It can be a part of the body, a material or type of clothing, or a scenario. The most common theory about fetishes is that they stem from childhood experiences, where the item brought on a feeling of sexual excitement or comfort.

I consider my obsession with jelly to be a fetish. I loved it as a kid, and the delight of how it looks, feels and moves continued into adulthood. Jelly brings me joy in non-sexual ways, but it took me a while to acknowledge that it also has the very real power to turn me on. It's an aspect of my sexuality that I'm still in the early stages of exploring, and I love how it adds another playful string to my sexual bow. My ultimate fantasy is to be set inside a giant jelly – something about being cast inside that wobbly texture, the bondage element in having to hold still as the jelly sets around me, and then the possibility of being eaten out of it, ticks a lot of my sexual boxes.

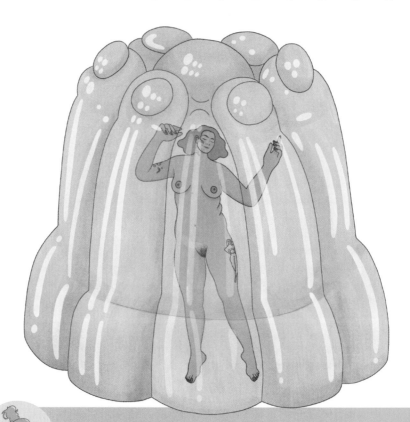

Take a moment to consider what you'd want to explore if there was no expectation of what should be considered 'sexy'. Is there anything that surprises you or would surprise other people? Rather than squash those desires down, giving them space to grow helps to shed shame – and it teaches you about a whole new way you can enjoy experiencing pleasure.

If you're not in the kink scene, it's easy to think of fetish as something separate from your sex life, but I'm a big believer that we all have fetishes of some sort. It's just that many of us are scared to voice them out loud, or think about them in the first place.

It took me years to go from 'jelly's so fun to eat' to 'it's actually kind of sexy' to 'OK, now I'm fantasising about being encased in a bath of jelly and spending far too much time googling how to make this a reality'. Much like my bisexuality, I dismissed my interest in jelly for so long because it didn't fit into any of the ideas about 'normal' sex I'd received. Unpicking this and embracing this weird and wonderful facet of my sexuality has been a joy – if there's something that pushes your buttons, give yourself permission to explore it, it could lead to something beautiful.

Bringing up kink with partners

If you have an interest in BDSM, or a particular fetish, you might feel nervous raising this with a partner. Not everyone is kinky, but there's a good chance that your partner also has some kinky things they'd like to explore, and they may be just as nervous raising it with you. If you're asking your partner to participate in one of your kinks, give space for them to have a think about it on their own before they give you an answer.

I don't tend to talk about my kinks in the initial consent conversations I have with partners, because I like to build a sexual relationship with someone before incorporating that into the dynamic. But it's good to allude to the fact that it's something you'd be interested in exploring. Just as you shouldn't kink-shame a partner for being into something you're not into, you also can't put pressure on a partner to do something that they're not comfortable with.

Kink-shaming

There can be a lot of shame associated with kink. Many make the judgement that just because they think bondage/furries/feet are weird, it's wrong for someone else to enjoy it. There's a lovely acronym in the kink community: YKINMKBYKIOK. It stands for 'your kink is not my kink but your kink is OK'. Provided this kink is being practised in safe, adult, consensual environments, please refrain from making someone feel like a freak for being into something (unless, of course, they're into humiliation, in which case you saying that to them is probably turning them on).

You may have some kinks you want to keep private, engaging with them through solo sex but not with partners, which is absolutely OK.

Remember that your kinks are valid, and you deserve to explore them in safe environments without shame. At the end of the day, we're all perverts in one way or another.

Tantric Sex

Tantric sex as we know it is over 1,500 years old and, like yoga, originated in India. It's rooted in the spiritual belief that the more fully we can experience our sexual energy, the closer we are to reaching enlightenment. These aspects of tantra can be rewarding for some, but if you aren't interested in the spiritual aspects you can still get a lot out of the practice itself.

I've dabbled in tantric practices in the past and have found it very rewarding. There are lots of ethical communities of people practicing tantra, with online resources and real-life events across the country. But a word of warning: I've come across some people whose teaching felt a bit culty. Do your research on practitioners and groups before diving in head first.

Tantra takes the focus away from orgasms. That's not to say you can't experience orgasms through tantric practices, but they're not seen as the aim, and they don't symbolise the success rate or end of sex. Like BDSM, aspects of tantra can feed into our sex lives, often without us even realising. The guidance I gave earlier in the book about connecting with your breath comes from a combination of mindfulness and tantric practices. Another big player in tantra is intentional touch, often practised through massage. By touching with greater consciousness, be that on yourself or others, you can experience more intense sensations.

Another big aspect of tantra, and something many are curious about, is separating orgasm and ejaculation. Most people with vulvas experience orgasm and ejaculation as separate things within their body, whereas the opposite is true for most people with penises. Because ejaculation and orgasm happen simultaneously, they're considered to be the same thing. In unlearning this approach and practising through solo and partnered sex, you can experience orgasm without ejaculation.

There are entire books dedicated to this practice, so if you're interested I recommend you read up on this separately, but the rough idea is that by identifying 'the point of no return' – the moment when you can no longer control your climax – and training yourself to stop just before reaching that point, through breath, refocusing the sexual energy in the body and using different forms of touch, you can prevent ejaculation. This can result in longer-

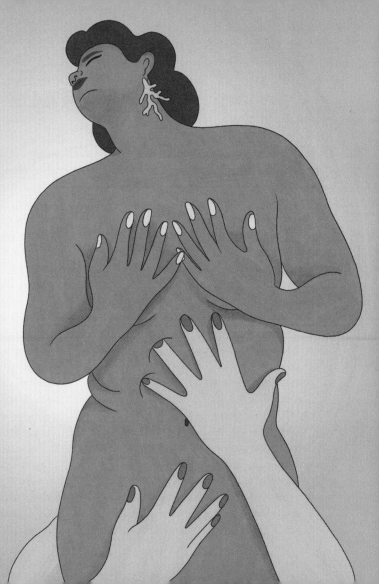

lasting pleasure, and allows you to experience a number of orgasms in quick succession, or waves. For some, it can be a cool party trick, while for others it's a deep spiritual and emotional experience.

66 *Tantric practices allow me to process trauma in a way that psychotherapy was unable to. For so long I felt disempowered and passive — not only during sex — but in many aspects of my life. Tantra allowed me to work through this in a safe and nurturing way. It brings together sex and spirituality in a way that makes perfect sense to me. It's given me a joyful spiritual practice that liberates me in ways that are impossible to put into words. In tantra, I am home."*

Threesomes

Some of the most rewarding sexual experiences I've had have been threesomes. Not because it was a 'bucket list' moment, but because the connection was so strong. My first threesome was arguably the best-timed event in the world: not only was it my first threesome, it was my debut into queer sex, and it happened on London Pride, which also coincided with my birthday! It doesn't get much better than that.

Threesomes are great, but navigating them can be tricky, and our expectations often get in the way of us having a really good time.

- ◆ Acknowledge threesome sex is not the same as sex with two people: there are more limbs to coordinate, more bodies to pleasure, and more emotions to consider. In my experience, real-life threesomes rarely look like the stuff that you see in mainstream porn.

- ◆ There's the expectation that in order for a threesome to be successful, you need to be touching someone or being touched at all times. But it can be fun to sit back and watch, and it shouldn't mean you feel any less involved in the action. If you are feeling left out, though, use your words! Like with all types of sex, there is always the option of pausing to regroup, have a cuddle and discuss how you can all feel included.

- ◆ I recommend avoiding penetrative sex during threesomes as they are two-person-centric acts, and when you're getting to know two other bodies it's logistically easier to focus on all the lovely things you can do with your hands and mouths.

- ◆ If you're in a couple, talk about why you both want to explore threesomes, and get on solid ground with your boundaries and what you want to get out of the experience before bringing in a third. It's not fair to invite someone into a hostile or unstable dynamic. Neither is it fair to push the idea of a threesome on to your partner. There is no greater boner-killer than a nonplussed participant in a threesome. It's your responsibility to create a safe and welcoming environment. Your third is not a unicorn there to fulfil your fantasies!

For those not in the know, 'unicorns' are typically bi/pansexual women who are into sleeping with couples, called unicorns because of their supposed rarity. I've done my fair share of unicorning in the past. It can be a lovely experience, but if the couple make you feel like your sexuality's been boiled down to 'threesome provider', it gets draining and the fun stops really fast. This is known as unicorn-hunting, and if you're a couple looking for a threesome, please avoid this by treating potential partners with care and respect. Instead of seeing the third as a service provider, think of yourself as a team dedicated to lavishing this sexy new person with attention.

Sex Parties

Sex parties are events where several people come together to create a space for sexual play. They can be wild, debaucherous affairs, or spaces for nurture and connection. Attending a sex party is an experience you can't replicate on your own, and opens up a whole host of sexual possibilities. But with more people involved, there's also more risk of building up expectations and miscommunication.

Lots of sex parties have a system called PAL in place (which stands for Pervy Activity Liaison, lol), which means you can't rock up on your own. You need to come along with a friend or partner you can vouch for, and if either of you violate the guidelines, you'll both be held accountable.

There are sex parties that are designed for specific groups, whether that be sexualities, fetishes or relationship styles. Some are quite high-end affairs, while others feel more like you're in the middle of a festival; some are super slow and sensual and others are very silly. All these spaces create a different atmosphere, so if it's something you're interested in it's worth doing the research to find an event that suits you. It's all down to personal preference.

The sense of community you can experience in these spaces is remarkable:

> 66 *I've met some of my closest friends through play parties. I now help run sex parties, and while it's amazing to have a large group of friends I can play with when I attend, I'm most excited about making connections that aren't explicitly sexual: naked dancing, talking about the shit week we've had, and generally feeling seen, accepted, valued and desired."*

If you've not been to a sex party before, I bet you're thinking they're all FUCKING WILD! They definitely can be – I've been to a few orgies that would rival the Romans' – but the reality is that they're often more mundane than you'd think. Like all parties, there's small talk, there's queueing for a wee, there's figuring out if it's worth getting the bus home or splashing out on an Uber.

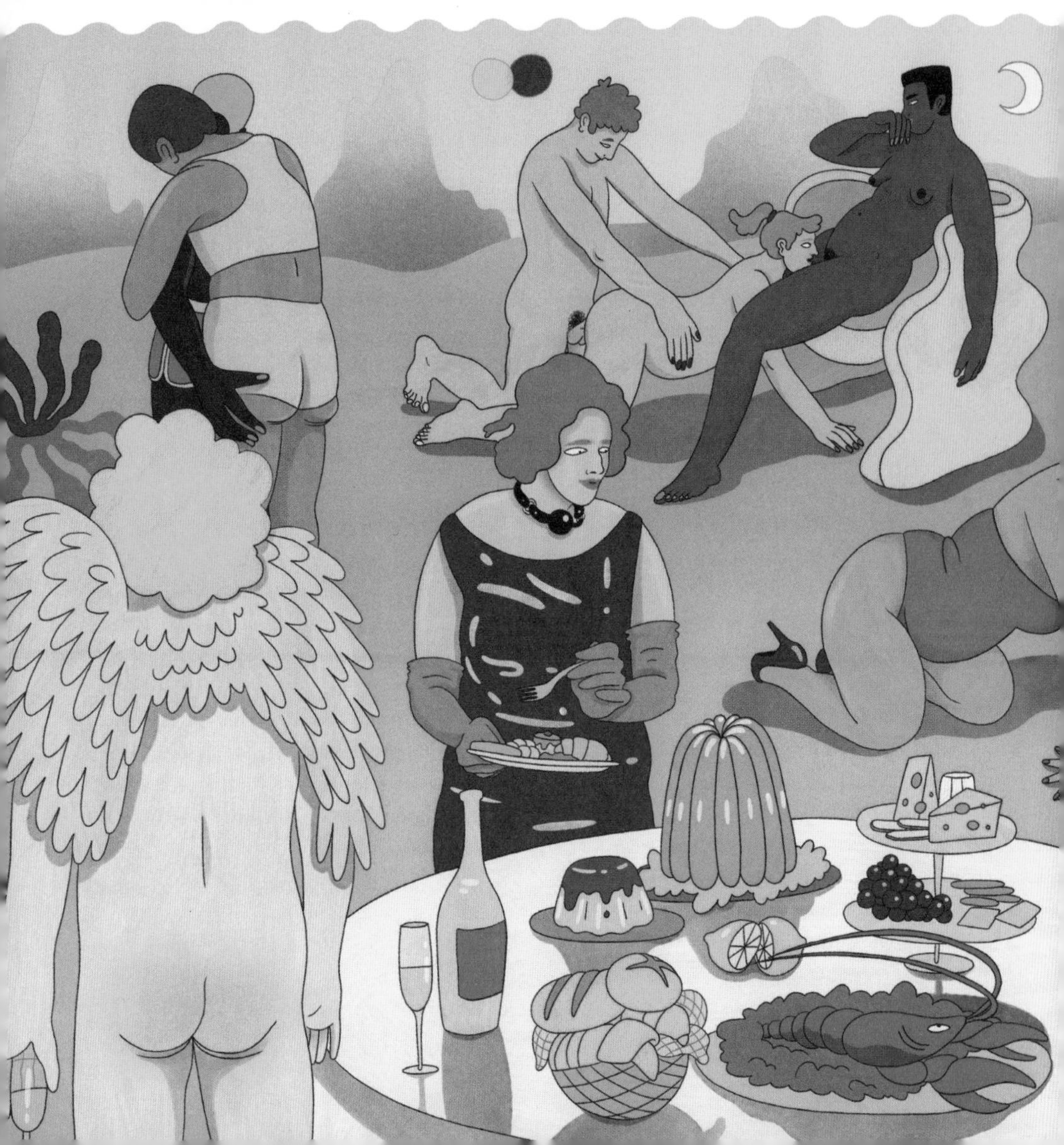

Wholesome sex party experiences:

◆ I have friends who host small parties at their house, and even though it's so nice to have sex in that space with friends I love, my favourite thing about their parties is always the food. They put on such a good spread, and you'll often find me helping myself to a third portion at 2 a.m., quietly eating my plate of dhal and pitta bread in the corner of the living room while I watch my friends frolic. This blend of mundane and sexy is my happy place.

◆ At a queer play party, I was chatting away with some friends, and it took us ages to realise there was a full gang bang happening next to us, with a guy knelt down servicing a circle of hunky men, loving life. There was something warm and fuzzy about watching people having a brilliant sexy time and being themselves – it felt wholesome more than being an explicit turn-on. We cheered them on, and then just kept chatting.

Going to a party

Acknowledge your expectations ahead of time, and think about what you're looking for and your boundaries, so you don't end up just going along with what's happening around you. Communicate this with whoever you're going with, so you can look out for each other during the party.

Condoms and lube are provided at most parties, but it's always worth bringing your own. And in most spaces you're invited to bring along any toys you might like to use (just remember to use condoms if you're sharing toys).

If you're going to a sex party with a partner for the first time, you may decide to stick to playing with each other initially, while you get used to the space around you. Check in with

66
Try to avoid fixed expectations of what's going to happen. Every party should be approached as an opportunity for personal growth, and that includes the possibility of really challenging or uncomfortable experiences alongside easy or joyful ones!"

how you're both doing throughout the party, and carve out time the next day to have a proper debrief, going over what you loved, what you didn't enjoy as much and anything you'd like to do differently if you go again.

Consent

Communicating consent clearly is so important. I know we want to be terribly British about things and avoid directly declining anything, but a sex party is not the place for avoidance tactics. Be kind but be clear communicating what you want – and firm communicating what you don't. If anyone makes you feel uncomfortable or breaches the guidelines of the party, please inform one of the organisers. And if you hear a no from someone, know that it's really not about you. Isn't it way better to hear a no from someone rather than get into a sexual situation with them where they're feeling uncomfortable? The benefit of being at a party is that you're surrounded by other people who may be interested in playing with you!

The final sexy nutshell:

- ◆ Sex online, in all its glorious forms, can be a lot of fun. Be playful with it, but only do things you're comfortable with. In order to get one good nude, you need to take 30+ photos.
- ◆ BDSM and tantric practices push the boundaries of what sex can be. There's a good chance there are elements of both already in your sex life, but if it's something you want to explore further then there are whole communities for you to learn from and become part of.
- ◆ Group sex is a whole different experience to solo and partnered sex. Remember it often doesn't look like the stuff you see in porn, and the more people involved, the more time you'll need to spend on communicating consent and boundaries.
- ◆ This is just the tip of the iceberg – if you're interested in exploring more, there are so many great resources out there to expand your sexual horizons. It's up to you how you choose to dive in.

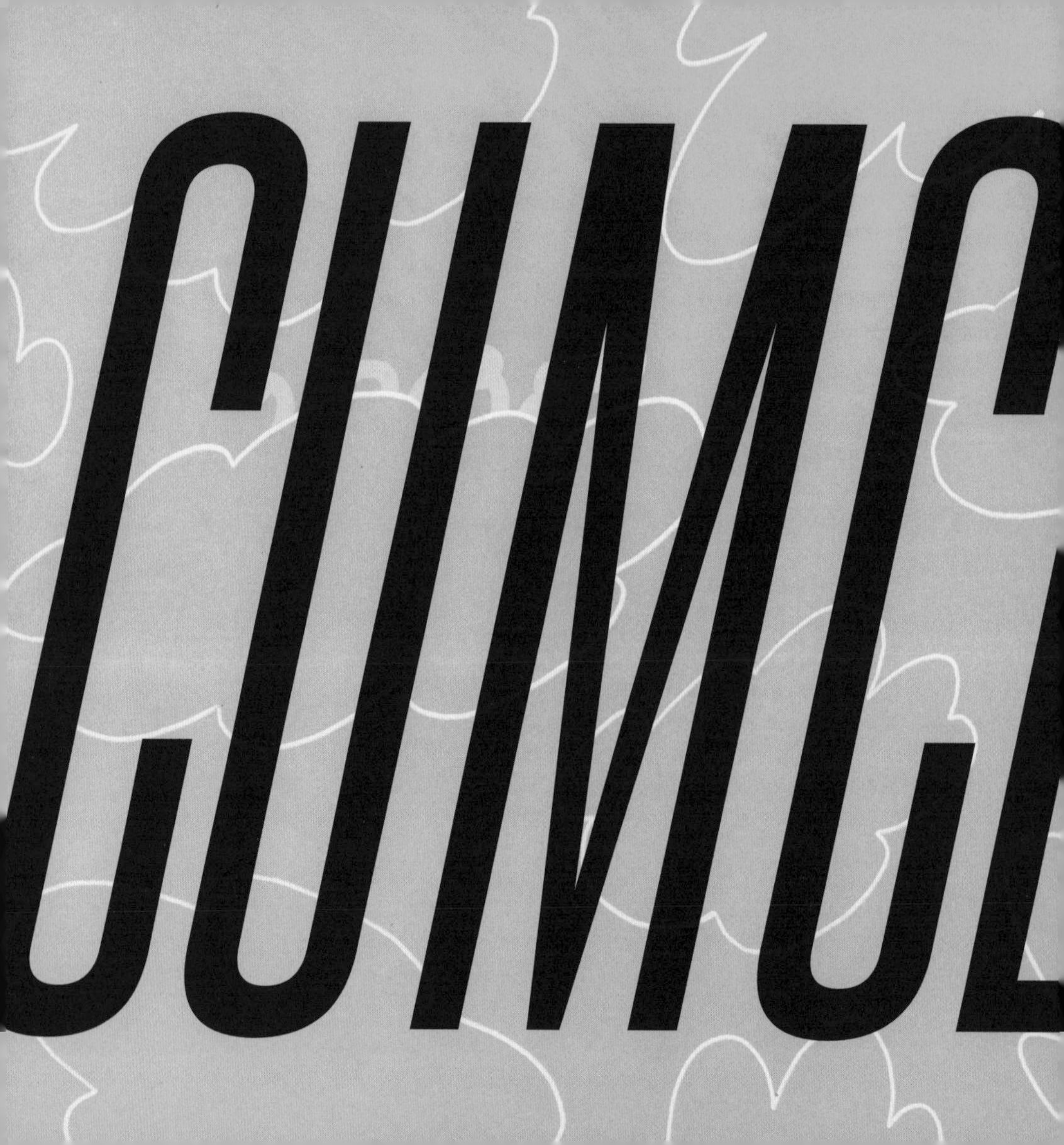

USION

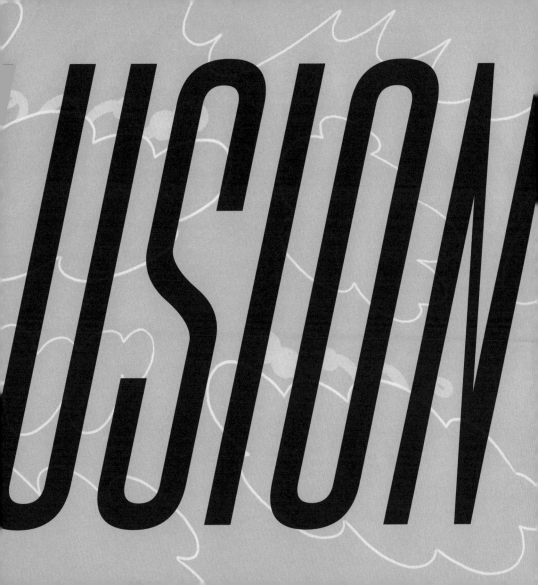

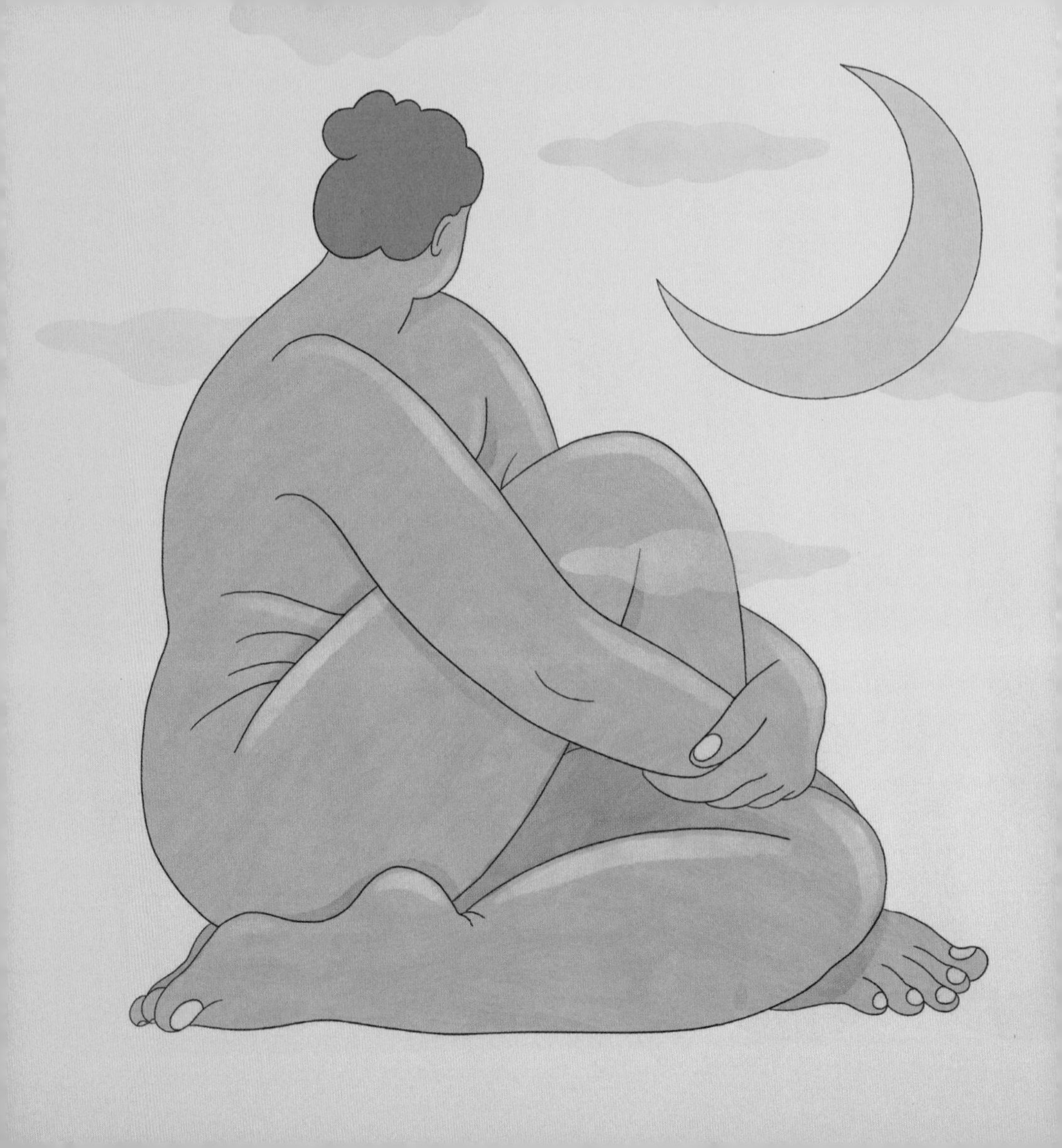

So here we are. We've reached the end, and hopefully we're parting ways with you feeling satisfied, appreciated, encouraged and seen – like any good sexual experience!

I hope you've had fun reading this book. I hope you've learnt new things about your body, your genitals, your desire and the endless ways you can have sex, and I hope you're feeling less alone when it comes to the challenges you face. There are so many layers of negativity and shame to shed. It's a big task, but once you strip away those layers, you can embrace the pleasure you actually want, rather than being limited to what you were taught you *should* want.

Our relationship with sex is a key part of our identity, and without clear, inclusive information, it's easy to limit our own desires. I feel lucky to have found the sex-positive community, to have learnt how to communicate confidently and embrace the queer, non-monogamous, occasionally kinky sex I actually want to have.

This book isn't a one-night stand situation – you're welcome to return to these pages again and again whenever you're in need of a pep talk or looking to scrub up on your sexual knowledge.

Or perhaps my tales of non-monogamous group sex have rubbed off on you, and rather than keep this between you and me you'd like to share this book with someone else! It could be a great way to open up more honest conversations. By talking about sex with friends, we become more informed and gain the confidence to navigate consent and experience the pleasure we deserve.

All of this is a learning process: think about the sex you were having five years ago, and compare it to the sex you're having now. There's a good chance a lot's changed in that time, and it's likely there'll be a similar amount of change in the five years ahead. What that change looks like is up to you. The endless possibilities are something to feel excited about.

Above all, I hope this book encourages you to invest time in your sexual pleasure. Your relationship to sex has the potential to impact your whole life, and it's worth putting the time in to learn and explore.

So be brave, stay curious and communicate with yourself and those around you. Never forget that you are worthy of respect, love, pleasure and FUN.

Further Reading

Bodies
× *Happy Fat*, Sofie Hagen
× *Body Positive Power*,
  Megan Jayne Crabbe
× Laura Dodsworth's
  Bare Reality series

Desire
× *Come As You Are*,
  Emily Nagoski

LGBTQI+
× *Queer Sex: A Trans
  and Non-Binary Guide
  to Intimacy, Pleasure and
  Relationships*, Juno Roche
× *Beyond the Gender Binary*,
  Alok Vaid-Menon
× Stonewall.org.uk

Kink
× *The Ultimate Guide to Kink:
  BDSM, Role Play and the
  Erotic*, Tristan Taormino

Sexual Violence
× *Sexual Healing Journey:
  A Guide for Survivors of
  Sexual Abuse*, Wendy Maltz
× Rapecrisis.org.uk

Porn
× *The Feminist Porn Book*
  (ed. Tristan Taormino et al.)
× makelovenotporn.tv/
× literotica.com/
× *The Butterfly Effect*,
  podcast by Jon Ronson

Sex Work
× *Revolting Prostitutes*,
Juno Mac and Molly Smith
× swarmcollective.org/

Sexual Health
× Brook.org.uk

Abortion
× Mariestopes.org.uk

Sex Toys
× sh-womenstore.com

Therapy
× The College of Sexual and
  Relationship Therapists,
  cosrt.org.uk

Tantra
× *Urban Tantra: Sacred Sex
  for the Twenty-First Century*,
  Barbara Carrellas

Acknowledgements

Thanks to everyone at Bloomsbury for their enthusiasm about this book, in particular my editor Lauren Whybrow and designer Pooja Desai, to my lovely agent Nicola Barr, and to Sofie Birkin, for bringing this book to life and sharing my love of peignoirs.

Thank you to the queer and sex positive communities that I call home, and to my past lovers (even the crappy ones), who have taught me so much.

Thank you to my friends, who read through endless drafts of sexual ramblings and helped banish my imposter syndrome. Special shoutout to Molly, Soraya, Adrita, Disney, and Bronwyn. And to the friends who've shared their stories – I'm so grateful to you for contributing to this book in such an honest, open way.

To everyone at Brook, where I earned my sexual health stripes. Thank you for encouraging me to learn and thrive, and for your continued support. This book wouldn't exist without you. To my sex nerd colleagues in the Hackney office – I miss talking about fisting over lunch.

To Rosy, my dear friend and Body Love Sketch Club co-founder. Running around naked together never fails to relax me.

To my parents, thanks for being so cool about me talking about sex for a living. Your love and support has made me the tiny woman I am today.

To Alex, for being so incredibly lovely and weird. You make my heart happy.

And to Maya – my psychic sidekick sissa. Thank you for writing to Mrs Vag in Year 4 and creating an icon, and for simply being my favourite person in the world. My life is infinitely better with you in it.

About the Author

Ruby Rare is a sex educator on a mission to get people talking more confidently and inclusively. Her work is influenced by her experiences as a queer, non-monogamous, dual-heritage woman. She lives in London with her obscene collection of sex toys and vintage peignoirs, and her happy place is on page 47.

She's an ambassador for Brook, the UK's leading sexual health charity for young people, where she worked for five years earning her sexual health stripes. She taught relationship and sex education (RSE) to thousands of young people, and managed a national period equality project – the youngest person to hold a position at this level in the organisation.

Ruby talks about all things sex and body positive on her Instagram (@RubyRare) and at live events internationally, and runs monthly sell-out workshops in London. She's written for *Gal-dem*, *Huffington Post*, and *Polyester magazine*, and has spoken on BBC4's Woman's Hour. *Sex Ed* is her first book.

About the Illustrator

Sofie Birkin is a queer British illustrator who left the mice of London behind to elope to Denver, Colorado, with her partner Erika, where they now live with two enormous dogs, Sir Arthur and Rupert Bear. She celebrates bold characters in contemporary and playful illustrations, and prioritises inclusive, empowering representation. Sofie has worked with a wide range of international clients, such as *Cosmopolitan*, *Playboy* and *The Body Shop*, and uses her work to promote the gay agenda whenever possible. She likes drawing nipples more than anything else, thinks her sexiest possession is her 1930s bedframe, and once got a bit turned on by a poached egg. This is her second book, and she would like to live on page 52, please.

BLOOMSBURY PUBLISHING
Bloomsbury Publishing Plc
50 Bedford Square, London, WC1B 3DP, UK

BLOOMSBURY, BLOOMSBURY PUBLISHING and the
Diana logo are trademarks of Bloomsbury Publishing Plc

First published in Great Britain 2020

A catalogue record for this book is available from the British Library

ISBN: HB: 978-1-5266-2837-4; eBook: 978-1-5266-2838-1

2 4 6 8 10 9 7 5 3 1

This book was commissioned by Lauren Whybrow and brought together by Pooja Desai on Design,
Helen Szirtes on Copyediting, Saba Ahmed on Proofreading and Laura Brodie on Production.

Printed and bound in Italy by L.E.G.O. SpA

This book is produced using paper that is made from wood grown in well managed forests and other
controlled sources.

To find out more about our authors and books visit www.bloomsbury.com and sign up for our newsletters.

MIX
Paper from
responsible sources
FSC® C023419